SHIPPING BUSINESS

Institute of Chartered Shipbrokers

Errata

Page	Text reference	Change
6	1.6 Reference to Appendix 3	The reference to 'Appendix 3: Organisation Chart' is incorrect as this appendix has not been included in the book.
24	2.10 Reference to Appendix 9	This is an incorrect reference and should read 'Appendix 4' which is a copy of Shell's time charter form.
95	8.15 The Principle of Average	The second sentence should read 'The concept of partial loss may be subdivided into particular average and general average'.

Published by the

Institute of Chartered Shipbrokers

85 Gracechurch Street

London

EC3V 0AA

United Kingdom

Telephone: +44 (0)20 7623 1111

Email: books@ics.org.uk

www.ics.org.uk

First published 2013, second revised edition 2013

ISBN 978-1-908833-36-5

© Institute of Chartered Shipbrokers 2013

Printed and bound in the UK by Latimer Trend, Plymouth PL6 7PY

Artwork production by Jacamar (www.jacamar.co.uk)

Front cover image: Portpictures.nl

Front cover design by Mark Clubb (www.theclubb.co.uk)

Foreword

By DP World chairman, HE Sultan Ahmed Bin Sulayem

Sultan Ahmed bin Sulayem is one of the most prominent businessmen in Dubai. He was responsible for the establishment of the tax-free Jebel Ali Free Zone in 1985 and since then has served on the boards of many high-profile companies and organisations in Dubai. He is the former chairman of Dubai World.

The study of shipping intrinsically brings with it the knowledge and understanding of the components of the fascinating and complex world of maritime transport and the role it plays in supporting and facilitating international trade. To place this education in a 21st century context is even more crucial in view of the technological undercurrents that are rapidly changing the way the entire supply chain industry, including shipping, works.

As one of the original drivers of human civilisation and commerce, maritime transport has seen many transformational developments over the ages. From the simple oar to sail and steam engines, to electric and nuclear power, it has been a long journey in search of efficiency and excellence. Today we are on the cusp of another paradigm shift in the efficient management and seamless running of the supply chain across borders and around the world. This change is powered by information technology and the internet.

In today's technological age, as we know, information is power. The flow of information that supports the efficient management and smooth running of the maritime transport and logistics sectors is defining the way the industry functions, with far-reaching impacts on global trade and national economies. New generation container liners and marine terminals are already using IT-driven solutions such as gate automation, RFID tags to track container units, and sophisticated control tower operations that integrate everything from berthing ships to matching men and machines in the port area.

Increasingly, too, we are seeing road, rail and air connections linked to ports, with business parks springing up close by, making the port very much a hub and a gateway for trade. A prime example of this model is in Dubai with the Dubai Logistics Corridor, which opened in 2010. Jebel Ali Port, which handles more than 11 million TEU a year, and the connected Jebel Ali Free Zone, home to more than 6,500 international companies, is directly linked to Al Maktoum International Airport. Cargo from the seaport can move to the airport in just 20 minutes. Meanwhile, sophisticated and interlinked IT eliminates paperwork, provides visibility of shipments, monitors carrier and supply performance, automates customs entry and gate exits, and maximises yard space on wharves and slot space on ships. The platform is accessed by supply chain operators through Dubai Trade, an e-service provider that has won praise from the World Bank for enabling 'trading across borders', globalisation's core mantra.

The same integrated model is being replicated at our new development, DP World London Gateway, where we have built a brand-new port on the Thames, with adjacent business park, both connected with efficient road and rail links directly to the UK's biggest market, London, and empowered by IT.

As a global connector and facilitator of trade, the maritime shipping business enjoys influence that often extends beyond ships and terminals. DP World's experience is that efficient infrastructure stimulates trade by reducing supply chain complexity and cost, which has a knock-on benefit for local communities – and of course for those involved in supply chain management. This means that increasingly, marine terminal operators are being seen as long-term strategic innovation partners.

The rise of sustainability as an issue is linked directly to this trend. Demands for greater reliability, agility, and lower costs are exerting positive pressure on the industry's operating model. Superior sustainability performance is no longer an option but a necessity for stakeholders across the supply chain.

In this context, the effective and efficient management of risks and opportunities demands strategies that can deliver continuous improvement in baseline business, social and environmental performance that validate sustainability. Tactical investments in innovation, technology and collaboration will define the way the industry progresses in the future.

Shipping is one of the oldest commercial activities in the world and it continues to be a major force in global trade. The world's merchant fleet still carries 90% of international trade by volume, accounts for more than a third of the value of global trade and generates millions of jobs.

As the world becomes more competitive, professional and personal development assumes greater importance as a career growth engine. This book published by the Institute of Chartered Shipbrokers opens the door to a world of possibilities and opportunities in the truly global business of shipping.

Acknowledgements

First and foremost we would like to thank HE Sultan Ahmed Bin Sulayem for his inspirational support in the revision of this book. We also need to acknowledge the contribution of several industry professionals, but special thanks are in order for Paul Wogan, Stephen Spark and Bridget Hogan.

Also special thanks to Andrew Lansdale and Victoria Grillo for their unrelenting efforts to improve the content of the book.

The illustrations have been sourced from across the industry but with particular thanks to DP World and Danny Cornelissen, whose pictures keep inspiring and belie his modesty as an artist.

We must also thank BIMCO for its support with charter parties and contract copies.

Technical editor

Andrew Lansdale

The Institute's technical editor comes from a naval family. His father served in capital ships in the Royal Navy. Andrew Lansdale served aboard the three-masted training ship HMS *Worcester* before going to sea, serving as a cadet and deck officer in the British Merchant Navy. He came ashore and started in the Shipbroking sector of the shipping industry. He passed the Institute examinations in October 1972.

He has worked in dry cargo chartering and in tanker chartering as well as in ship management and in shipping research. He has plied his trade in London, in Tokyo and in Hong Kong. Ten years ago, he turned to journalism and has worked as markets editor for *Fairplay* and as a freelance journalist for *Lloyd's List* and *TradeWinds*. He was presented with the News Journalist of the Year Award in 2006.

In July 2012, he completed 50 years of service in the shipping industry.

Apart from writing, his hobbies include navigating his small sailing yacht around the south coast of England. He is Commodore of the Old Worcester's Yacht Club.

Technical copy editor

Victoria Grillo

Victoria read law at the University of Leicester and practised at a City law firm before moving into the shipping industry. She moved to the marine insurance sector and joined an International Group P&I Club as a claims adjuster in the Far East team. She passed her Institute exams in 2012 and has sat on the London-branch committee for more than two years. The Institute is fortunate to be able to take advantage of her knowledge of our industry in the production of this book and in other projects.

Contents

Contents

Contents

Francis Drake – English explorer and circumnavigator 1540–1596

Chapter 1

· ·

The business entity

1.1   INTRODUCTION

With the exception of cruise liners, shipping is what economists call a *'derived demand'*. Ships only exist to provide the means to transfer goods between a buyer and seller. Nevertheless, shipping is a business like any other and understanding the basic elements of how a business is run is vital.

Whether large or small, the tasks undertaken in business are largely the same. A large organisation may have separate departments undertaking discrete tasks while in a small firm they are likely to be different tasks undertaken by a small number of staff.

1.2   THE SOLE TRADER

A sole trader is a person who enters business on their own account, contributing the capital to start the business, working in it with or without the assistance of employees and receiving as a reward the profits or proceeds.

No formal procedure is required to set up such a business, though the trading name may have to be registered, and some businesses may require a licence to operate.

The sole trader is completely independent and can make their own decisions and put them into effect quickly. Personal supervision, individual attention to customers' and clients' requirements and low overhead costs can make this most basic of organisations a very effective business unit in specialised areas of shipping business. It is not uncommon to find marine surveyors, consultants and even small port agency and brokers' businesses operating as sole traders.

The sole trader, apart from making certain confidential disclosures for tax purposes, need not reveal the details of the business to anyone.

The sole trader's status carries with it a number of disadvantages, however, not the least of which is the unlimited liability. This means that they are personally liable to the full extent of their private wealth for the debts of the business. Insolvency in such circumstances may lead to the loss of virtually all possessions to satisfy the business's creditors.

It can also be difficult to regulate working hours and to take time off for holidays. Similarly the business could quickly get into difficulties if the proprietor were to fall ill and be unable to work.

It may also be difficult for the sole trader to expand the business without a loss of independence.

1.3   PARTNERSHIPS

One alternative available to a sole trader wishing to expand is to take one or more business partners. The firm (as a partnership is usually called) is then owned by the partners, and has the benefit of increased capital, allowing the business to expand. The former owner can now share the responsibility for control with the other partners, who may also bring with them wider experience and the opportunity for the business to specialise. The private nature of the business is preserved.

However, the partners are still fully responsible for the debts they incur. In addition, all business decisions must be taken with the full agreement of both (or all) the partners. Disagreement may lead to the breaking up of the partnership, and the death of any one of the partners could make it difficult for the firm to continue if the deceased partner's share of the business has to be withdrawn to settle their estate.

Some countries also sanction a type of 'limited partnership' designed to protect non-executive partners (i.e. those who are merely providing capital for the firm) by limiting their liability to the extent of their financial participation in the firm. These 'hybrid' organisations are beyond the scope of this text.

1.4   LIMITED LIABILITY COMPANIES

The most significant difference between the types of business entity considered so far and their larger counterparts is the concept of limited liability. In the United Kingdom the limited liability company can be identified by the abbreviation Ltd (limited company) or plc (public limited company) following the company's name. Company law is complex and differs from country to country, but broadly speaking the private limited company and the public limited company can easily be distinguished in any part of the world.

A limited liability company is owned by shareholders and each shareholder is liable for the company's debts only up to the value of the shares they hold. This means that, in the unfortunate event of the company becoming insolvent, the shareholders may find their shares are worthless but they are not required to provide additional funds to pay the balance of the company's indebtedness. (The exception is when the shareholders have only subscribed part of the cost of their shares, in which case they would have to pay the remaining instalment to the liquidator in the event of insolvency). Anybody who has granted credit to the failed company will receive only a proportion (occasionally only a small proportion) of the amount owed to them.

This may sound as though a limited liability company provides a licence for the directors and staff to use other peoples' money without any responsibility. This, of course, is not so and in every country there are laws that give protection to the shareholders generally, and in particular to minority shareholders against the majority. Some protection for creditors is afforded by the requirement for limited companies to have their accounts carefully checked (audited) by an independent professional accountant. When the auditor is satisfied, a profit and loss account (which sets out the company's income and expenditure for the last year) and a balance sheet (which shows what assets and liabilities the company had at the end of that year) have to be distributed to every shareholder and also lodged with a government agency. In the UK this is the Registrar of Companies and, for a nominal sum, anyone may obtain comprehensive details of any limited company's structure as well as copies of its annual accounts. However, it has been said that what a company's annual accounts reveal is interesting but what they conceal is vital. In other words, there is no substitute for prudence when dealing with a limited liability company because large as well as small companies have been known to become insolvent.

When we refer to shareholders 'owning' the company, what do we mean? Simply it is those people who have supplied the 'capital' to run the concern. Regardless of size, a business must be provided with some money at the beginning to enable it to start and it will continue to need more money throughout its life. The shareholders supply this money in the expectation of receiving income (dividends) and in the hope that this income will be better than placing their money on deposit with a bank. Furthermore, they hope that the company will continue to grow so that the value of their shares will also increase.

Capital within the company is divided into two categories. The first is that which is used to purchase items called fixed assets, needed for the company to operate and likely to last for many years. For a shipowner, this is the ship, for the smallest broker, perhaps a desk and telephone. The second category, called working capital, is needed to pay for such things as rent, wages and items with a short life span, such as bunkers for a shipowning company or stationery for a small broking firm. All of these will have to be paid for before any profit can be identified.

These two types of capital and more details of how money is used and accounted for will be discussed later in the book.

In the organisation chart of a typical UK group of companies, at the top is the parent company, which is the public limited company (plc). A public limited company, as the name implies, is one in which any member of the public may hold shares. Such a company's shares are usually quoted on the Stock Exchange and, in most instances, they have hundreds, even thousands, of shareholders (although English law only requires a minimum of two).

The other type of limited liability company in the UK is the one that has Limited (Ltd) after its name. This indicates that it is a private company whose shares may not be offered to the public at large.

Such a company could be a relatively small concern, rather like a partnership, but where the owners have decided to incorporate the company. Exceptionally, however, there are some quite large private limited companies where the shareholders have managed to keep the shareholding 'within the family'. The other case where one encounters 'Ltd' rather than 'Plc' is where the company is a subsidiary of a parent, which owns 'all' the shares in its 'daughter'.

In the UK, and many other countries, the parent would not own all the shares because company law requires a minimum of two shareholders in a limited company. This is usually overcome by having one qualifying share either owned by another subsidiary in the group or owned in the name of an individual director or staff member.

When a company is incorporated, the owners of it (or 'members' as the law always calls them) in effect create an artificial person. It becomes an entity in its own right which will, unlike a sole trader or a partnership, continue even after the death of the original founder and will remain in existence until it is formally wound up.

Remember that a partnership theoretically comes to an end when one of the partners dies because a partnership is, in effect, nothing more than an agreement among two or more persons to work together. In practice, partnership agreements usually make provision for the firm to continue even after members have died or retired. However, in a partnership it is not possible to sell one's place in it to another person.

This is quite different in a limited company where any shareholder can, theoretically, sell all or part of their shares to a third party. Unlike a partnership, even a major shareholder need not necessarily be on the board of directors, although they may have a voice in deciding who should be on the board. Conversely, a member of the board is not bound by English law to be a shareholder.

The qualification 'theoretically' was used at the beginning of the previous paragraph because, in the case of many private companies, the founders want to pick and choose who should be a part of their venture. They would, therefore, protect themselves by writing specific clauses into the documents creating the company (called the memorandum of association and articles of association in the UK). Such clauses, called 'pre-emption clauses', would set out the procedure to be followed should a shareholder wish to sell their shares or upon the death of a shareholder. Usually this would insist on the shares being first offered to other existing shareholders, with details as to how their value should be calculated.

Such pre-emption clauses are only usually found in private companies and it would be most unusual for there to be any restriction as to who may or may not hold shares in a plc. Many countries do, however, make it obligatory for anyone acquiring an interest in more than a certain percentage of a public limited company (5% in the UK) to disclose this fact.

What determines whether a small group should form a partnership or incorporate themselves into a limited liability company? One would assume that being able to limit one's liabilities would be irresistible as it is possible to start a limited company with only two £1 shares being issued. The working capital in such a company could be provided by loans (from a bank or the directors or their friends and relatives) which would be paid back as soon as the profit allowed. However, a company with such a tiny 'asset base' would not be attractive to anyone who was expected to grant extended credit.

If the proprietors of a new company go to a bank for a loan, the bank will want some sort of security and this usually is in the form of personal guarantees from the directors. As this means the directors are virtually placed in the same position as if they were partners they may well decide to dispense with the expense and formalities of incorporation and simply form a partnership. In many cases the decision to be a partnership or a limited company will be strongly affected by whichever form produces the smaller liability for income or corporation tax.

In a normal organisation chart, you will see several divisions subordinate to the parent. In such a group, the main function of the parent would be the control of capital and each of the subsidiaries would have to convince the parent board of directors of the viability of any enterprise, which required the investment of capital. The parent company might also run certain central services common to all divisions (eg human resources, training, information technology (IT) etc) where an economy of scale can be achieved.

Many companies are engaged in a number of apparently unrelated activities, each within its own division. These type of companies are often referred to as conglomerates.

Within some of the divisions there is more than one subsidiary company; for example in the shipping division where there is a shipowning company quite separate from the company dealing with shipping services (agency, chartering etc). Similarly, in the building services division, the company manufacturing bricks is quite separate from the heating and air-treatment company.

In the case of the oil-storage division, you will see that there are sub-subsidiaries to cover the situation where it is more convenient (or obligatory) for an overseas branch to be separately incorporated in the country concerned.

Why should an already established company be concerned about being 'attractive to the investing public'? First, remember the company belongs to the shareholders who have the right to attend the company's annual general meeting, which the company is obliged to hold each year. Those shareholders technically have the right to dismiss any member of the board of directors and although, this rarely happens, the possibility is there. Second, if the company wants to expand it will need extra capital beyond its own resources. Although borrowing from a bank could raise some of this, the company will need to have a prudent mix of debt and equity to ensure that it does not become unable to repay its debt in case of a downturn in business. It is therefore prudent to seek additional capital through a mixture of borrowing and by offering new shares on the market. The more efficient and profitable the company, the easier it will be to raise the additional money. Finally, of course, the directors of any company need some external measure of their success (or otherwise) and what the stock market thinks is clearly shown by the price being offered for its shares.

A lengthy discussion on how stock markets operate is well beyond the scope of this book but readers should study the financial pages of their newspapers from time to time. Look for the names of companies you know something about and note how the price of its shares have 'moved'. Most financial sections of the newspapers show this by indicating whether the price has gone up or down during the previous day's trading.

It is not unusual to find shares that have been around for a long time to have a par value of, say, 50 pence now being quoted at 350 pence. One needs to study a company's share price over a period of time and to compare it with the general trend (eg the Financial Times Index or the Dow Jones Index) in order to assess what the market thinks of how that particular company is being run.

The value of a share is, theoretically, a measure of the expectation of the size of the dividend that the company will pay out over time. Much of the market fluctuation is, however, the result of investors seeking to make profits from trading in the shares rather than owning shares simply for the income they provide.

1.5 HORIZONTAL AND VERTICAL INTEGRATION

Conglomerates consist of a number of differing businesses operating in a variety of sectors of industry and commerce, and have generally grown from a smaller, single-activity company. Other businesses have been acquired over a period of time for a variety of reasons. They may simply have been attractive, profitable private limited companies that could not develop further without the resources of a larger organisation. On the other hand, they may have been struggling enterprises that the conglomerate's board of directors considered could be bought cheaply and, with careful management, turned into valuable, profitable businesses.

Whatever the original reason for their acquisition, the component companies of such a conglomerate provide a good example of *horizontal integration*. The diverse and seemingly unrelated nature of their activities provides the group with a broad base of operation in a number of businesses, industries, countries and even continents.

Conglomerates are now largely out of favour with investors as they prefer companies to focus on a core business and in fact diverse companies today often suffer from a 'conglomerate discount' where the aggregate value of the individual businesses on a standalone basis is higher than for the conglomerate as a whole.

Before we leave the subject of conglomerates there is, of course the opposite to such a diverse group, that being a 'vertically integrated' company. This is, literally, integration from top to bottom within a particular industry. This could be where the one company in the group owns, for example, some forest land, another company owns sawmills, a third is a furniture manufacturing company and a fourth is a chain of retail furniture shops. The major international oil companies are a good example of complex vertical integration.

1.6   COMPANY ORGANISATION AND MANAGEMENT

Now look at **Appendix 3**, which is the organisation chart for the 'shipping services' company in the shipping division of our company example. This enables us to look not only at the operating departments (agency, chartering etc) but also at the service departments. The functions of the service departments are vital even in a firm of a couple of partners and a total of three other staff. The only difference is that the company we are looking at is large enough to need separate departments, while in the small firm or company the tasks would be taken on by the partners or delegated to staff members as part of their duties.

The secretariat

This is vital in any company. In several countries the company secretary is the only member of the company that the law recognises. It is he (or she) who is responsible for complying with all the legal requirements imposed on limited companies. One might find this strange when in real life the secretary is subordinate to the directors. However, directors can theoretically, be dismissed by the shareholders at any annual general meeting of the company and so a more permanent person has to be the point of contact for the authorities such as the tax collectors and registrar of companies.

In the example company we are studying, the secretariat also contains the human resources or personnel department and the importance of this function cannot be over-stated.

In almost every country in the world there are laws relating to employment. In the UK there are employment protection acts and redundancy payment acts as well as other statutes relating to sexual, racial and disability discrimination.

There are legal curbs such as 'constructive dismissal', that prevent an employer from making changes to an employee's working conditions that go to the root of the contract of employment. For example in most countries, an employer cannot suddenly decide to switch its agency staff from an overtime scheme to a shift-working system without their consent. In essence, large or small, a business entity must take its selection, employment and promotion of its staff very seriously indeed.

The accounts department

This is another non-operational section and details of the more mechanical side of the work done by accountants will be discussed later in the text. In the context of company structure, however, it is important to realise that there is more to an accounts department than simply counting and recording money coming in and going out. Money is as much a resource as any other raw material and its proper management can be a significant factor in the profitability of the enterprise.

You may recall from the ICS publication *Introduction to Shipping* how the downfall of many companies that have failed has not been so much an adverse difference between income and expenditure but more that of simply running out of money, i.e. poor cash-flow control.

Credit control

Particularly in countries where high interest rates are the norm, credit control is a vital element in commercial survival. The credit controller's duties go far beyond the relatively simple task of debt-chasing. Deciding who should be granted credit, how much and for how long is the constructive side of the controller's work. Despatching 'final demands' or, worse still, issuing 'writs' to recover debts should be looked on as a failure in credit-control rather than a routine task.

Credit control is only one side of controlling cash flow. In the absence of a better expression, 'debit control' is just as important. One never wants one's firm or company to acquire the reputation of being 'bad payers'. However, many suppliers build into their price structure an element based upon the fact that their customers will not settle invoices until they have received a statement at the end of the month. Some suppliers even offer a discount for payment within a shorter time. Taking advantage of discounts and/or not settling before the appropriate date are essential parts of general cash-flow control.

At the other end of the scale, having large sums of money for long periods earning a low level of interest at the bank or, worse still, sitting idly in a current account, is inefficient commercial practice.

1.7   MANAGEMENT ACCOUNTS

While it was noted above that "there is more to an accounts department than simply counting and recording money coming in and going out", although that in itself is a vital function. Apart from those accounts which a company is obliged to maintain in order to satisfy the auditors, the accounts department's other role is to produce 'management accounts'. These will vary in the level of formality and complexity depending upon the size of the enterprise, but the purpose is always the same, namely to let the operational members of the company know to what extent their labours are profitable. Your first reaction to that statement may be to say "How ridiculous", as if it were not quite obvious that if you fix ships in a chartering department and earn brokerage, it must be profitable. This may not necessarily be the case because there are such things as 'overheads', the costs which have to be borne whether brokerages are being earned or not. Such things as office rents and salaries have to be paid and the problem does not end with these 'fixed costs'. The other costs incurred in running an office (like telephone and internet charges) are just as important and can affect the profitability of a business.

Remember also that overheads have to be paid at specific times regardless of when brokerages, fees and commissions are collectable, so that the accounting information supplied by the accounts department will show not only whether what a company is doing is profitable, but also whether the cash-flow position is under control.

Even such things as economies of scale are not automatic. Take, for example, a port agency operation where the staff is almost at full stretch with holiday or sickness absence having to be covered by a level of overtime working by the other staff that could not be sustained indefinitely. The natural instinct in a commercial situation is always to try to get more business, but in the situation just described, if a new client with four or five small ships a month came along it would not necessarily mean more profit. What it would probably entail is the hiring of an additional staff member, but would the extra income cover that new person's salary?

Managers therefore not only need accounting information, but also need to use it sensibly. The head of that port agency department would have to decide whether they turn down the new business or whether they have sufficient faith in their marketing ability to feel confident of finding yet more agencies so that the new person more than pays for the additional salary costs incurred.

The opposite of that situation is an enterprise which is comfortably profitable and has spare capacity in terms of accommodation, equipment and especially in staff time. In this situation the 'marginal cost' of taking new business is negligible as it would not add to the overheads. The new business should be highly profitable for the company, because once the direct costs of doing that business are covered, the rest is profit.

However, taking business on a marginal costing basis without being sure that it will not affect overheads and so be a loss-maker is a recipe for commercial disaster. Supermarkets often have 'loss-leaders' to tempt people into the store in the expectation that such customers will then buy other things, but this seldom works in a shipping situation.

Some pieces of business are retained simply for the contribution they make to the overheads leaving other activities to supply the profit. However, it is important to ensure that such pieces of business really are being kept for the contribution they make to the fixed costs and not for the sentimental reason that an agent never 'fires' a principal.

Budgetary control

This function shows that there is a great deal more to management accounting. Experience enables a reasonable estimate to be made of the more volatile elements of an expense budget and the possible income. No matter how far out the actual result may prove to be, at least with a budget in place for comparison, it will be possible to see where the variances arose. If these are due entirely to the vagaries of the market, that would have to be accepted, but if the differences are in items that can be controlled then remedial measures can and should be taken.

1.8 STATUTORY ACCOUNTS

It is important, for many reasons, for readers to understand what can be gleaned from the published accounts of a limited company.

Even allowing for the comment earlier in this chapter that "what is revealed is interesting but what is concealed is vital", statutory accounts (those that the government insists upon being produced, audited and made available to the public) can tell the reader a great deal about the company's size and health. The law does not permit them to be deliberately misleading and if you know what to look for, you can learn a lot.

The law may differ from country to country as to the precise form that the published accounts must take, but the basic pattern is almost the same all over the world. There has to be a record of the year's trading and a statement of what the company owns. The first is generally called a **profit and loss account** but it may be entitled 'trading account', 'income and expenditure account', or some other similar name.

Such an account will show the total income (often called 'turnover'). This may be broken down to show income from trading separately from that earned from other sources, such as investment income, profit from sale of assets etc.

Next it will show trading and overhead expenses and take one from the other to show a trading profit (or loss), although many companies simply show the trading profit. It is usual to show the interest paid on bank loans (overdrafts) or other means of borrowing money other than the issue of shares separately from the trading expenses. The resulting figure is the company's profit before tax and when comparing one year against another or one company against another, it is the convention to look at the pre-tax profit.

In the accounts, however, one has to show the tax (which may be called corporation tax, profit tax, income tax or some other similar name) and this provides the net profit figure for the year.

Theoretically this could all be shared out among the owners of the company, but this seldom happens. The more normal procedure is for some of the profit to be retained so that the profit and loss (P&L) account will show the amount of profit being retained, any amount that has already been paid to shareholders as an **interim dividend** during the year, plus the amount of the **final dividend** that the company proposes to pay. It puts it this way because the shareholders own the company and it is for them to agree (or otherwise) to the proposed dividend at the annual general meeting.

There can be more than one type (or class) of share in a company. We have so far been talking about **ordinary** shares but there are also **preference** shares. As the name implies, they have a prior claim on any profits available for dividend because the company is not obliged to pay a dividend to its ordinary shareholders. If it has been a very bad year, the company may decide to recommend no dividend but it may be obliged to pay one to the preference shareholders. It should be noted that most ordinary shares have voting rights in how the company is run while it is unusual for preference shares to have any voting rights.

Another way to own part of a company is to hold **debentures**. These usually have a fixed rate of interest and often are directly related to the company's fixed assets and so would have first claim on the proceeds of these being sold if the company was wound up. The interest on debentures has to be paid before any dividends are even considered. Interest payable to debenture holders, to mortgagees and on bank loans is usually shown separately from the trading figures.

There are many variations on these three basic types of share but such details are outside the scope of this book.

As mentioned earlier, some of the company's profits may be retained either because the company wishes to expand and deems it better to use profits to finance the new activity (either to buy new equipment or simply to provide extra working capital) rather than borrow more money to do so or to create reserves for an expense that only happens infrequently. For example, a shipowner will place money in reserve for the five-yearly survey. Even a small firm will need a reserve if its lease stipulates that the building it occupies has to be redecorated every few years. A very important reserve for a company that has to grant credit in order to trade is the bad debt reserve. If a customer is unable or unwilling to pay its debts then the company will need to have a bad debt reserve and experience will be used to decide how much should be put in reserve for this eventuality.

A prudent company, especially in an unusually good year, will put some profits into reserve with no specific purpose in mind. Such a reserve is then available if an opportunity requiring capital crops up unexpectedly. Furthermore, having money in reserve (which would be sensibly invested) would enable the company to survive a temporary recession in trade, even pay a dividend in a bad year, which is why you may occasionally see a company distributing more in dividends than it made in profits in that particular year.

Published accounts are not obliged to go into more detail than discussed in the foregoing sections, although most companies will append notes explaining certain items in the accounts. Current company law in the UK requires some specific statements to be included in the notes (e.g. details of salaries to higher paid directors/employees).

Readers should also remember that the P&L account is a record of the company's trading activities during the preceding year and its title usually includes the words "For the year ended".

Published alongside the P&L account is the **balance sheet.** This has different words in its title, namely "As at". The balance sheet gives a picture (some describe it as a 'snapshot') of what is owned and what is owed (to and by the company) on that particular day.

The things a company owns are called **assets**, which are divided into two classes. The first are fixed assets, which again are sub-divided into two. The word 'fixed' speaks for itself, as does the word 'tangible' used to describe one of the divisions of fixed assets. A fixed, tangible asset to a shipowner would be a ship or a freehold building. Smaller items like cars, desks and computers come under this heading, so a small firm is just as concerned with fixed assets as a big company.

As a rule of thumb, anything of a permanent nature that can be sold to raise money were the company to cease trading, is a fixed asset, and that definition indicates a problem with fixed assets. Most people know to their cost how something like a car is not worth nearly as much at the beginning of its second year as it was when brand new. This applies equally to ships and desks, so the value they have in the balance sheet has to be adjusted accordingly.

Such adjustments are made by a process of depreciation, which means that the asset's value is reduced by a specific percentage each year. Cars are usually reckoned to have a five-year life and so they would be depreciated by 20% per year. At one time, ships were expected to last 20 years and so were depreciated by 5% per year. The precise amounts by which assets are depreciated are agreed with the auditors, whose job it is to look after shareholders' interests, so that the company is neither over nor undervalued. The amounts by which assets are depreciated become an 'expense' in the P&L account.

Some physical (or tangible), assets (literally assets that can be touched), such as freehold land, can actually increase rather than decrease in value. To show a correct picture, these have to be revalued periodically. This is always a careful balancing act for the chief accountant because one yardstick for measuring a company's health is its 'return on capital employed', meaning that if assets are overvalued it will give an apparently poor result. Conversely, if assets are undervalued, the company will be too attractive to 'predatory' takeover bids.

The other types of fixed (but not tangible) assets are investments. You will recall mention of the fact that a prudent company puts money into reserve for different purposes and that money is invested so that it is kept 'working' while not being used for the company's own business. Of course, a parent of a group of companies would show the value of its subsidiaries as investments.

Quite separately from fixed assets will be **current assets**. These are usually under three headings. One of these will be any cash the company has in its bank accounts.

Another will be **stock** which, although it is tangible, is by no means fixed because the whole idea is to either sell or use the stock in the process of manufacturing whatever the company makes. Stock can be either raw materials, 'work in progress' or finished goods in inventory, and there has to be another balancing act here. After all, to the company as a going concern, that stock has a fairly clearly defined value, give or take some fluctuation in the profit margin. If, however, the company were to cease trading, it is most unlikely that it would be possible to sell that stock at the same price as its value to the active company.

At the beginning of this section we mentioned that the balance sheet contained what was owed (to or by the company) as well as what was owned. It is in the list of current assets that the **debtors are recorded**, the value of that debt being owed to the company.

The company's chief accountant and financial director will already have studied the details of outstanding debts, and will have decided what proportion of these may never be paid. Provision for these will have been made in a reserve for 'bad debts'. The remaining sums will be paid to the company in the fullness of time, and therefore represent part of the company's value.

On the other side of the company's balance sheet to the assets are the **liabilities**, which are what the company owes to others. Here there are two basic headings. One is the value of what is owed to people who have lent the company money. It is not unusual for a small company to prefer to borrow money at an agreed rate of interest (often referred to as 'loan capital') rather than sell shares and, therefore, part of the ownership of the company. Similarly, a big company may decide to borrow money from a bank rather than go 'to the market' to raise capital. That is usually fine as long as the profits come in to pay off the loan, but it must always be remembered that lenders usually insist on some security for loans, particularly banks. This means that if disaster should strike, the banks will be the ones who have first claim on what is left.

When looking at the financial stability of a company, one of the factors to watch is the relationship between loans/overdrafts and share capital, which is referred to as 'gearing'. If a company becomes too highly geared (more and more loans rather than an increase in share capital) the company could be at risk should there be a downturn in trading conditions.

High gearing is not always a sign of poor company health because lenders will not lend without a reasonable hope (near certainty) of getting their money back, but always remember that the lenders will probably have ensured that they get priority should the worst happen.

The other item under the current liabilities heading is what the company owes to its **creditors** and it is the study of these in comparison with the debtors which will give an immediate clue to how well the company is managing its cash flow. **Cash flow** is simply having funds available for all those items that need to be paid for at a defined time. If those who owe you money take longer to pay than the rate at which you have to pay those to whom you owe money, it is only a matter of time before you run out of cash. It does not matter how profitable a company may appear on paper. If it has run out of cash, it cannot carry on.

It is not easy to calculate accurately how a company is managing its cash flow from the sparse information given in published accounts. However, as a general rule, one obviously wants to see current assets being more than current liabilities, but within the detail it is likely to be a healthy sign if the creditors are slightly more in number than the debtors.

As well as current liabilities, most companies will have further amounts to take away from the assets, such as a provision for **contingent liabilities**. For example, if the company were in the middle of defending a legal claim, no matter how confident it might feel about the outcome, the dispute would not exist without the other side also being hopeful of winning. Under such circumstances the auditors would insist on an amount of money being set aside against the possibility of an adverse decision by the court.

At about this stage you may well be asking why this piece of accounting is called a balance sheet. What is presented is a substantial net figure of total assets minus current liabilities. Where then are the rest of the liabilities to establish the balance? You should remember that the original definition of a balance sheet was a listing of what was owned and what was owed, and there is no clearer instance of what the company owes than that money which the shareholders put up as owners of the enterprise. Consequently, the other side of the balance sheet will always be shown as **shareholders funds**.

1.9   QUALITY MANAGEMENT

The needs of customers will only be met if a business has control of the factors that affect the quality of its service. These may be human, administrative or technical factors and can only be controlled if tasks, equipment and procedures are used in the same way every time. These methods can be documented and used to assess the operation. Regular audits have to be carried out to check that procedures are being followed and targets being met. Quality audits and reviews can therefore lead to suggestions for improvements in the way work is carried out to the benefit of the company's clients and thus to the business itself.

Companies may choose to demonstrate their commitment to quality by registration with a nationally or internationally recognised independent assessment body that can testify that the company's systems have achieved a certain international standard. for quality assurance. This process is known as *accreditation* and serves as evidence to the company's customers and to the world at large that it meets certain quality criteria.

Ship management companies were among the first shipping businesses to embrace the concept of quality assurance, as the services they provide to shipowners in a highly competitive field lend themselves documented processes. In recent years the International Safety Management (ISM) Code has adopted a number of documented procedures relating to safety at sea and in effect turned these into a mandatory quality management system.

ISO 9001 is a series of international standards for measuring quality systems. In Britain this was formerly known as British Standard (BS) 5750, and companies that are registered and have achieved the required benchmarks can display the standard designation symbol.

To register, companies have to document their business procedures, prepare a quality manual, and assess their quality management systems. They are then assessed by an independent body, which will measure their performance against the internationally defined standards. Interestingly, this process lends itself to skills and expertise of organisations such as classification societies, whose work in the shipping business routinely requires them to provide independent confirmation of the seaworthiness of ships. As a result, many businesses both within and outside shipping can be seen to display accreditation of their quality systems by Lloyd's Register, Bureau Veritas, Det Norske Veritas and other familiar names.

After the initial assessment and award, businesses are visited at regular intervals by the accrediting body to ensure ongoing compliance. It is absolutely necessary that everyone in the organisation follow the procedures outlined in the quality manual.

The concept of quality is, however, a moving target. What may be of acceptable quality today may not be so in the future as customers' perceptions change. Although most businesses benefit from introducing quality initiatives, there can be problems associated with their implementation, such as:

- costs of inspection, training and material
- time required by both management and staff to make the system work
- different viewpoints on short-term costs and long-term results. Quality initiatives require a long-term view and benefits can be difficult to measure
- changes in culture are not easy and may be resisted.

Therefore an organisation (and its personnel) must be absolutely committed to the concept of quality management if its introduction is to be a success. Likewise the system will need to be reviewed at regular intervals in order to ensure that it is still serving its purpose.

Chemical tanker

Gerardus Mercator – Flemish cartographer 1512–1594

Chapter 2

The practitioners in shipping business

2.1 INTRODUCTION

This chapter and the following two will summarise the main activities within the six disciplines into which the Institute of Chartered Shipbrokers divides shipping business.

To remind you these are:

Dry cargo chartering

Tanker chartering

Sale and purchase

Ship management

Port agency

Liner trades.

You will note that there is an obvious element of inter-relationship between some of them, just as certain matters are exclusive to each one.

Before embarking upon the elements peculiar to each discipline within what might be described as 'our own' part of the shipping industry, it is important to look at one aspect that sometimes gets overlooked.

2.2 THE MERCHANT

It is important for all practitioners in the shipping business to remind themselves on a regular basis that the demand for shipping is a derived demand.

If the buyers and sellers of goods reduce their level of business, the demand for shipping reduces. We have seen this effect clearly in recent years with recessions affecting significant areas of world trade and these effects have often been compounded by the fact that they occurred when there was an over-supply of merchant shipping.

Later we will study some of the mechanisms of international trade, whereas at this stage we are only concerned with those that directly impinge upon our own six disciplines.

If your principal is the merchant, such as a charterer, knowledge of how this business works is vital.

2.3 THE CHARTERING MARKETS

2.3.1 The dry cargo market

In the dry cargo markets, most contracts are for the carriage of bulk raw materials. There are exceptions and we shall look at some of them later.

The traditional contract of carriage for the movement of such materials is the **charter party**. Incidentally, you may well find in other publications, especially in law books, the expression 'contract of affreightment' rather than 'contract of carriage'. However, 'contract of affreightment' has, among the chartering fraternity, taken on a meaning describing a specific type of contract. To avoid confusion, the term 'contract of carriage' is used in the following sections.

A chartering contract is probably one of the clearest examples of a transaction entirely governed by market forces. It is negotiated in a free market, subject only to the laws of supply and demand. The relative bargaining strengths of the two parties will depend on the current state of the market. The shipowner and the charterer are able to negotiate terms entirely free from any statutory interference.

In practice they will almost certainly adopt a customary standard form of charter party that has been developed for the particular trade. Even so, that standard form will probably be littered with additions and deletions and added typed clauses. It will be among these amendments, as well as the rate itself, where the hard bargaining may take place, depending upon the state of the market.

2.4 DRY CARGO CHARTER PARTIES

Most standard forms began by being imposed on the market by the charterers for two reasons. First, they needed a charter party that fitted into their contracts of sale of the commodity itself. Secondly, the charterer would always tend to be in a somewhat stronger position when it came to terms and conditions because charterers are static and so find it easier to band together, even with competitors, to devise terms appropriate to the commodity and suitable to them all. Such strength against a single ship is likely to win the day. In some parts of the world individual charterers could even have a virtual monopoly.

The merchants did not have things all their own way for long. National bodies such as the United Kingdom Chamber of Shipping and international organisations such as the Baltic and International Maritime Council (BIMCO) formed rallying points for shipowners to fight against the more iniquitous charterers' forms. The result has been mutual agreement between the charterers and the owners so that the charterers' terms have been modified sufficiently for the owners' organisations to adopt them. In many cases it has been the owners' side that has eventually published the form for the trade. For example, whenever you see a charter party form the code name for which ends in 'CON' (for CONtract) it is almost certain that it was published by or with the collaboration of BIMCO, which is renowned to this day for its active and successful documentary committee.

Even in cases where the charterers have not had their forms adopted by the owners' organisations, the compilers have been sensible enough to avoid a form too heavily weighted in the charterers' favour.

The existence of standard forms, which command worldwide recognition, obviously facilitates negotiations in which the parties are able to include the phrase 'otherwise con charter' in order to save much time. The printed clauses in so many cases have stood the test of time with legal precedent ensuring that ambiguous wording is avoided.

Unfortunately, when an organisation tries to produce something that seeks to suit everybody it inevitably does not exactly suit anybody and some of the convenience of standard forms is lost due to the amendments and/or additional typed clauses demanded by one side or the other in order to make it fit their precise circumstances. In some trades, the standard form has now become nothing more than a framework on which to hang dozens of extra clauses.

A classic example of this is the GENCON charter. As its name suggests, it is a general-purpose form intended for cargoes or trades for which no specific form exists. As printed, it is heavily weighted in the owners' favour and large areas tend to get deleted and replaced with typed clauses. Such is the conservatism of the chartering world that both sides seem to prefer using a radically amended GENCON than to move over to the more modern and more even -handed Multiform charter published by FONASBA (the Federation of National Associations of Ship Brokers and Agents).

So far we have been considering single **voyage charters** where the ship agrees to go to A to load a cargo of an agreed quantity of a commodity and carry it to B for which the consideration will be a rate of freight probably calculated on a per tonne basis.

Many charterers, however, have more than just one cargo to move and in consequence, may find it convenient (particularly with an eye to fixing their costs) to contract with an owner for the ship to make a series of **consecutive voyages**. This procedure lends itself especially well to trades where it is usual for the ship to make the passage to loading port in ballast.

However, an alternative to consecutive voyages may be needed, especially when the frequency of loading does not coincide with the consecutive voyages of the one ship, or in trades where returning in ballast is not the norm. In such a case the method would be for the charterer and owner to agree parameters covering the frequency of loading, the ranges of size of the ships to be employed and the total quantity to be lifted within a given period. This leaves the owner a considerable degree of flexibility so that they can keep their ships as fully employed as the market will allow, even nominating other people's ships chartered-in by the owner should they not have one of their own in the right position. It is such contracts as these which are known colloquially as **contracts of affreightment**.

Where, however, the charterer's commodity is drawn from a variety of places and sold to several buyers in different locations, neither consecutive voyages nor a contract of affreightment will give the merchant the flexibility they require. This is especially the case if there are marked differences in the speed of loading/discharging at the different places involved. The charterer may overcome this problem by moving entirely away from a contract of carriage based on a rate of freight per tonne of cargo carried and instead, hire the ship on a contract based on time. Not surprisingly , this is called a **time charter.**

In this type of contract, the ship-owner still remains responsible for the technical operation of the vessel and the crew remain its employees. But the commercial direction of the ship is transferred to the time charterer. The charterer now decides where the ship will load and discharge and the time and expense of doing so becomes its concern. All the incidental expenses directly resulting from the commercial trading of the ship will be for the time charterer's account including port expenses. The biggest item of expenditure, after the hire payment, will be the cost of bunker fuel.

The charterer may simply want the ship on time charter for just one voyage but needs the flexibility of a time charter. Such a time charter is often referred to as a 'trip time charter'. On the other hand, the charterer may want the vessel to be at their disposal for several months even years. Over this period the time charterer acts almost as if the ship belonged to them. In fact in law, they will be described as the 'disponent owner'.

One advantage of a time charter, unless the wording is extremely restrictive, is that if the charterer's own business does not require the ship for any part of the period, they can sublet it either on a time or a voyage basis to a third party.

There is, of course, one other form of charter party known in chartering circles as a **bareboat** charter, although lawyers prefer the expression '**demise**' because that word is more akin to such words as 'transfer' or even 'abdicate'. As the name suggests, a bareboat charter transfers the entire job of operating the ship to the charterer so that it is fair to equate this to the original owner abdicating their responsibilities. It is quite usual for the charterer even to change the ship's port of registry and flag for the period of the charter. Such a contract can best be compared to a long-term lease of a house or an office block. To all intents and purposes the bareboat charterer acts as the owner and the outside world sees them as such.

In most cases a bareboat charter is, in effect, an alternative way of financing where the charterer finds it more convenient or beneficial to pay a monthly hire out of revenue rather than raise the capital to buy a ship themselves. Bareboat charter parties are something of a rarity in the working life of the average chartering person and, paradoxically, when a broker does encounter one it is probably more likely to be in the sale and purchase department where some sort of sale-and-lease-back deal is involved.

2.5 THE ANATOMY OF CHARTER PARTIES

There are certain features common to all chartering contracts, a general knowledge of which is essential to any shipping professional.

2.6   VOYAGE CHARTERS

A reproduction of a GENCON (1994) charter party can be found in **Appendix I** – reproduced by kind permission of the Baltic & International Maritime Council (BIMCO). This is the latest revision of a long series of GENCON charter parties dating back to the 1920s. In common with many recently revised charter parties, this appears in what is known as 'box form'. The required information to be inserted in each fixture is conveniently allocated boxes on the front page, so that completing the charter party is relatively straightforward and the salient details can be seen at a glance.

The printed clauses, which are referred to in the top right-hand corner of each box, all appear in Part II, and are numbered 1 to 19.

It must be remembered that all charter parties emerge from negotiations between owners and charterers, usually through one or more brokers, and the resulting agreement may well require amendments to some of the printed clauses. In addition, as the GENCON is designed for non-specialised trades, both parties to the contract may well insist that certain additional clauses particular to their requirements are attached to the standard form.

As a general rule, all the details inserted in the boxes of Part I of the charter party are negotiable, and most will feature at some stage in the offers and counter offers that are traded back and forth during the negotiations. Although the most fiercely contested area may be that of the freight level, the dates and the time allowed for cargo operations may also be crucial to the fixture, as will be seen below. The terms agreed can be crucial to the profitability of a voyage for both the charterer and owner and great care should be taken in agreeing these terms.

By examining the boxes in Part I of the GENCON '94, the first thing to note after the broker's name and address is the date and place of when the 'fixture' (as a chartering agreement is called) was made. Next, there are boxes in which to enter the names of the parties and of course, the name of the ship and its details (registered tonnages, deadweight, and any other characteristics important to the fixture, for example cubic capacity or perhaps the size of the hatches).

Boxes 8 and 9 should not be overlooked. They describe the position of the ship relative to this particular charter. Everyone understands that ships do not run like trains and there are many factors that may affect the vessel's expected readiness to load. Nevertheless, this information should not be taken lightly. Because of the imponderables in terms of time that affect merchant ships, there is usually a span of some days between which the vessel may be presented for loading. If, however, the owner gives an expected readiness for box 9 and then subsequently takes on some intervening business that makes the ship much later than originally intended, they are guilty of misrepresentation. In extreme cases, such misrepresentation could be grounds for the charterer to cancel the contract, and the date when this could take effect is shown in box 21. Boxes 10, 11 and 12 address the loading and discharging ports and the type and quantity of cargo to be loaded. Note that the printed clause 1 to which these details relate qualifies the places of loading and discharging by the phrase "or so near thereto as she may safely get and lie always afloat". Some loading or discharging berths, especially those in tidal rivers where small coasters regularly load, do not have enough water alongside at low tide to allow ships to remain afloat. These are often referred to as 'NAABSA' berths (not always afloat but safe aground). If the ship is fixed for loading or discharging at such a place, this must be specifically agreed in the charter party, otherwise the owner has every right to refuse to put its vessel there.

As far as the cargo is concerned, the charterers are expected to give full details, and if they have fixed the ship for 'a full and complete cargo' they can expect the master and owners to demand sufficient to bring the ship down to its load-line or to fill the cargo space. If they fail to satisfy this request they will be liable to pay 'deadfreight' on the shortfall as if it had been loaded.

Boxes 13 and 14 give details of the freight payable, whether it be so much per tonne or a 'lumpsum' or on some other basis, and how, when and where it should be paid. The options in the printed clause 4 need to be carefully considered in conjunction with these details.

Then comes the all-important clause setting out the rate of freight including how, when and where it is to be paid.

A crucial question in connection with the freight is which party should be responsible for the costs (and risks) of loading and discharging the cargo. The GENCON 1994 charter party only envisages a situation where the shippers pay for the loading and the consignees for the discharging. These are known as FIO terms (free in and out) implying that both loading and discharging operations are free of expense to the shipowners. There are still trades where it is customary for the ship to pay for (or contribute to) the cost of loading and/or discharging and if the GENCON 1994 form was used for such a cargo then a typed clause would have to replace part of clause 5. In the case of a ship having its own cranes or derricks (cargo handling gear often simply referred to as 'gear', for charterers or their shippers/receivers), provision is made to make use of it in loading or discharging, provided that this is expressly agreed in advance by a note in box 15. Note also from the printed clause that the owners expect the charterers to be responsible for putting right any stevedore damage noted by the master during cargo handling operations.

The next clause (clause 6, boxes 16, 17 and 18) introduces a word that is exclusive to the world of chartering, 'laytime', which refers to the time allowed for loading or discharging of the cargo.

This clause may seem surprisingly long to the uninitiated, dealing as it does with when the ship is ready to load/discharge and how long the operations may take. The fact remains that large sections of maritime law books are devoted to 'time counting' disputes and legal arguments about the 'arrived ship' have enriched many maritime lawyers and will no doubt continue to do so. In addition, there are many ways in which laytime can be expressed. In terms of hours or days, as so many tonnes per day, as separate periods for loading and discharging or a total time span for both operations, whether or not time stops counting for bad weather and so on.

The GENCON clause has been refined over the years in the light of successive legal and commercial disputes to avoid all the usual pitfalls, but in reality there will always be scope for further argument.

Linked to when time starts to count and the amount of time allowed for loading and discharging is the penalty for exceeding the agreed limits. A ship only earns income when at sea, not when lying idle in a port. A shipowner is, therefore, anxious to keep the time spent in loading and discharging to a minimum. If the charterers exceed the agreed time, then the owner wants compensation, which is covered by including a rate of 'demurrage' for every day or part of a day by which the agreed time is exceeded. The sum negotiated for this is inserted in box 20 and governed by clause 7.

In some dry cargo trades the converse may also apply, in that the charterers can earn a bonus if they load/discharge the ship in **less** time than agreed. This is termed 'despatch money' and if such an agreement is made it must be inserted as a typed clause in the GENCON 1994 form.

So clauses 5, 6 and 7 cover this dispute-prone area of time in port. Within these clauses there are perhaps a few words and expressions that may be new to you, as below.

Trimming

This applies to bulk cargoes such as coal, where the surface of the loaded cargo needs to be levelled out to make best use of the space available and to minimise the danger of the cargo shifting in the hold during the voyage.

Dunnage

This is timber used to prevent metal to metal contact between cargo and the ship's hold or between (for example) steel plates, and to stop loose items from moving around in the hold during the voyage.

Tallying

This is the name given to the procedure of checking the number of packages, as they are loaded/discharged.

Stevedores

Although technically the name for those working on the ship itself during the loading/discharging, it is often used to describe all the loading/discharging labour.

Agents

The agents referred to in Clause 6 (boxes 18 and 19) are not the port agents who will be appointed by the owners to look after the ship's interests at the loading and discharge ports, but the agents of the charterers who will be responsible for co-ordinating the cargo operations at each end. The appointment of port agents is dealt with in clause 14, and they may be named in a typed clause attached to the charter party.

Clause 8 (the Lien Clause) is designed to protect shipowners from non-payment of freight, demurrage and other such sums due to them.

Remember the date given in box 5 when the ship was expected to be ready to load? The cancelling date (Box 21, clause 9) defines the other end of this period, known as the 'laydays', after which the charterers have the option to cancel the charter party if the ship has still not presented itself for loading. Cancellation tends to be a last resort in most instances, as the charterers are then faced with having to find another suitable vessel to carry the cargo, probably at short notice. Similarly, the owners will have to find other employment for their ship, which may already be on its way to the expected loading port. However, excessive delays may force the charterers to use this sanction.

The remaining clauses deal with such eventualities as collisions, strikes, war and ice, and establish the jurisdiction that will apply in the case of legal disputes or arbitration, an important consideration in international trading.

You will note that clause 12 covers **general average**. This is another expression with a long history and is now covered by an international convention (the York-Antwerp Rules). In essence, general average (GA) is the procedure where if the ship is involved in extraordinary expense to avoid damage to the ship and its cargo owner/s, then the cargo as well as the shipowner contribute to that expenditure. The formal wording reads "preserving from peril the property involved in the common maritime venture". The York-Antwerp Rules lay down how the various parties' contributions will be calculated, a procedure known as average adjusting. All prudent merchants are careful to include general average in their insurance cover.

Brokerage (clause 15) is the commission due to the broker or brokers involved in the fixture, and is their reward for succeeding in bringing the negotiations to a satisfactory conclusion. The amount of brokerage involved is usually between $1\frac{1}{4}\%$ and $2\frac{1}{2}\%$ of the gross freight, depending on whether one or more brokers are involved. Most charter parties, including GENCON 94, now include brokerage on demurrage and on deadfreight (freight paid on cargo not supplied by the charterers, which should have been).

To sum up, a voyage charter will have a 'skeleton', the bones of which are:

- date
- names of the parties
- name of the ship including a description
- loading port
- cargo nature and quantity
- discharging port

- laydays and cancelling dates
- rate of freight and manner of payment
- loading/discharging costs
- speed of loading and discharging (laytime)
- demurrage rate
- brokerages (commissions).

2.7 TIME CHARTERS

Before the days of containerisation, the most prolific time charterers were the liner companies that used time charter to supplement their fleets of ships when demand in the general cargo market exceeded their own resources. In those days the BIMCO-adopted BALTIME charter was most popular. Today the most popular time charter form is the New York Produce Exchange Form, commonly known as either the NYPE or Produce 46. The number refers to the fact that this form has not been revised since 1946, but such is the conservatism of the chartering market that charterers still prefer to use it. This is despite the fact that in 1981 an updated version was compiled and called the ASBATIME. The compiler was the Association of Ship Brokers and Agents (USA) Inc and the text of an ASBATIME is reproduced with its kind permission (**Appendix 2**). Although this is not the most used form, its straightforward clauses and comparatively recent compilation makes it more convenient for the study of generalities of a time charter.

As was mentioned earlier, the objective of a time charter is to transfer the commercial direction of the ship to the charterer while still leaving the technical control with its owners.

Having worked your way through a voyage charter you will find no difficulty with the wording of ASBATIME. You will note that the names of the parties and the ship are similar to a voyage form but the first difference is the inclusion in the ship's particulars of speed and fuel consumption. As the cost of fuel is the charterer's largest item of expenditure after the hire itself, this is a vital component of the agreement.

The duration of the charter comes next. This can be set out in months (even years) or may be for a trip, when the areas of starting and finishing will be entered with an approximation of the time likely to be involved.

Then instead of a loading port there is a place of delivery, again with the stipulation that the ship be "tight, staunch, strong and in every way etc". While the intention is to pass the commercial control of the ship and the risk of the voyage to the charterer, there may well be some dangerous or otherwise unpleasant commodities which the owner does not want the ship to carry. There may also be places that (usually for political reasons) the owner does not want the ship to visit and provision is made to prohibit these.

Those things that the owner will continue to provide and those things that the charterer must provide are clearly set out.

Critically, because bunker fuel is a major item, it is important for the charterers to pay for the fuel they take over on delivery and for the owners to do the same on redelivery.

Then the all-important clause appears that states the daily rate of hire with the stipulation that it shall be paid semi-monthly in advance. Somewhat illogically, the place of redelivery is interposed between the rate of hire and the terms of payment.

One harsh condition relating to hire payment gives the owner the right to withdraw the ship from the charterer's service if the hire payment is not punctually made. In the past, owners have been known to take their ships away to take advantage of an improved market when the hire has been delayed by no more than a day due to a hold-up in the banking system. It is usual, nowadays, to include a 'technicality' clause so that the charterer is given a little time to rectify such a situation.

Like the voyage charter, there is a clause stipulating when time shall start to count. Although not such a problem-prone area as it is in the voyage world, it is still important to give the charterer a few hours to 'take over the reins'. Again, like a voyage charter, there is also a laydays/cancelling clause.

An important point that has to be covered is that of suspending hire payments for any time the vessel is not available to the charterer – the 'off-hire' clause. The usual reason for a ship to go off-hire is some temporary technical breakdown. On a long period charter, however, the ship may have to go off-hire in order to keep up to date with routine maintenance. The off-hire clause covers all of this, including the consumption of bunker fuel reverting to owner's account while the ship is off-hire.

The other clauses are fairly straightforward, ranging from what happens in the event of a war down to the charterer's right to paint its own colours on the funnel so long as they repaint it at the end of the charter.

You are advised to read the entire wording carefully and pay particular attention to those clauses that clearly describe the manner in which the master (captain) of the vessel has to comply with the instruction of the charterer. It is quite a balancing act for a captain on time charter, who has to co-operate fully with the charterer without ever losing sight of their primary loyalty to the owner.

To summarise, the basic elements of a time charter include:

- date
- names of the parties
- ship's name and particulars
- speed and fuel consumption
- duration
- places of delivery and redelivery
- trading area/limitations
- rate of hire
- laydays/cancelling
- commissions.

2.8 INTERNATIONAL CHARTERING MARKET AT WORK

Dry cargo chartering takes place in many cities throughout the world but the London market still holds a dominant position, partly because of its geographical position. Brokers and traders in London can do business with Asian countries during the morning and with the Americas during the afternoon. The steady improvement in communications systems over recent years has meant that chartering is no longer carried out face to face as it was in the past through institutions like London's Baltic Exchange, where once brokers and traders met daily on the 'floor' to do business.

Intelligence that once was gathered by brokers on the Exchange is now reported through networked computer systems, internet-based information pages and of course from telephone conversations between brokers, who still depend on their network of contacts to keep in touch with the market.

Many practitioners regret the disappearance of face-to-face contact in the shipbroking world. The idea of personal contact tended to reinforce the sense of a business community and markets such as that presided over by the Baltic Exchange in London were regulated by a code of ethics. This code served as a guarantee of certain standards of commercial behaviour to all those whose business was transacted there.

The Baltic Exchange still exists, even though its role as a marketplace is no longer pre-eminent, and the ethical code it represents is as important in today's shipping business as it always was.

Who are the practitioners in the shipping communities of London and the other shipping centres of the world? We have already talked about charterers and their agents, owners and their brokers, but it is important to understand that agents and brokers can have a variety of roles. At one end of the scale, the agent or broker may be a member of the charterer's (or respectively owner's) own staff. Most of the major grain 'houses' for example have their own chartering departments as do many of the Greek shipowners who have their bases in London and New York as well as Piraeus.

Next comes the 'exclusive' broker. A charterer or owner who selects one firm or company through which to place all their business on the market could well have the best of both worlds. Such a broker may have several clients, which enables them to acquire a wide range of market intelligence from which they are able to advise their principal while ensuring that there is no conflict of interest that might interfere with other loyalties to principals.

Finally there is the 'competitive' broker. Some principals are confident of their own ability to assess the market and, instead of advice from their brokers, they want speed. To achieve this they place their business on the market through several brokers who are in competition with each other to bring suitable business to the principal. The advantage of this system is the ability to cover the market in the shortest possible time, while the disadvantage is human nature. Even the most ethical broker is likely to shy away from advising the principal to hold off while the market moves more in their favour if the risk is that the business may be done by a competitor.

In the area of competitive broking it is important not to overlook the intermediate broker. Markets such as London and New York may well be bringing together principals in two other countries, each with their own local broker or agent. The intermediate broker must, of course, walk a very narrow path because he or she does not represent either of the parties and so must take care to be strictly even-handed. The role of the intermediate broker is coming under threat from improvements in modern communications that mean a principal can speak directly to brokers in many different countries and time zones.

2.9   THE TANKER MARKET

This market may justifiably be described as highly specialised. Not only does its specialisation make it clearly separate from the dry cargo markets but also tanker chartering itself sub-divides into separate specialities.

Crude oil

The first market-within-a-market is the movement of crude oil. This is the trade that often hits the news whenever there is political unrest. It is also prone to be in the headlines from time to time because of the catastrophic pollution problems that can arise when one of these giant ships becomes a casualty and spills its cargo along a coast.

It is the carriage of crude oil where one can see ship size as the economy of scale in its simplest form. More or less the only limiting factor is the depth of water needed to accommodate the draught of these giant ships. It was probably the closure of the Suez Canal during one of the earlier Middle East conflicts which forced tankers to go round the Cape of Good Hope, that proved the viability of ignoring the canal's size limitations and building the biggest ships that yards could produce. Even when the Suez Canal reopened, very large crude carriers (VLCCs) were still profitable to run in competition with those tankers small enough to transit Suez. The VLCCs were in the region of 150,000–200,000 tonnes and such was the success of such vessels that ultra large crude carriers (ULCCs) of around 300,000 tonnes followed them.

Several naval architects designed a million-tonne tanker, but none has ever been built, and the largest tanker ever to trade was 555,843 tonnes dwt. Three things finally conspired to stop the continuing upward trend in tanker sizes. The first was draught, as there was some doubt about the sense of building ships which, for example, could not proceed up the English Channel (although plans to overcome this local difficulty were well under way). Furthermore, many voices were being raised against a vessel capable of polluting huge stretches of coastline, that needed more than 1.5 nautical miles to effect an emergency stop.

Second, the economy of scale idea was being questioned because the sheer size of ships was taking designers into areas of pure theory. Some ships had developed cracks and other signs of strain in unexpected places and to build-in the additional strength required was likely to increase rather than reduce the price per deadweight tonne of construction.

Finally, the economic recessions of the 1980s and 1990s created a slump in the demand for oil and the notion of 'big is beautiful' ceased among crude carriers. Nevertheless, the largest ships afloat are still tankers in the crude-oil trade.

Petroleum products

The second tanker market is that for refined petroleum products. The oil-consuming world quickly found that the most economical system was to site the refineries near the end-users. This is another example of making the economies of scale work in shipping. In simple terms, if a quantity of crude oil is to be refined into different products then it makes sense for the largest carrier (crude) to make the longest voyage. The science of refining has developed considerably over the last few decades and continues to do so, resulting in an ever-increasing variety of by-products from the original crude oil.

Refined petroleum products are those products extracted from crude oil and they range from jet fuel and gasoline through ever more viscous liquids such as gas oil and diesel, to the heaviest of fuel oils, which are almost black in colour and often have to be heated to ensure that they are at the correct viscosity to be pumped. Oil products are often categorised as 'clean' or 'dirty'. Clean petroleum products require particular care in handling and need to be carried in clean tanks to ensure they do not suffer contamination. They include products such as petrol (gasoline), aviation spirit, kerosene (paraffin), naphtha and lubricating oils.

Chemicals and other products

Many will argue that to combine all the rest into one category is quite wrong as there are indeed several specialities remaining.

Chemicals comprise the main part of this third category, most of which are among the more sophisticated by-products from oil refining, including solvents, feedstock for manufacturing plastics etc. Some are particularly volatile, and others highly toxic, even to the extent that quite a small amount inhaled or touching the skin can be serious or fatal.

One thing these cargoes have in common is the need for absolute cleanliness of the ship's tanks' Generally, the materials do not undergo any further refining so a cargo that is 'off-spec' (not up to specification) could be rendered useless to the buyer.

One source of impurity can be the surface of the tanks themselves and chemical carrier tanks normally have epoxy or zinc coatings. However, the coatings can also contain a source of impurities if previous cargoes have leached into the coating, and the most sensitive of cargoes are often shipped in stainless-steel tanks.

Chemicals can be shipped as full cargoes but more often they are shipped in smaller quantities by parcel tankers. As the name implies, these ships are designed to carry many different consignments in separate tanks, which require highly complex and sophisticated pipework and pumping arrangements.

By-products from the petroleum industry are not the only liquids to move in parcel tankers. Sulphuric acid and liquid ammonia are regularly moved in bulk, as are vegetable oils and wine.

Probably the most highly specialised tankers are those constructed for the carriage of liquefied natural gas (LNG) or liquefied petroleum gases (LPG), such as butane and propane.

2.10 TANKER CHARTER PARTIES

The tanker market has its single voyage and consecutive voyage charters as well as time charterers and contracts of affreightment. The last-named are probably even more common in the liquid trades than in dry cargo.

Tankers require quite different charter parties from dry cargo and many of these have been compiled by the major oil companies such as Shell, BP and Exxon for their own use. Independent bodies such as Intertanko (the trade association representing independent tanker owners) and ASBA (the US based Association of Ship Brokers and Agents) have compiled forms for others to use.

Appendix 3 is a copy of SHELLVOY 6, the latest edition of Shell's tanker voyage charter party, launched worldwide by Shell International Shipping and Trading in 2005. SHELLVOY 6 consolidates the additional clauses and amendments used by Shell since the previous version was published in 1987 and introduces some new provisions relevant to the current trading environment.

Appendix 9 is a copy of Shell's time charter form.

The basic construction of a tanker charter is the same as for dry cargo and, in some respects, the clauses are simpler. This is partly due to the fact that oil installations are almost invariably set well apart from port complexes so that 'readiness to load' and 'time counting' clauses are far less complicated.

It is common for oil installations to work 24 hours a day, 365 days a year. As a result, it is not uncommon for a loading/discharging clause in a tanker charter to be no more than three or four lines.

Commonly, 72 hours is often the total time allowed for loading and discharging, to a large extent regardless of the size of the ship because tankers are usually equipped with pumps commensurate with the size of vessel. Demurrage works in the same way in tanker charters but despatch is seldom if ever encountered.

One major difference between voyage charters for dry cargo and those for tankers is in the way the rate of freight is expressed. In dry cargo charters it is usual for the rate to be expressed as so many dollars or other unit of currency per tonne of cargo carried. With crude oil, the requirements of producers and refiners can change very quickly so that flexibility in the choice of loading and discharging places is highly desirable, even in a single voyage charter, and essential in a charter for more than one cargo.

To cover this problem a system was evolved after the Second World War to have an agreed schedule of nominal rates covering every combination of loading and discharging ports for crude oil. This enabled a charterer to fix a ship naming, for example, the whole of Indonesia as the loading area and the whole of Europe for discharge, with the scale sorting out the precise rate for the finally nominated loading and discharging places. The fluctuations in the market were accommodated by agreeing the scale plus or minus a percentage.

Originally there were two scales, one published in the USA and another in the UK, but after suffering this complication for over a decade the two bodies came together and produced Worldscale. Although the scale has undergone amendments, it is still in use today and will probably continue far into the future.

As an example, a fixture at Worldscale 90 would imply that the charterers and owners have agreed that whatever the eventual loading and discharging ports might be, the freight will be 90% of the Worldscale rate for that voyage.

The Worldscale organisation has calculated a standard freight rate (in US dollars per tonne) for a 'standard' tanker for almost every conceivable voyage on which crude oil can be carried. These are reviewed at regular intervals, and subscribers to the service can access the relevant rate at any time. In the unlikely event that a rate for the voyage has not been calculated, Worldscale will produce one.

By studying reported crude oil fixtures, it is straightforward to see how the crude oil freight market fluctuates and reacts to market forces. Forecasting it is a much more difficult task.

2.11 TANKER MARKET AT WORK

The tanker market is dominated by the oil majors (Shell, BP, Exxon, Total), by oil traders and by state-owned oil companies such as Saudi Aramco.

At one time, the oil majors owned large fleets, supplemented by many ships on long-term time charter. In recent years the trend has been for the companies to reduce their owned fleets and to depend more on chartering ships from the independent tanker owners.

Companies will have their own chartering departments and so it is quite usual for only one broker to be involved between the owner and the charterer. The principal skills of such brokers are their knowledge of which ships are open and where and their speed of transmitting information of cargoes coming into the market and quickly placing the right ships before the charterers.

The wide fluctuations in prices following the oil crisis in the 1970s saw an increase in speculators and, as a result, oil traders appearing as charterers have become commonplace.

Naturally the charterers in the chemical trades are many and varied, while the charterers for the less usual cargoes such as gas, vegetable oils, wine etc tend to be fewer in number.

The way in which the trade itself is divided into specialities is clearly reflected among the brokers. It is by no means unusual to find individuals who have spent most of their working life in a particular market such as crude oil, refined products, chemicals or vegetable oils.

Car carriers

26

Chapter 3

· ·

Shipping sectors

3.1 SHIP SALE AND PURCHASE

There are three distinct sectors of the sale and purchase market: newbuilds, secondhand and demolition.

The most active market is the trade in secondhand ships, as it is rare for a ship to stay with the same owner from builder's yard to scrapyard. A ship can have an active life in excess of 20 years, although a depressed freight market can shorten a vessel's economic life as newer more economical ships get preference from the charterers. In such a timespan the requirements of a ship operator can vary considerably.

Unlike the chartering markets, where the principals are clearly specialists in their respective fields of activity, any shipowner is at some time a buyer or a seller. Selling may be motivated by the need to dispose of ships made redundant by changing patterns of trade, or ships becoming obsolescent in a particular owner's fleet and sold to make way for more modern additions, or simply as a way for the owner to make money through the buying and selling of the shipping asset.

3.2 SCRAPPING

The final incentive to sell is when a ship becomes too old or uneconomic to keep in a trading condition at which point the only course left is to sell it for scrap.

Age, unfortunately, is not always the reason for scrapping, as was seen during the oil crises of the late 1970s and 1980s. Just prior to that period, there seemed to be no limit to the demand for crude oil carriers and every yard that could build VLCCs or ULCCs had full berths and bulging orderbooks. Then came the recession and with it an inevitable massive reduction in the demand for oil, resulting in some tankers going straight from the builder's slipway to a lay-up berth. In such a situation, many owners could find no prospect of trade for their ships and no funds to pay for 'mothballing' them, so demolition was the only course left.

It is not unusual for a shipowner to sell an obsolescent ship for scrapping even though there may be buyers at a better price wanting the ship for trading. There are two reasons for such apparently paradoxical behaviour. The first is the fact that under some fiscal regimes, obtaining a high price for a ship near the end of its life may actually be disadvantageous from a taxation point of view.

The second reason is if a ship should be sold for trading to make room for a new addition to that owner's fleet, there would now be two ships where there used to be only one. Ships naturally tend to be suitable for particular trades, so there is the risk that the seller would be creating problems for themselves by providing a competitor with a ship with very low capital cost to amortise. Such an owner may decide that selling the redundant ship for trading rather than for scrap could risk increasing the amount of competition against the newly acquired ship.

3.3 NEWBUILDS

At the opposite end of the time spectrum is the purchase of a new ship.

There are various stages at which the shipyard and the owner may sign a new build contract. The parties may agree to a contract based on a very general specification with clauses to take into consideration variations, which come about as the detailed drawings are produced. Often the builders will produce models of the hull and try them out in testing tanks. After such tests, quite appreciable changes may be agreed. For example the tank-test may prove that the ship will perform even better if it is made longer than originally contemplated. This could be a bonus for the buyer if length is not critical because of the extra cargo that can be carried but it may not feasible if the additional length of the vessel means that it will not be able to trade to some of the important ports.

The buyers may employ their own naval architects to produce detailed drawings of the desired ship and then approach several shipyards and ask each to tender for building the design.

Some yards offer standard designs. This was a very popular trend towards the end of the 1950s when owners were looking for a general-purpose ship to replace the second World War 'Liberties'. Such vessels as 'Freedom' types and the very successful SD14 (14,000 ton, 14kt Standard Design) built in the Sunderland yard of Austin & Pickersgill. Today there are no standard designs with a brand name, but several yards have off-the-shelf designs for such things as Panamax bulk carriers.

The obvious advantage of a standard design, or indeed accepting the design of a ship built for another owner, is not only the saving of a great proportion of design costs but also the fact that many of the bugs will have been eliminated the first time round.

Naval architecture is a highly developed art, but the problems of the forces of sea and weather cannot entirely be simulated in the laboratory.

Some ship designers now argue that the economy of scale in ship sizes has reached its limit. They consider that any further increase in size will require so much additional reinforcement to cope with the stresses that the cost per deadweight ton will increase rather than decrease.

3.4 SECONDHAND TONNAGE

By far the majority of transactions in the sale and purchase market are for secondhand ships and, as mentioned earlier, it is in this sector where sale and purchase brokers are most active.

Brokers tend to build up connections with potential buyers and sellers and also with other brokers. As with dry cargo chartering, it is more the rule than the exception for the buyers and the sellers to have their separate brokers.

Invariably, S&P brokers produce and circulate particulars sheets for the vessels that they are trying to sell to brokers of potential buyers.

The strength of any S&P broker's office lies in the maintenance of records of all ships currently available for sale and an extensive database of vessels for sale can be a competitive advantage.

The following is a brief outline of the process of selling a ship.

Once the potential buyer's requirements are known, the particulars of ships that meet their criteria are submitted. These particulars are compiled from information supplied by the owners (or their brokers) and augmented by details shown in Lloyd's Register or the books of other classification societies, such as Bureau Veritas, Germanischer Lloyd, Det Norske Veritas or American Bureau of Shipping.

The most important features are: deadweight and draught, the year and place of build, dimensions, cubic capacities, cargo handling appliances, arrangements of decks, water ballast capacities, numbers of holds and hatches, details of machinery and its builders, engine power, speed and consumption, bunker capacity, classification and special survey position. This will be followed, as far as specialised ships are concerned, with matters such as numbers of passengers, details of refrigerating machinery, pumping capacity of tankers and container and car/trailer capacities.

In the case of ships that are being sold for scrap it is desirable to give information regarding the light displacement, whether the propeller and spare propeller are of bronze or iron and whether there is a spare tail-shaft on board.

Then come two very important features, the price and the position for inspection and delivery.

Nowadays the vessels particulars are usually sent electronically, but the forms (see **Appendix 6**) that brokers normally use for supplying these details should always have on them wording such as "These particulars are believed correct but no guarantee is given of their accuracy."

A buyer who is interested in a ship will normally ask for a capacity plan to see the arrangements for carrying cargo and probably also a general arrangement plan giving such details as the accommodation, requirements for which vary from country to country.

It is not the function of the broker to express an opinion regarding the condition of a ship except to state should they know for a fact that something is wrong with it. Usually either the buyer's superintendent or possibly a firm of consulting surveyors deals with the inspection. One of the most important things to do when buying a ship is to inspect the classification records ,as these give the full history of the ship during the time it was under construction and also give details of damage it may have suffered, together with the classification surveyor's requirements at its various periodical surveys. With a little experience it is very easy to see where the weak spots are and these will naturally be very carefully examined by whoever carries out the physical inspection of the ship.

Sometimes the inspection takes place before the negotiations and sometimes offers are made subject to the examination of the ship. It rarely happens that the ship is drydocked at the time of this initial inspection.

A firm offer for a ship for running purposes is normally made with a time limit on the following lines: "*£X less commission, delivery at such and such a port on or about a certain date, with the buyer's option to cancel the agreement if it is not delivered by a later date, the ship's class at the time of delivery is to be maintained without qualification.*" (In other words, repairs which have already been deferred for a specific period with the consent of the classification society, together with any further repairs that could be placed in the same category, are to be put right). Then there is the question of damage, which is not within the province of the classification society. Surprisingly enough, a ship's class can be fully maintained even if its accommodation has been completely burned out and all its lifeboats washed overboard.

Formerly this matter was dealt with by using the words "free of average" but owing to a decision a few years ago in the commercial court, it is now more usual to use a phrase such as "free of damage recovering from underwriters", or words to that effect.

Another very important condition is that dealing with additional payment for stores on board and bunkers. It is also usual to stipulate that all the vessel's trading certificates shall be valid at the time of delivery. Where it applies it is usual to insert a condition regarding government permission either to buy or sell the ship.

Finally there is the matter of drydocking and a typical clause might read:

"The sellers shall place the vessel in drydock at port of delivery and if rudder, propeller, bottom or other underwater part or parts be found broken, damaged or defective so as to affect the vessel's clean certificate of class, same shall be made good at the sellers' expense to classification society's satisfaction to retain vessel's class without qualification.

"While the vessel is in drydock and if required by the buyers the tail-end shaft shall be drawn. Should same be condemned or found defective so as to affect the vessel's clean certificate of class it shall be renewed or made good at the seller's expense to the classification society's satisfaction to retain vessel's class without qualification. The cost of drawing and replacing tail-end shaft shall be borne by the buyers unless classification society requires tail-end shaft to be renewed or made good.

"The expense of putting in and taking out of drydock and the drydock dues shall be paid by the buyers unless rudder propeller bottom other underwater part(s) or tail-end shaft be found broken damaged or defective as aforesaid in which event the sellers shall pay these expenses.

"Sellers shall pay all costs of transporting the vessel to the drydock and from the drydock to the place of delivery."

The best way to explain this clause is to imagine the actual drydocking of a ship for inspection prior to delivery.

First, it is the responsibility of the sellers to bring the vessel to the drydock ready for docking and subsequently from the drydock to the berth or place of delivery. The expenses involved in doing this, including tugs and pilot (if required) are for sellers' account and these expenses should not be confused with those involved in actually putting the vessel in and out of drydock and the drydock dues.

Once the ship is in the drydock, an inspection of the underwater parts will be carried out by the classification society's surveyors who are, in effect, neutral referees and cannot be influenced by either sellers' or buyers' technical representatives, except to the extent that if a repair is called for the method of carrying it out may be discussed.

If the classification surveyor requires any work to be done on the underwater parts, the cost of putting the ship in and taking out of drydock and the drydock dues will be paid by the sellers. On the other hand, if there are no such repairs affecting the ship's class, these expenses are for the buyer's account.

As a separate matter buyers have the option of having the tail-end shaft drawn. This is the shaft that finally connects up the main engine with the propeller. If they elect to have it drawn for examination it is done at the buyer's expense unless it is condemned or found defective so as to affect the ship's clean certificate of class. If it is condemned or defective, sellers would not only have to pay the cost of drawing and replacing the shaft plus the repairs thereto, but also the drydocking costs even though no other repairs were required on the other underwater parts.

You will perhaps understand the importance of this clause, particularly to a buyer, if you appreciate that they have, as a rule, bought the ship without seeing what it is like below the waterline and consequently must have adequate safeguards against the unexpected.

Generally there is a certain amount of haggling in the matter of price and conditions, but when agreement has been reached it is the seller's brokers' duty to draw up a memorandum of agreement. This usually consists of clauses as follows:

1. A preamble giving the names of the buyers and the sellers, the name of the ship and a brief description of her.

2. Price and times for payment. Payment is normally made by a 10% deposit on signing memorandum of agreement in joint names of buyers and sellers or their agents and the balance together with the release of this deposit is paid on delivery, which is usually within three days after readiness for delivery.

3. Conditions of sale, also time and place for delivery.

4. Drydocking clause.

5. Additional payment for bunkers and stores.

6. Exclusion of hired items such as radio, satellite communication equipment and radar, if not the ship's property, and particularly in passenger ships it is usual to exclude badged articles.

7. All plans and classification certificates to be handed to buyers.

8. Ship to be at seller's risk until time of delivery.

9. A caveat emptor clause, absolving sellers from all faults or deficiencies of any description after delivery subject, of course, to the conditions of the contract being fulfilled.

10. Clauses dealing with default on either side. If the buyers default the sellers can cancel the contract, retain the deposit (which will normally be held in an escrow account) and obtain compensation for any further loss, all expenses, plus interest thereon. If the sellers should default, buyers may cancel the contract and the deposit will be returned with interest. In addition sellers would be required to make due compensation for any loss caused to the buyers.

11. Automatic cancellation of the contract and return of the deposit to the buyer in the event of the loss of the ship before delivery.

12. An undertaking to change the ship's name and funnel marking before trading under new ownership.

13. Arbitration clause.

14. A clause providing for commission to be paid to the brokers concerned.

In addition, this agreement contains all other terms of the firm offer finally accepted.

In general international use there is a printed form called the Norwegian Shipbrokers' Association Memorandum of Agreement SALEFORM 1993 (see **Appendix 7**) This is reproduced with kind permission of the Norwegian Shipbrokers' Association.

When the time comes for delivery of the ship, this is carried out by the execution and delivery of a bill of sale, which (under English law) must be executed under seal.

The bill of sale is handed over against a letter releasing the deposit and a banker's draft for the balance of the price. If extra payment for bunkers and stores is provided for, this is dealt with at the same time.

As insurance runs from noon to noon this is usually the time selected for delivery.

The broker should make sure that the new owner has attached insurance and also ascertain whether the following documents are being handed over either on board or on shore:

Certificate of registry

Load line certificate

Deratisation certificate

Safety construction certificate

Safety radio certificate

Safety equipment

Certificate classification

Certificates plans.

Occasionally the broker is asked to register the vessel in the new owner's name, in which case they have to go to the registrar with the following documents:

Bill of sale

Declaration of ownership

Appointment of managing owner or ship's husband

and in addition if the buyer has not previously owned a ship:

Articles of association

Certificates of incorporation

Appointment of public officer.

In many instances, the bill of sale must be signed before a notary public and bear the visa of the buyer's consul.

Sales for demolition are, of course, much simpler with no problems about drydocking registration or classification, but may require the arrangement of towage contracts or cargo voyages to the ultimate port of destination.

3.5   FINANCING THE PURCHASE

In addition to the technical and commercial aspects of sale and purchase, it is essential for the S&P broker to understand the problems a buyer faces in finding the money to pay for the ship.

Large companies may do this from their own resources or by increasing their share capital, but a common method of financing the purchase of a ship is via a bank loan secured by a mortgage.

The prudent buyer will have entered into preliminary negotiations with their bank so that the general principles will have been covered. These mainly involve the bank satisfying itself that the ship will be able to earn enough money to repay the loan and the interest. One subject that may delay concluding negotiations could be the time it takes for the buyer's bank to ensure that the proposed ship complies with the business plan originally agreed between the lender and borrower.

In the case of newbuilds, it is customary for progress'payments to be made. There may be five or six of these, the first on signing the contract, another when the keel is laid and so on until the final payment at the time when the ship is handed over after successful sea trials have been carried out.

Loans for the purchase of newbuilds can in some cases be negotiated with the banks through the shipbuilders themselves.

Normally, credit arrangements for newbuilds follow international agreement, which stipulates that up to 80% of the purchase price may be advanced with the buyer providing the other 20% out of their own resources.

3.6   VALUATIONS

Many S&P brokers have built up a sufficiently good reputation for their services to be engaged to act as valuers. There are several purposes for which an independent expert opinion of a ship's value at a specific time may be required such as:

Law cases and arbitration

General average (where the ship's value is needed to determine the owner's contribution to the average settlement)

Salvage awards

Insurance claims

An independent check when the purchase is being made by a government

Revaluing assets in a company's accounts

Loan to value covenants under bank financing.

Such valuations establish the market value of the vessel at a particular time and should not be confused with a survey. The valuations given by S&P brokers are always given with the qualification that it is assumed the vessel is in good trading condition appropriate to its age.

Valuation is by no means easy, as the S&P market fluctuates like the freight market and it is seldom that two ships are identical. A high degree of expertise is needed when giving an expert opinion that can be substantiated if required.

3.7   SHIP MANAGERS

Although reference to 'ship managers' tends to make one think of one of the many independent companies offering management services, the most obvious place to find ship management is in a shipowner's office. Whether it is a shipowner's department or a separate organisation, the job is the same.

In some owners' offices, it may be difficult to see just where the chartering department ends and the operational elements of management begin. In others the management is kept entirely separate, which permits, in several cases, shipowners to offer a management service to ships of other owners in addition to their own, so maximising the output of the different sections.

For the purpose of this section we will look at the task undertaken by independent ship management companies. These can vary widely depending upon the shipowner's requirements. The most complete service arises where the ship has been bought as an investment and the owner wishes to have no actual part in running it. In such a case (sometimes referred to as 'total management'), the manager treats the ship as if it were part of their own fleet, including making the commercial decisions about the trades in which it will operate and what freight rates to accept.

At the other end of the scale the owner may simply wish to subcontract one element of management such as the technical department. Today the part of management most often subcontracted is that of crewing.

3.8   CREWING

Owners managing all other aspects of their ships will still often subcontract the supply and management of crew.

The most obvious reason for this practice is cost, and it should be recognised that this is a practice adopted by many reputable owners, not just unscrupulous owners of substandard ships. Owners often 'flag-out' to other countries, which enables the ships to be managed from the original country while being crewed in accordance with the laws of the flag country. The benefits of this can include reduced tax on company earnings, lower registry fees, bilateral and multilateral trading agreements, limits on owner liability, reduced ship survey fees and fewer restrictions within the flag requirements on ownership qualifications.

It is important to remember that shipping is an international trade in which the ships of different countries compete in a common market, irrespective of the cost of living of individual countries. Salaries for jobs ashore will be higher in wealthier countries and, to attract crews from that country, the owners often have to match or exceed shore wages. In some cases, the situation is further complicated by trade unions that have negotiated higher wages. Going to sea is often no longer considered an attractive career option, with demographics increasingly making it difficult to source officers and crew from within the home country.

A typical situation may be a US owner with ships under the Liberian flag and crew supplied by contractors in the Philippines. British ships have discovered they can have, to some extent, the best of both worlds by changing flag to the Isle of Man. Under the Isle of Man registry, ships fly the British flag, but do not come under English law. Owners are not obliged to collect or contribute to social security payments or collect personal income tax from their employees.

Contracting overseas agencies for ships crew is not a new practice and for many developing countries the supply of international crew has become a major invisible trade export.

There will always be more unscrupulous shipowners who wish to operate at an absolute minimum cost and level of conditions, regardless of the effect on welfare and safety. However, there are three forces acting to counter such practices.

1.   The natural reluctance among most charterers/shippers to entrust their goods to sub-standard operators.

2.   The international agreements to operate port state control that allows any country to immobilise ships in ports if they are patently unsafe.

3.   The safeguard against undue exploitation of ship's crews exercised by the International Transport Workers' Federation (ITF).

Almost all transport unions throughout the world are affiliated to the ITF, which is dedicated to ensuring that seafarers receive adequate wages and conditions. This means that, should the ITF decide a ship should be immobilised until a suitable pay and conditions agreement is agreed between employer and crew, it can easily ensure the ship is held up by the labour unions in the port.

3.9 TOTAL MANAGEMENT

At the other end of the scale from simply providing crews is the task of providing a complete service. This activity is substantially the same whether it is for the company's own ships or for outside clients. In addition to crewing, ship management can generally be divided into a further three parts.

3.9.1 Technical

In this department will be found senior shore-based masters and chief engineers often referred to as marine and engineer superintendents. Their jobs include ensuring that stores and spares are properly purchased and directed to the ships. They have to react quickly to any sort of accident or technical issue, often flying out to the scene of a problem in order to oversee repairs. Their most important routine task is to do all that is necessary to ensure the ships are maintained to the standards set by the classification society including monitoring the ships through their special surveys and ensuring the safe management of the vessel.

3.9.2 Operations

Once a decision has been made as to the ship's employment, it is this department that has to make it happen. It will of course have to be involved before the decisions are made, because it is in the operations department that the ship's capabilities are known.

Operations departments in shipowners' offices may often include the decision-makers. Those who determine what business will be negotiated and what rate of freight or hire will be accepted; it will be they who 'authorise' the brokers to make firm offers. To do this effectively they will have to be highly skilled in the art of voyage estimating, the specialised form of budgeting that enables the value of different pieces of business on offer to be compared one with another and each with the running costs of the ship concerned. They and the technical department must always liaise closely. For example, it could be ruinous if a drydocking were to be due and the operations staff committed the ship to the other side of the world from where the drydock was stemmed.

3.9.3 Administration

This third section deals with all the essential administration such as insurance and cargo claims and the all-important task of accounting. In the same way as the technical people and operations have to liase closely, so too do the accounts personnel have to have a close cooperation with both the others.

Not the least of this is the comparison of the actual outcome of a particular voyage with the estimate which was made at the time it was fixed; wide differences will need investigating and the data for future estimates adjusted if necessary.

3.10 THE CONTRACT

Owners and managers are, of course, free to draw up a contract between them in any way they wish but BIMCO (the Baltic and International Maritime Council) has produced a standard ship management agreement, SHIPMAN 2009, which is reproduced by kind permission of BIMCO, see **Appendix 9**. It is rare for such a form to be used without some amendment or addition but it serves as an excellent checklist to ensure that both parties cover all the necessary points.

Later we will explore the legal relationship between a shipbroker and their principal and in almost all other cases it is one of pure agency. In ship management there are some areas where the managers could well be contractors (ie principals themselves), yet agents in others, all in the same contract.

At this stage it is not necessary for you to consider this aspect in detail but you should be aware of it when reading the terms and conditions in the contract form.

Discharging 'in the stream'

Chapter 4

Shipping sectors (continued)

4.1   PORT AGENTS

A senior ship's captain once described the duties of his port agent in one simple sentence. Pointing along the length of this ship he said, "When I am at sea, all this is my responsibility; when I reach port I am looking for someone with whom to share that responsibility."

In the first part of the chapter we will be looking at the agent for tramps, tankers and similar ships. These types of ship normally trade under a charter party (rather than in a liner service) and for which the agent's remuneration is almost invariably an agency fee.

Regardless of whether the ship is a dry cargo tramp vessel, tanker, liner, container or one of the many other specialised types of ship, the reason for an agent is the same. The precise duties will naturally be different depending on the ship, the cargo and of course the locality, but the reason why the agent is there will always be the same. That is, to look after all the needs of the ship and its personnel while it is arriving at, staying in and departing from the port.

The first thing to clarify is that we are talking about an *agent* and where there is an agent there has to be a *principal*. Identifying the principal is a vital first step for the port agent for many reasons. The agent will be expected to expend substantial amounts of money during the time the ship is in port and establishing where this money is coming from has to be a priority.

To the outside world the agent will be seen as representing the ship and in going about this work the agent will generally feel themselves to be in this role.

You may at this stage wonder if this all sounds too easy, and that the agent's principal must obviously be the owner of the ship. In most cases that is likely to be true, but what happens if the ship is on time charter? Time charters invariably include, in the clause about who pays for what, such words as "charterers shall provide and pay for all fuel, towage and pilotage and shall pay *agency fees*, port charges". Legal parlance can be helpful here because you will often encounter the expression disponent owner in the preamble of a charter party for instance, and this title includes time charterers.

So you should now be getting a clearer picture because the principal for whom the agent is acting must be the one who pays the agency fee. But the actual owner may want things done for which the time charterer is in no way responsible (such as repairs or crew changes) and we have already visualised the agent representing the ship. It definitely presents a dilemma at times. The time charterer is expected to instruct their agent to act in all ways as if their principal was in fact the owner of the ship, but it is not always as easy as that.

When the time charterer makes the appointment, there is no direct contractual relationship between the agent and the actual owner. This may not be too important when such duties as the agent carries out for the ship (which are not the time charterer's concern) are matters that any agent would consider to be purely routine. It becomes rather different if such tasks are extensive and complex. In such cases a direct contract is more appropriate from the legal point of view and, on the purely commercial side, when the expenditure of the agent's time and expertise goeswell beyond the value of the fee agreed between the time charterer and the agent.

Of course there is a remedy. The range of tasks can be spelled out and an appropriate fee agreed between the actual owner and the agent appointed by the time charterer. But what if the instructions from the actual owner create a conflict of interest with the time charterer? A skilful agent can often handle such a situation without causing either party any distress but both sides need be made aware of the agent's position.

If necessary the agent has to revert to working exclusively for their principal (the time charterer) and the actual owner will have to appoint a separate agent.

By now readers who have had some dealings with charter parties will be asking, what about charterer's agents? It is true that in some badly drafted voyage charter forms you will encounter the words "vessel to be consigned to charterer's agents at port of loading (or discharging)."

What the more responsible compilers of charter forms put is: "Owners to appoint agents nominated by the charterers at port of (etc)".

Legally, the agent always represents the owner or disponent owner, so why should there be so many cases where charterers stipulate that they should nominate the agents at loading or discharging port, or both?

There are several different reasons. Take, for example, some tanker charters where it is not unusual to find a charterers' agents clause. Major refinery jetties cost many millions of dollars to operate and the companies are keen to have the ships using them represented by agents who understand the trade. By nominating an agent expert in tanker agency the company is sure of receiving communications it can trust, and it will be dealing with someone who 'knows the language'. Ship owners seldom try to resist such appointments, because they also benefit through being represented by an agent who is an expert in the trade.

Another reason could be the need to protect trade secrets. This has, for example, been particularly noticeable in the coal trade. Many agents where coal is imported are connected with one of the importers. No charterer would want to risk an owner appointing one of the charterer's competitors as the ship's agent, so they insist on the right to nominate who shall be appointed. It is normal for owners to agree to this, but they would usually include an amendment to the charter party stating that they will accept the agent provided they are competitive, to ensure that the agent cannot charge them an exorbitant fee.

Inevitably, the charterer expects a quid pro quo from the agent being nominated, which is usually in the form of keeping a supervisory eye on the charterer's interests.

There is seldom, if ever, any contractual relationship between the charterer and the agent they nominate, although there are cases where the charterer demands a share of the agent's fee as an introductory commission.

Once again, the agent who is nominated by a charterer has to ensure there is no conflict of interest and, if there is an area of possible dispute between charterer and owner, that the agent maintains a completely even-handed approach. In many cases the owners are by no means satisfied with the agent's ability to avoid favouring the nominating charterer. In this situation the owner may appoint a 'supervisory' or 'protecting' agent to look after the owner's interest. In this case the supervisory agent would expect to deal with the 'domestic' requirements of the ship, such as stores, cash snd crew travel, They will also need to keep in close contact with the 'charterers' agents' over such matters as working times and statements of fact to ensure the owner's interests are protected.

Except in those trades such as tankers (where the owners would probably be just as happy to appoint the expert agent even if they were not nominated by the charterer), owners generally dislike the stipulation of charterer's agents.

One of the many reasons why an owner may dislike charterers' agents clauses is that there may be no opportunity to check on the financial stability of the nominated agent, but the owner is still expected to remit a substantial sum of money in advance of the ship's call.

4.2 THE AGENT'S FEE

Although it may seem strange to introduce the subject of remuneration before considering the agent's tasks, there is some logic to discussing the question of fees directly after having covered the subject of the methods of appointment.

In most countries the agents have formed themselves into some sort of association. In Britain they did this in 1911 when the association that eventually became the Institute of Chartered Shipbrokers was formed. Most associations produce some sort of tariff of agency fees and at one time such a tariff or scale of minimum agency charges was mandatory upon all members of the association concerned. This is rarely the case today as the mandatory nature of such scales is now illegal in many countries. The USA has had its anti-trust laws since the end of the last century. The United Kingdom extended its Restrictive Trade Practices Act to cover services during the latter part of the 1970s and this prohibition of mandatory scales of charges is reinforced by the free competition clauses in the Treaty of Rome, which created the European Community. The argument in support of outlawing mandatory scales is that they protect the sub-standard agent and deter the better ones from striving for greater efficiency. Those in favour of tariffs argue that keeping the fees the same but competing in quality of service provides protection enough for the consumer.

Owners still seem to welcome some sort of tariff for agency fees (just as much as they do for tugs and pilots) so that they can more quickly calculate their voyage estimates. Most tariffs, even when only advisory rather than mandatory, tend to have some form of sliding scale based upon the size of the ship from which the basic fee is calculated with variations (usually additions) for non-standard tasks.

There is an argument that says what agents are selling is their time and that the same amount of time is expended on a 50,000 tonner as on a ship of 150,000 tonnes. The converse of this does not work, however, because you could take the same argument down perhaps to a 15,000 tonner, the owner of which would heartily object to paying the sort of fee appropriate to the responsibility involved in attending a ship 10 times bigger. The consequence is that most agency fees scales are based on a delicate balance of time, responsibility and size, the last being, in reality, a question of what the market will bear.

Under most anti-competition laws it is not an offence to base your charges on the scale. The offence would be for two or more agents to agree among themselves to charge the same, or for the institution publishing the scale to attempt to make it obligatory.

Whether a tariff is in existence or not, except in those few countries where there is a mandatory scale, it is important for the agent to agree the fee before the ship arrives. Almost invariably the fee does not include the agent's out-of-pocket expenses, such as the cost of communicating with the owner; cables, telex, faxes, telephone, the cost of travelling to and from the ship, (cab-fares or a car mileage charge) and similar items. These will be charged to the owner but will have to be justified in exactly the same way as any other items in the disbursement account.

Some ships require the expenditure of more time and effort than others but, except in the case of truly extraordinary circumstances, the same fee is charged for the same size/type of ship. The differences mean the agent takes the rough with the smooth in the hope that things average out in the end.

4.3   THE AGENT'S DUTIES

These were referred to at the beginning of the chapter as that of looking after all the needs of the ship and its personnel while it is arriving at, staying in and departing from the ports, but perhaps it is time to be a little more specific.

Before arrival

The first thing the agent must do is to acknowledge the appointment. At this stage there are two vital things to be done. First, establish whether the appointee is to be responsible for settling the disbursement account. This is not as elementary as it may sound because there have, sadly, been many cases where the appointment has been made by the ship's managers. Then when the actual owner has fallen into financial difficulty the managers have averred that they were only agents and have successfully avoided settling outstanding items.

Of course the intimation may come from the charterers and it is then up to the agent to contact the owners.

The second vital action is to provide the owner with a *pro forma* disbursement account, which will include the intended agency fee. The *pro forma* at this stage need only be in round sums under the main headings of expenditure, but the object is to receive advance funding from the owner.

Other tasks before the ship's arrival will include liaising with the shippers or consignees to determine where the ship is to berth and to maintain contact with them so that the necessary labour and equipment is ready at the appropriate time. Pilots, tugs and boatmen (for mooring) will all need advance warning.

During this time contact will be made with the ship itself not only to establish its expected time of arrival and to give berthing details but also to learn in advance of any urgent requirements,. The most common request of which is a supply of cash in local currency.

On arrival

A good agent meets all ships on arrival unless the captain asks to delay this meeting. At this first meeting, which may include the first officer and the stevedores, all requirements in connection with the cargo, the ship and its personnel will be discussed. Apart from the actual cargo operations the ship may need some repair work and members of the crew may need medical or dental treatment. The agent must always ensure they bring the captain's cash and the crew's mail to this first meeting.

Remember that in some ports, the agent is not allowed to set foot on board until the port health and/or the customs officials have boarded it. In many ports today, however, the ship may obtain *free pratique* by radio, confirming that none of the ship's personnel is suffering from an infectious disease, after which the health authority grants permission to enter the port and make contact with people from the shore.

It will be around this time that the agent will have to lodge various forms with such authorities as the customs, the port authority and the administration of lighthouses. To some of these the agent will have to pay (or commit themselves to pay) substantial sums of money. The largest proportion of the ship's disbursements (except for stevedoring) is committed at this stage, which is why advance funding is vital.

The vital action in the commercial area that the agent has to take at this stage is to ensure that the written **notice of readiness** is properly tendered to the shippers or consignees. There are more arbitration and court battles about time counting than any other single area of dispute.

This chapter is not the place to explore the finer points of what constitutes a **ready ship**, with all the complexities of demurrage and despatch claims. The tendering of the notice of readiness is the thing that 'starts the meter ticking' for the calculation of laytime, and possibly the consequent demurrage or despatch. This should be looked upon quite separately from when loading/discharging actually started.

At least once a day, or more frequently if circumstances so dictate, the agent should advise the owner of the ship's progress and prospects.

Upon departure

The liaison with the ship will continue throughout the ship's stay at whatever frequency the circumstances require, and a careful note of the progress of loading/discharging will be kept in the agent's office. This will particularly record any stoppages caused by bad weather, machinery faults, strikes etc.

When the loading/discharging is finished, the agent will be in a position to complete a statement of facts, a *pro forma* of which is included as **Appendix 10**. Ideally, if time permits, the agent should get the captain to check their own log against the **statement of facts** and add their signature to the latter. The signature of the loading/discharging terminal manager should also be sought and the statement should be sent to the owner without delay.

It is upon this statement of facts that any claim either for demurrage or for despatch will be based. It is not for the agent to debate the legal niceties as to whether demurrage is due or despatch earned – they simply have to ensure that the facts are 100% accurate.

In good time to coincide with the ship being ready to cast off, boatmen, tugs and pilots need to be called up and when the ship sails the owners and the agents at the next port of call have to be notified.

After departure

The job now is to gather together the invoices or other vouchers for all the expenditure made on the ship's behalf. Then, when they are all to hand, a disbursement account is produced. **Appendix 11** is a typical example of the way such an account should be laid out. A voucher for every item of expenditure will accompany the account. There will be a balance in favour either of the owner or the agent. In the former case, the balance should be sent back to the owner without delay while an agent should lose no time in seeking any balance due to them.

4.4   LINER AGENCY

In the Institute's materials, this discipline is entitled **liner trades** because the work is the same whether it is carried out by an independent agent or by departments within the liner operator's own company. For simplicity, however, this chapter will look at the tasks as they are found in the office of an independent agent.

The other headings under which we have so far looked at in *Shipping business* – the different jobs that fall under the general term of shipbroking – have all tended to be tasks done by individuals or small teams. Even ship management with its various departments will tend to comprise several small groups of people. Liner work is the only form of shipbroking that can be called labour-intensive'.

In addition to employing a larger number of people, liner work involves a wide variety and different levels of skill. There are some tasks that are purely clerical in nature while others require an ability to 'think on one's feet' within the legal aspects of the contract of carriage between the liner and its users. Perhaps the easiest way to tackle this part of the chapter is briefly to examine the different skills that the liner trades demand.

4.5   DEALING WITH THE SHIP

Liner agency is not always port-based, but more will be said about that later. This section will focus on the agent whose appointment also includes attending the ship in port.

Obviously, much of what was covered in the first part of this chapter will apply as much to liners as tramps and tankers. Dealing with customs, health and port authorities on behalf of the ship and looking after the requirements of the personnel are much the same.

The major difference is that with a chartered ship it is probable that the cargo is all one commodity and the loading/discharging arrangements will have been made at the time of the charter. With a liner there may well be many hundreds of separate consignments so that discussions with stevedores have to start well before the ship arrives. Arranging the stowage to ensure safe trim as well as having the right cargo accessible at each discharging port is obviously the responsibility of the ship's command but the agent has to ensure that all the information about what cargo has been booked is provided as early as possible.

Long before the ship arrives, a suitable berth has to be arranged; if the liner is carrying break-bulk or non-containerised cargo the berth has to be one with a suitable transit shed in which to accommodate the cargo discharged from the ship (imports) and to assemble the cargo that will be loaded on board the ship for export.

Container carriers have to go to a dedicated container berth and much of the stowage decisions will have to be made before the ship arrives. This tends to be a job for an expert with a good computer program to assist.

4.6 DEALING WITH OUTWARD CARGO – MARKETING

Although liners adhere to a schedule (or try to do so) the many hundreds of shippers and their forwarding agents have to be made aware of which ship is due at what time and for which destinations. This usually means some form of advertising plus active salesmanship. Unlike all other aspects of the shipping business we have studied, the marketing of space in liners is almost like selling an actual physical product. Competition is usually fierce, so that a sales force, often full time representatives (in the past called 'canvassers') have to be on-the-road all the time.

While dealing with more than one principal in the same trade is seldom a problem in the tramp/ tanker agency world, it is considered impossible for an agent to canvass for more than one liner service in the same trade. Potential conflict of interest is a serious consideration for a principal when choosing an agent. With an increase in the number of liners operating in some of the major trades, it is becoming difficult for principals to find a good quality agent who is not already committed in certain of these trades.

The outward freight department personnel not only take the bookings but also have to provide information about when and where the cargo should be delivered to the port and answer any other queries from the shipper. Most importantly, they have to calculate and quote the freighting cost to each potential shipper – and liner freight tariffs are notoriously complicated.

In law it is the shipper's responsibility to declare dangerous goods (explosive, inflammable, toxic etc) but no law book protects a ship from catching fire or the crew from being poisoned. Therefore, liner agency personnel also need to be able to recognise potentially hazardous cargo and cross check any suspect material with the shippers and with the IMO's code on the carriage of dangerous goods (the IMDG Code).

4.7 DEALING WITH OUTWARD CARGO – DOCUMENTATION

The amount of paper used in the liner business must be responsible for the decimation of more forests than all the rest of shipping business put together. Every consignment will have a **mate's receipt** handed by the shipper to the exporter when the cargo is first taken on board. A standard shipping note may precede this or **dangerous goods note** if the cargo is first delivered to the port authority, terminal operator or whoever controls the transit sheds.

In the meantime, the shipper has to present a set of **bills of lading (B/Ls)** to the liner's agents, which will be signed by or on behalf of the captain when the mate's receipt shows that the cargo has been shipped on board. A set of B/Ls can comprise three originals and anything up to a dozen copies.

The liner's agent retains at least one of the copies and data from it is used to complete the **manifest**, which is a comprehensive list of all the cargo in the ship. This will be produced in several copies, for the file, the owner, the ship, the customs and, of course, the discharging port.

Before being signed, each B/L has to be checked against the mate's receipt to ensure that the description and quantity in the B/L agrees with what has actually been shipped and then it has to be freighted or calculating the freight due.

If the freight is to be paid at the loading port it is customary for a **freight account** to be produced and unless there is an arrangement for the shipper to be granted credit, the B/Ls are not passed back to the shipper (with the all-important 'Freight Paid' endorsement) until the money is handed over. If the freight is to be collected at discharging port then the amount due is entered on the B/Ls.

Therefore, it is not unusual for as many as 20 sheets of paper to be involved for a single consignment and there can well be a thousand consignments in a deepsea liner. Widespread use of computer systems at least ensures that several documents are produced from the same input of data, which eliminates some of the manual checking, but even so there still has to be a very large human as well as paper component in the movement of liner cargo.

4.8 DEALING WITH OUTWARD CARGO – CONTAINERS

The process described so far relates to cargo loaded directly into the ship often referred to as break-bulk cargo or conventional cargo to differentiate it from cargo in freight containers.

The introduction of containerisation moved a great deal of manual work off the quayside, and moved a substantial amount of extra work into the liner agent's office.

With conventional cargo, the agent simply takes the booking and advises the shipper to which transit shed the cargo should be delivered. The stevedores can then load it on the ship. With containerisation, the agent takes the booking, then arranges for the necessary container(s) to be available for the shipper. All such container movements to the shipper and then to the docks have to be monitored so that the agent now needs a **container control** department. If the shipper elects to use the door-to-door service then it is the agent's responsibility to arrange for the container to move from the depot to the shipper's premises and then to the docks, which means that the agent also needs a **transport** department.

The foregoing assumes the shipper to have sufficient cargo for a full container load (FCL) but if this is not the case and the shipper has less than a container load (LCL), they present this to a nominated depot as if it were conventional cargo.

The line will usually have contracts with depots to put such LCL cargo into containers. The agent will of course have to monitor the depot's work and ensure that the LCL containers duly reach the ship at the right time, together with a packing list (like a miniature manifest) for each LCL container.

4.9 DEALING WITH INWARD CARGO

Before a liner is due at the agent's port it is normal for a manifest of cargo for discharge to be received by the agent well in advance of the ship's arrival. The manifest details include both the name and address of the consignee for each item of cargo, or the name and address of a 'notify party'. The latter situation is usually when the cargo has been sold with payment via a letter of credit and the notify party is probably the eventual consignee, the bill of lading has been issued to 'order' rather than to a named consignee. The purpose of this is to 'open' the bill of lading (like a cheque drawn to cash) and this enables the banks involved in the payment transaction to hold the bills of lading as security until payment is in fact made.

Although the notify party is often the actual consignee this is not always the case, and indeed even the consignee named in the manifest may no longer be the consignee when the ship arrives. One role of a bill of lading is that of a document of title. This not only enables an 'order' bill of lading to be held as security for payment, but even a bill of lading to a named consignee may be endorsed to another party (this can happen an infinite number of times). That party then has title to the goods described in the bill of lading and can claim them when they arrive.

On receipt of the manifest the agent will notify all the parties or consignees (although, paradoxically, they are not legally obliged to do so) and the bill of lading holders will present their documents at the agent's office. Where freight is payable at destination they will also be required to make payment before their goods are released. In most cases these days, the agent issues a **delivery order** in exchange for the bill of lading. Such an order is an instruction to the ship, port authority or terminal operator to deliver the consignment to the person named in the order.

The department doing this work is probably the most vulnerable spot in the whole of the liner agent's organisation. There may be scores, possibly hundreds, of consignments on each vessel, and probably 99.9% of them will require only routine handling. Yet the inward freight department always has to be alert to the risk of releasing cargo without receiving an original bill of lading and may encounter the occasional forgery. The point is that it is not simply the amount of freight that is at risk but the total value of the cargo. If fraud is being attempted it will tend to be for high-value goods.

The agent will have arranged transit shed space before the ship's arrival if the cargo is break-bulk. With containers requiring more or less the reverse of the loading procedure, it involves special attention being paid to ensuring that the empty container is returned ('resituated' is the container expression) to the correct depot.

One further duty for the inward liner agent is that of dealing with any cargo claims. These are less prevalent in containerised traffic, but with break-bulk cargo there are often a few cases of cargo damaged in transit or less cargo delivered than is stated on the bill of lading. A cargo claims department is inevitably an unproductive part of the organisation, but when done professionally it makes for good public relations. After all, its sole purpose is to establish as painlessly as possible whose insurance company pays for loss or damage and the Hague/Hague-Visby Rules are there to determine the degree of liability that the ship has to bear.

4.10 DEALING WITH THE PRINCIPAL

When a liner has sailed away, the task of reconciling the financial account is a highly complex affair. Apart from normal disbursements, there will be substantial stevedoring charges, tallying costs, transit shed rental etc. If containers are involved there will also be road/rail haulage accounts and depot handling charges to be processed.

The ship owner obviously wants the balance in their bank as quickly as possible and will, therefore, expect the agent's accounts department to be just as efficient as all other parts of the agent's organisation.

The gross amount of money collected by the agent for a liner's call can be substantial and a prudent principal takes good care to investigate the financial stability as well as the reputation of any agents they appoint.

4.11 THE LINER AGENT REMOTE FROM THE PORT

Countries with no coast line of their own still export and import goods and liner companies will want a sales organisation there. Sometimes lines operating to countries that do have their own ports may find it convenient to have the marketing in the 'hinterland' carried out by a different agent from that handling the ship itself. Even in the UK where it is impossible to live more than 80 miles (130km) from the sea, it was by no means unusual for the ship to be looked after by one agent and the cargo to be obtained by a 'loading broker'.

The duties of such agents will vary from case to case: some may simply take the booking and leave all the documentation to the agent at the port. While in other cases the hinterland agent will complete all the documentation while often also acting as a forwarder to get the cargo to the port.

4.12 THE AGENCY CONTRACT

In many cases the contract between the owner and the agent for a tramp/tanker agency may be no more than one line in the appointment email. Generally, however, the duties of a liner agent have to be spelled out in more detail. Furthermore, an agent has to 'staff-up' to handle a liner service and so needs a contract of reasonable duration in order to justify the commitment to take on several additional employees.

There is no set pattern for a liner agency contract but the Federation of National Associations of Ship Brokers and Agents (FONASBA) has produced a printed draft in the form of their Standard Liner and General Agency Agreement a copy of this is reproduced with FONASBA's kind permission as **Appendix 12**.

A study of the clauses helps in understanding the range of different duties a liner agent may be expected to perform, and the way in which they can expect to be remunerated for them.

Safe alongside

Ferdinand Magellan – Portuguese explorer 1480–1521

Chapter 5

• •

Business ethics

5.1 WHAT ARE ETHICS?

Everyone knows what ethics are until you ask them to define them. The word itself comes from the Greek language and it translates almost exactly into the Latin word for morals. Philosophers have been writing learned theses on these subjects since the written word emerged. Some equate ethics to the difference between good and evil or right and wrong or virtue and vice, but not *exactly* any of these.

So not only is ethical behaviour tricky to define, it is also a moving target. We are prepared to accept some business practices today that would have been considered quite unethical a hundred years ago. In some parts of the world the practice of unofficial payments made to individuals to obtain preferential treatment is accepted, if not entirely approved of. In other countries this would be utterly condemned.

We tend to gain our understanding of ethics from the environment in which we work, from our colleagues and competitors alike and from the business community of which we are a part of.

5.2 ETHICS IN SHIPPING BUSINESS

The law looks after the problems of crime, tort or breaches of contract but one needs the mutual trust of the unwritten law in order to keep the wheels of our particular industry turning.

Examples are probably the easiest way to look at the subject. Take a chartering situation where several brokers are competing with one another to get the charterer to work through one of them. The sure way for this to come about is if a suitable owner opens the bidding with a firm offer. One way of achieving this would be for a broker to present to the owner a fabricated offer, pretending that this emanated from the charterer. They would, of course, ensure that the pseudo offer was not one where there was any risk of the owner accepting 'clean' but attractive enough for the owner to make a counter offer which the deceitful broker can then carry to the charterer as if the owner had started the negotiations. That sort of procedure is clearly unethical.

That example also shows the clear division between what is unlawful and what is unethical. If the fabricated offer had indeed been accepted clean, the charterer whose name had been used would almost certainly repudiate the contract and the owner would then have had a clear legal case against the errant broker for 'breach of warranty of authority'. As, however, the unethical broker was cunning enough to make sure their offer would not be acceptable, there is no contract to repudiate, no damages to claim so no legal case to bring against them.

Ethics in shipping go much further than this one example because principals must be able to trust their agents and brokers and vice versa and brokers have to be able to trust each other.

You will hear in your legal studies how a B/L is *evidence* of a contract, the contract almost always being only what is discussed in a telephone conversation.

Ethics demand that one resists the temptation simply to take the easy way out and to use lies to explain away situations where one knows that no contrary proof is possible. That sort of temptation, not to exert oneself to do the best possible, can occur in any aspect of shipping business.

The Baltic Exchange, in London, has always been especially particular about ethical behaviour. It is perhaps in a fortunate position because of the examples set in the days of daily, face-to-face contact among those using that market place. It is much more difficult to do a 'dirty trick' to a fellow broker when you are likely to meet them and/or their friends the very next day. Furthermore, the Baltic's attitude to ethical behaviour enabled its governing board to discipline members for a breach of ethics. It did not have to wait until a law had been broken or a contract breached.

The Baltic is one of the few organisations to have produced a written code of ethical behaviour, which members must adopt in order to be accepted. Naturally enough, the Baltic's Code concerns itself specifically with shipbroking and concentrates on carefully defined areas of behaviour that are deemed to be unacceptable. To flout any of these rules is to risk expulsion and loss of reputation.

While the world outside the Baltic Exchange does not have the same ability to exert discipline, the shipping world is a fairly tight-knit community and persistent breakers of the unwritten laws eventually become known and find they either have to mend their ways or risk isolation. It is fair to say that self-regulation in ethical behaviour throughout shipping business depends as much on the fear of loss of reputation and loss of livelihood as on the altruistic observance of business ethics for the good of the profession.

The one definition of ethics is that which is summed up so succinctly in the motto of the Institute of Chartered Shipbrokers: 'Our Word Our Bond'.

5.3 MARITIME FRAUD

Fraudulent practice in one form or another is common to many areas of commerce, and imposes a considerable cost on the law-abiding community in terms of losses directly attributable to fraud and the price of precautionary measures taken to try to prevent it.

The shipping business is the perfect vehicle for a number of fraudulent practices that tend to take advantage of the high degree of trust upon which the industry depends.

5.4 INSURANCE FRAUD

Unscrupulous shipowners, in league with dishonest merchants, have been known to over-insure a ship and its cargo and subsequently arrange for it to sink in bad weather in a remote location, claiming far more than the ship or its contents were worth.

The celebrated case of the tanker *Salem* illustrates a large-scale fraud that almost succeeded. Under the name *South Sun*, it loaded 195,000 tonnes of crude oil in Kuwait for an innocent Italian charterer in Genoa. On passage through the Indian Ocean the vessel's name was quietly changed to *Lema*. It anchored off Durban and illegally discharged its cargo (which had since been sold to another oil company for $56 million), refilling its tanks with seawater to give the impression of being still fully laden.

Continuing on its illicit voyage, now under the name *Salem* it mysteriously sank after an explosion off the coast of Senegal. Had it not been for the fact that the officers and crew, when picked up from their lifeboats by the rescue services, had their suitcases with them the intended claim for the loss of the ship and her now non-existent cargo might well have been met.

Insurance companies have their own investigators to make enquiries into any suspicious losses, but even though they may save their underwriters from fraudulent claims, it may be difficult to track down and prosecute the perpetrators. Insurance frauds are not, as some dishonest parties might claim, 'victimless' crimes. The insurance companies and their underwriters may eventually recover their losses through the premiums paid, but the burden is borne at the end of the day by all those honest parties who take out insurance and pay their premiums in the first place.

5.5 DOCUMENTARY FRAUD

We are all aware of what a B/L looks like and the important role it plays in international trade as proof that goods have been loaded on a ship as a document of title to those goods, and as a form of security.

We are also probably aware that in our own offices there are drawers full of blank B/L forms of various types, any one of which could be typed up, signed, stamped ORIGINAL and would be indistinguishable to the unpractised eye from a genuine bill representing real cargo. How are we expected to know that the signature is not that of the master or their authorised agent?

The ease with which documents in shipping business can be forged, altered, fabricated or otherwise adulterated is not lost upon the criminal fraternity, giving rise to a series of fraudulent documents presented to banks in support of letters of credit or to shipping companies for release of cargo or to innocent individuals as documents of title, all of which are calculated to obtain funds or goods by deception.

5.6   OTHER AREAS OF FRAUD

Major incidents of fraud tend to make the headlines, but there are far more frequent incidents, that may never be detected. Even though the figures involved for each individual may be small they are nonetheless damaging to the business of shipping and collectively amount to millions of lost dollars a year.

As many liner operators are aware, shippers are frequently tempted, when booking cargo, to 'under-measure', reducing the volume of their cargo upon which they will eventually pay freight. In some cases this will only be discovered by sharp-eyed deck officers during loading operations, or if the company carries out spot checks on the dimensions of cargo delivered to the port in advance of shipment. Such fraudsters are trading on the fact that their under-declaration will not be noticed, and that even if it is they will simply claim that this was an innocent error. The cost to the carrier of carrying out such checks of course eventually rebounds upon the innocent as well as the guilty. In this way it can be seen that the victims of fraud are not simply those who are the prime target of dishonest behaviour but the wider shipping community.

Another example, in which parties may collude quite innocently, is the so-called 'letter of indemnity' or 'back letter' issued by a disreputable shipper of cargo to a master or his owners in exchange for a clean bill of lading. For example, if, a cargo of chemicals in drums on pallets is loaded, and the chief officer of the ship notices that many of the drums are secondhand, rusty, dented and leaking, the master is unlikely to sign a bill of lading without insisting that it should bear a clause to this effect. If they do not, they and their owners can be held responsible for the condition of the drums upon discharge. In order to secure a 'clean' bill of lading to obtain full payment from the consignee (whether through a letter of credit or otherwise), the shippers may offer to indemnify the master and owners against any claim for damaged cargo, issuing them a letter accordingly. This may indeed protect the owners from any subsequent claim, but it has the effect of giving the shippers a bill of lading that misrepresents the condition of the cargo. The bank, the consignee, or an innocent third party, may then be induced to part with payment for the cargo as described in the bill of lading. Had they been aware that it was in fact in leaky, rusted, dented and secondhand drums, they may well have decided not to do so and are thereby the victims of a fraud.

5.7   OTHER CRIMINAL ACTIVITIES

Students should be aware of a range of criminal activities involving shipping business which, whilst they may not be classified as fraud, are nonetheless illegal and a threat to the reputation and integrity of the shipping community. Among these are such activities as smuggling, where contraband goods, arms or drugs may be concealed in cargo, or within the vessel itself – often without the knowledge of the cargo or shipowners.

Illegal immigrants are also frequently smuggled by sea with or without the complicity of the carriers. In fact there have recently been a number of cases where bogus crewing agencies have attempted to obtain entry permits for illegal migrants by pretending that they are seafarers due to join a ship in the intended country of destination.

5.8 DETECTING AND AVOIDING FRAUD

International fraud connected with shipping business is a major problem, not simply for the victims but also for the business as a whole. However, the difficulties of detecting and preventing fraud are considerable.

International fraud is frequently very sophisticated. In cases where such activity has been discovered, it has often been found that the fraud has been perpetrated over a long period of time without the victims even realising.

Even when companies discover that they have been the victims of a fraud, they are frequently reluctant to admit the fact, as it does not reflect well upon their reputations or their security systems. In one case a key staff member of a liner agency was found to have taken bookings from a number of shippers on a freight prepaid basis. However, he put the bookings through the system as 'freight collect' issued his own receipt (on company letterheads) to the shippers and pocketed the freight. He then made out duplicate bills of lading on the line's form, but stamped "Freight Paid" which he issued to the shippers, who were none the wiser. It was inevitable of course that rather irate consignees would demand to know why they should have to pay the freight twice to obtain the goods and would quickly alert the line. Not surprisingly, the subsequent investigations revealed that the employee had left with the proceeds of the deceit.

Without the assistance of the law-enforcement agencies such victims are unlikely to be able to track down the offender themselves, and so the criminal may go unpunished and be able to perpetrate the same fraud on another unsuspecting party.

Sophisticated criminals will frequently use to their advantage the protection of different jurisdictions worldwide, especially those where freedom of information is highly restricted, and from which extradition is difficult. This makes the pursuit of criminals both expensive and time-consuming, and is calculated to put off even the most determined victims.

There are, fortunately, a number of measures that companies (and individuals) can take to avoid becoming victims of fraud.

Checking the *bona-fides* of customers and clients is a straightforward precaution. Limited liability companies have their details filed in the public domain and credit checks can be carried out by a number of private agencies very speedily. Enquiries can also be made within the trade or profession, and names cross-checked in directories, or with chambers of commerce and other institutions.

Education and training are powerful weapons in the fight against fraud, and information is readily supplied by organisations such as the International Maritime Bureau (IMB, of which more later), BIMCO, insurance companies, banks and others to alert likely victims to the dangers which are posed by fraudsters and criminals. Customs, police and revenue authorities worldwide are of course also committed to preventing fraud and can be of great assistance in pursuing and prosecuting criminals in the public interest.

Passenger and vehicle ferry

52

Chapter 6

. . . .

The geography of trade

6.1   SEABORNE TRADE

Moving goods by sea or waterways is by far the most economic method of transport in terms of the cost per ton-mile (cargo volume multiplied by distance carried). It is estimated that more than 95% of the world's trade is carried by sea.

Shipping is a global business. Shipowners, operators, brokers, managers, agents, and other specialists within the business are ultimately concerned with transporting materials, equipment and people from one part of the world to another. It is vital, therefore, for all those engaged in the business of shipping to have a good working knowledge of maritime geography.

Sea transport plays a crucial part in international trade and improved efficiency in ships and cargo handling has helped to reduce the overall costs of sea transport in real terms year on year, encouraging world trade and the steady increase in the volume of cargo shipped.

It is of course important to know where oceans, seas, continents, countries, ports and waterways are situated and the best way to do that is by frequent reference to atlases. Try to develop a love of maps, and always look up places when you are unsure of where they are.

Students will find it useful in this context to have access to a maritime atlas such as *Lloyd's Maritime Atlas* or *The Ship's Atlas*.

The commodities that are moved in the largest volumes across the world's oceans are crude oil and oil products, coal, metal ores and grains. We shall look at each of these commodities and the trading patterns of each in greater detail.

6.2   OIL

Crude oil is undoubtedly the single most important commodity traded in the world today. We depend on oil products to power every form of transport, for heating, power generation and countless other uses. The world demand for oil continues to increase and in 2011 almost 3,995 million tonnes of crude oil and over 1,895 million tonnes of oil products were carried in ships.

Crude oil is a natural product, and significant oilfields have been discovered and exploited in various parts of the world – principally in the areas of the Middle East, the Caspian Sea, Equatorial West Africa, the Caribbean and US Gulf, the north and east of South America, the North Sea and other smaller production areas.

Economics dictate that the most cost-effective system is to transport the crude product to refineries close to the end users, so that the largest ships are usually the crude oil carriers and they also tend to travel the furthest distances.

The largest ships in the world are crude oil carriers, the size of which is limited principally by the restrictions at the principal loading and discharging points. These are not necessarily ports, as both loading and discharge terminals are often located offshore (such as LOOP – the Louisiana Offshore Oil Port, in the US Gulf), which all vessels with deeper draughts use to discharge in areas where the conventional harbours are draught restricted

Crude oil tankers are specifically designed for this purpose and rarely, if ever, used in any other trades.

6.3   COAL

Coal is an energy source used for both power generation and as a heat source in many industrial processes such as steel making. It is estimated that about 7,678 million tons of coal a year are mined and consumed. About 1,142 million tons were transported by sea in 2011, from the sources of production to the industrial centres of the world where most of the steel is made and power is consumed. In spite of the fact that burning coal is not a very environmentally friendly process, it is still used to generate around 40% of the world's electricity.

Coal is transported by bulk carriers, which may or may not be equipped with gear (cranes) for discharging. Loading is usually by conveyor from shore. Where deep water is available at both loading and discharging port, Capesize vessels (over 80,000 deadweight tons) can be used to take advantage of economies of scale. Where restrictions of one sort or another dictate smaller parcels, Panamax (60,000–80,000 tonnes) or the smaller handymax bulkers are employed.

Coal is often discharged by grab-fitted cranes, often at specialised terminals that serve steelworks or power stations.

6.4 ORES

Most of the world's metals are produced from smelting mineral ores, such as iron ore or bauxite from which aluminium is produced, and in most cases the smelting is carried out at some distance from the mine.

Iron ore, used for the production of iron and steel, is the single largest product traded within this group. In 2011 about 1.15 billion tons of iron ore were moved in ships.

Most ores are a good deal more dense than coal (coal has a stowage factor of around 50 cubic feet per tonne compared with about 14 cubic feet per tonne for a typical iron ore) and at one time ore was carried in specialised bulk carriers with relatively small holds on top of large double-bottom ballast tanks to cope with this characteristic.

Nowadays, ores are carried for the most part in general purpose bulk carriers, most of which have flexible ballasting arrangements and strengthened bulkheads to allow them to carry a much wider range of bulk cargoes.

Ores are normally loaded and discharged at specialised terminals. Typically, an ore-loading terminal will have deep water alongside, to allow large bulk carriers to be loaded and extensive stocking areas feeding cargo into the ship by a series of high-volume conveyors.

Specialised gantry-type grab-fitted cranes will usually carry out discharging, with cargo being removed from the quay by conveyor belts to storage compounds.

6.5 GRAINS

Most grains traded in bulk are destined for human or animal consumption, and include wheat, sorghum, soya, rice and the seeds of such crops as rape, sunflower, flax and cotton. Some have been further processed into pellets or meal.

Annual carriage by sea amount to some 350 million tons, in bulk carriers very similar to those used in the coal and ore trades.

Most grains have a similar stowage factor to that of coal (eg bulk wheat stows at about 45–50 cubic feet per tonne). If you look in the shipping press at the details of reported fixtures in the grain market, you will frequently see cargoes described as HSS. This is a shipping term referring to 'heavy grains, soyabeans and sorghums, which have a bulk stowage factor of about 50 cu ft per tonne.

Some grains and seeds carried in bulk can be dangerous as they are prone to shifting at sea. To avoid this problem, some ships have 'self-trimming' facilities or special wing tanks that 'bleed' cargo into the main hold to ensure that there is no space left in the hold to allow the cargo to shift. Alternatively, the free surface of bulk grain cargoes may have to be over-stowed with bagged grain to stabilise it.

Loading is usually by grain elevators from shore silos. As with all cargo handling, time is money, and sophisticated grain loading equipment is capable of loading ships at a rate in excess of 30,000 tons per day. Discharging facilities may vary considerably, the fastest and most efficient being the pneumatic suction systems in use at most of the world's major grain importing ports, though other methods include mechanical bucket or screw elevators and, in some cases, simply grabbing out with shore cranes.

Production of grain for export is concentrated in the fertile agricultural areas of the world, such as the Canadian and North American 'grain belt', Argentina, Uruguay and Brazil in South America, Australia, New Zealand, Thailand and its neighbours in the Far East and in Russia. Grains and seeds are purchased by the highly populated industrial areas of the world, but are also shipped to many developing countries as seed for planting, human or animal consumption or in the worst cases for famine relief.

Like all agricultural products, the volume of grain available for trading worldwide depends upon the quality of the harvest in different parts of the world. This will affect volumes, prices, availability and ultimately trading patterns to some extent.

6.6 OTHER DRY BULK CARGOES

In addition to the coal, ores and grains mentioned above, there is in excess of 1 billion tons of other dry bulk cargo moved by sea every year, that does not belong to any of these categories. These include commodities as steel, minerals, fertilizers, building materials, timber and manufactured goods.

Some of these products require specialised ships, such as refrigerated ('reefer') carriers for fruit, vegetables, fruit juices and meat products. These ships have insulated holds equipped with refrigeration equipment to keep the high-value cargoes at exactly the right temperature. They are also likely to be designed for a relatively high speed, so that the produce can be delivered quickly and in good condition.

Other types of specialised vessels include those for transporting motor vehicles and livestock.

6.7 UNITISED CARGO

Quite separate from the bulk and liquid trades identified above is the rapidly increasing sector of unitised or containerised cargo. However, in its wider sense, the unitised cargo also includes palletised goods, packaged timber, 'jumbo' bags and pre-slung cargo, as well as the specially designed lighters and barges used in LASH (lighter aboard ship) systems.

There is no doubt that the freight container has revolutionised the general cargo trade. Steady advances in technology in ship design and cargo handling equipment, heavy investment in terminal development, and the adaption of road, rail and inland waterway transport to allow for the transportation of the now familiar 20ft and 40ft containers has introduced a standardised multi-modal transport system. The ability to fill and empty containers at points remote from ports and terminals, the reduction in theft and damage and the use of multiple transport modes to allow a true door-to-door service has benefited many trades, especially in manufactured goods. Fierce competition in the major container routes has reduced freights in real terms and encouraged efficiency.

Establishing an integrated container service requires a very large capital investment in specialised ships, berth facilities, terminals and depots, handling equipment, road, rail and waterway connections, and of course the actual containers. As a result, such services from the very outset involved deepsea container vessels trading between major terminals with smaller container feeder vessels linking these with smaller ports and terminals in the area.

This 'hub and spoke' system has developed to the stage where container transit times are now fast and reliable. There are now few parts of the world from which door-to-door container services cannot be offered.

6.8 PORTS

Many traditional ports around the world have developed in step with the communities they serve. Originally, in many cases it was the presence of a natural harbour that encouraged people to settle in that area in the first place and thereafter the population and the port have often grown in unison. Many other ports owe their existence to the exploitation of an exportable commodity. Specialised grain ports in North and South America are typical examples while, more recently, new terminals in otherwise uninhabited regions have been built to allow for the export of minerals, such as coal or ore.

The extent to which a port will develop, stagnate or even fail to survive depends on many factors such as:

- depth of water
- protection from adverse weather
- space for cargo storage
- infrastructure (eg road/rail connections)
- availability of labour.

The location may dictate the extent to which a port will expand or contract. The ports of Liverpool and Felixstowe are good illustrations. Liverpool with otherwise excellent port facilities and with its densely populated and industrialised hinterland is not expanding. This is because modern container ships find it more economical to move cargo overland from the south or east coast rather than have the ship deviate from a voyage that will almost invariably include ports in western Europe. Felixstowe, with virtually no industry and only an agricultural hinterland, has expanded rapidly because it is so conveniently located on a route that includes continental ports.

It is almost impossible to classify a port into a particular category, as generally ports have many facilities available for numerous traffic activities. However, bearing in mind the simplification, it may be interesting to note some port categories:

Entrepot	Places where goods are transferred from one ship to another. These are usually large ports such as Rotterdam, where cargo arrives in large vessels and is transferred to smaller coastal vessels and/or barges for onward transit.
Naval ports	Home ports for national navies, such as Plymouth or Portsmouth in the UK, often chosen for strategic purposes.
Ferry ports	Terminals for shortsea routes such as Dover–Calais, Folkestone–Boulogne, where ferries ply the English Channel between England and France.
Outports	Often old-established ports on rivers that cannot accommodate the larger vessels and have been superseded by new ports nearer the sea. For example Tilbury and its neighbouring estuarial terminals have taken over most of the Thames shipping activity, that formerly used London, with its obsolete enclosed docks and greater distance from the sea.
Fishing ports	Smaller ports, that are the home ports of fishing fleets, usually located near recognised fishing grounds and that have good transport facilities inland for quick dispatch of the catch.
Goods/cargo	The large majority of ports will deal with cargo imports and/or exports. These cargoes will be very varied in nature. The larger ports will cover all aspects from bulk cargoes, such as grain, to container facilities, and oil terminals. One such example would be Rotterdam, but most of the major ports have these facilities.

Free zone   A free zone is an area of land that is considered for customs purposes to be outside the territory of its host country. Goods may be brought into the zone without import duties being paid. Duties are paid only if the goods are 'imported' from the zone to the territory of the host country. Enterprises operating in the zone are thus able to hold stock without adding the duty element to their working capital.

Free zones located at or near ports are often called 'Freeports'. In addition to having a suspended duty customs regime, some free zones offer incentives such as tax concessions or grants designed to encourage business. Zones may also be exempt from the operation of certain laws or regulations, which apply to the national territory. The concessions offered vary so widely that it is difficult to generalise about the potential benefits of free zones. The opportunities for a particular zone will depend on the exact nature of the regulations applying in the zone, and how these compare with conditions in the host country and in neighbouring countries.

The major shipping publishers produce directories of port information and a current edition are an of essential part of any shipping office library. However, always remember that the data could easily be over a year out of date so that anything that may be considered marginal should be checked with a local agent.

Communications about port restrictions inevitably use abbreviations or expressions, which should be clearly understood. Some of the most common are given below.

6.9   LOA

Length overall – the actual length of the vessel that is able to enter the port, berth or discharging place. In some cases the vessel will not be able to enter the port because of its length, either because may be due to meandering rivers, eg Rouen, or because the berth is too short, such as Alexandria (620ft/189m/LOA max.).

6.10   BEAM

The actual beam or width of the vessel becomes significant if there is a lock or a channel through which the vessel has to pass in order to get to the discharging/loading berth for example Avonmouth, for example, the vessel has to pass through locks to access the berths. The beam of the vessel is important at cargo installations where the outreach of the loading/discharging gear is a limiting factor. Often shipowners are requested to give additional information about the vessel such as the distance between ship's rail (side) and the hatch coaming (side of hatch). This is usually for the purpose of checking if the shore cargo installation can reach far enough to ensure efficient loading of discharging of the vessel.

6.11   DRAUGHT

If no draught restriction is stipulated and the load or discharge port is named in the charter party it is the owners' responsibility to ensure that the vessel can meet the draught restrictions at that port. If, however, the vessel is fixed to a range of discharge ports, the responsibility remains with the charterers who will need to know the arrival draught of the vessel before they can nominate a safe berth.

The charterer may also require more information about the vessel, such as the height from the waterline to the top of the hatch coaming in fully ballasted condition; this will be to ensure that the vessel can remain beneath the shore facilities during the entire loading/ discharging operation.

6.11.1 Air draught

Sometimes the term used to describe the distance from a vessel's waterline to the top of hatch-coamings. Otherwise, this is the distance between the waterline and the highest fixed point on the vessel (usually the radar mast, although this may be hinged) in fully ballasted condition. This is usually required when, for example, an empty, ballasted vessel is to load in a berth where, to reach the berth, she must pass under a bridge (eg Toledo in Lake Erie). Alternatively, it can be required in a different set of circumstances such as in Genoa where there is an airport close to the berths and the port authority restricts the air draught of vessels to a certain height so as not to interfere with the approach path of an aircraft.

6.11.2 SWAD

This means salt water arrival draught and is the maximum draught that a vessel in a loaded condition should draw upon arrival at a port of discharge (variable according to the port).

6.11.3 FWAD

Fresh water arrival draught for those upriver ports that have fresh rather than seawater (for example, Warri 21ft FWAD and Matadi 22ft FWAD in West Africa).

6.11.4 BWAD

Brackish water arrival draught. In general terms, this type of water is usually where the rivers meet the sea and is a mixture of the two waters (eg Tampa, in Florida).

Vessels have a greater draught in fresh water than in seawater because of the water's specific gravity (SG), while draught in brackish water will be somewhere between the two. The SG of fresh water is 1.000, while salt is normally 1.025.

6.11.5 Bar draught

Where river silt builds up, bars may form that force vessels to load up-river to a draught able to pass safely over the bar and then to 'top-off' in other ports. In South America, the Martin Garcia Bar requires vessels to load up River Parana, topping-off at Buenos Aires; similarly loading in Bangkok requires completing in Kosichang.

In some ports, there may be a combination of factors for the owner to consider. In Buenaventura, Colombia, there is one wharf/berth, which is divided into imports and exports. The depth of water at low tide is 24 feet and consequently charterers of the ship and/or receivers of the cargo always need the vessel to agree to NAABSA (not always afloat but safely aground) terms. For additional protection the shipowner may add the words "where it is customary for vessels of similar size to lie aground"' An additional problem at Buenaventura is that there is a bar at the entrance to the port that can only be crossed by vessels with a maximum draught of 28 feet, one hour before until one hour after high tide.

Other restrictions that may cause a shipowner to reconsider calling at a port include weather conditions (including ice, which will be discussed later in this section), which may cause restrictions on entry at certain times of the year.

War zones or piracy areas naturally cause owners to consider the safety of their ship and crew and the extra insurance premiums payable.

In addition to the restrictions mentioned above, some ports and areas depend on canals and waterways for access.

The problem with waterways is always one of size. On rivers such as the Thames in London, the increase in ship sizes to achieve economies of scale has caused docks nearer to the city to fall into disuse, whereas those farther downstream that have fewer restrictions are being developed.

The problem of size is even more apparent when looking at manmade waterways that have been built to create or improve access. What may have seemed more than big enough at the time of construction can be very restricting to modern ships.

A good example of this is the **St Lawrence Seaway**, which is a series of canals linking the North American Great Lakes to the sea. The lakes themselves are very deep, but when they were built a decision had to be taken on the dimensions of the canal locks. The locks were an enormous undertaking, bearing in mind the height that the locks have to lift ships (from Lake Ontario to Lake Erie). Eventually, a compromise between ships' requirements and civil engineering constraints resulted in a limitation of 26ft fresh water maximum draught with 222.5m maximum length and 23.16m maximum beam. In practice this means that the largest ships the Seaway can accept are about 30,000 tons deadweight and can load up to about 18,000 tons of cargo on the Seaway draught of 26ft and then complete ('top-off') at Montreal. Because of the complexity of the different canals and locks, ships need to possess equipment such as special fairleads for mooring lines, onboard sewage systems to avoid polluting the lakes, extra lighting etc. Managers of ships intending to enter the lakes are advised to make their preparations well in advance.

Despite these restrictions and the almost complete shut-down of the Great Lakes during three of the winter months because of ice, the St Lawrence Seaway is still a very valuable link to the grain and industrial heartlands of the USA and Canada.

The Panama Canal, which opened in 1914, links the Atlantic and the Pacific oceans, saving many days of steaming round the southern tip of South America. So important is this link, especially to Japan, that the Canal is presently being widened and deepened to allow larger ships to transit.

The locks in the present canal can accept ships up to 274.3m long, 32.3m maximum beam. So long as rainfall has been reasonable a draught of just less than 40ft fresh water may be accommodated. Many shipowners consider the Panama Canal restrictions when ordering ships and the description 'Panamax' to describe a design incorporating the maximum dimensions that the canal can accept is now firmly implanted in the shipping vocabulary.

Just as famous and even older is the Suez Canal, which when it was built in 1869 needed no locks as the levels of the Mediterranean and the Red Seas are the same. Because there are no locks, it has been possible to increase the dimensions of the Suez Canal as ships have increased in size. This now means that ships drawing as much as 53ft can be accepted, which allows ships of around 150,000 deadweight fully laden to use it and ships in ballast as large as 370,000 deadweight can be accommodated.

6.12 POLITICAL RESTRICTIONS

Physical restrictions and climate are not the only constraints on where a ship may trade. Trade between certain ports and countries maybe restricted for political reasons. Problems in this respect include countries such as Israel that is blacklisted by some Arab countries and vessels that are known to have traded to Israeli ports maybe banned from entering the ports of certain Arab countries.

Similarly, owners and operators of ships that have called at Cyprus ports under Turkish control can expect to be prevented from calling at Greek ports as a result of government policy.

6.13 TRADE UNION DISPUTES

You will recall from the 'crewing' section in Chapter 3 how the International Transport Workers' Federation (ITF) can 'black' a ship if it disagrees with the terms of the crew's contract of employment. The ITF tends to concentrate its efforts in certain areas, at the time of writing the union is particularly strong in Scandinavia and Australasia, where shore labour such as stevedores or tug crews may support seafarers in disputes and prevent vessels from entering ports or from sailing.

You are most likely to encounter reference to political exclusions in time charters in cases where the owner does not want to have their ship 'blacked' either now or at some later date. Therefore, the shipowner will seek to exclude such places from the list of countries or ports to which the ship may be traded by the time charterer. Voyage charter parties, too, carry clauses relating to strikes and 'lock-outs' as well as politically motivated blockades and warlike actions.

6.14 NATURAL PHENOMENA

6.14.1 Tides

Tides have a considerable effect on merchant shipping, regulating available draughts and in some cases, periods of maximum and minimum port use. They are caused by the gravitational attraction of the sun and the moon and although the sun is much bigger than the moon, the moon is much closer. As a result, the moon has more than twice the tidal effect of the sun. At times of a new and a full moon, the gravitational attractions of the sun and moon combine to provide an extra-high tide called a **spring tide** while, at times of a half moon, the two gravitational pulls cancel out to give more nearly equal, **neap tides**. As the moon's orbit is not quite circular, its distance and tide-forming capacity continually varies and tidal predictions are published to assist navigation at many locations. The illustration below shows how spring and neap tides are generated.

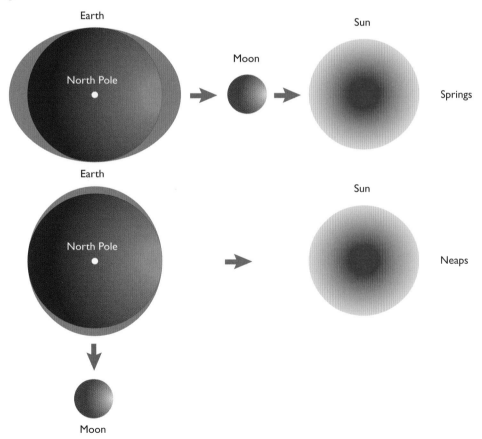

Spring and neap tides

It is also useful to know how long reasonable tidal levels will remain in order that cargo can be discharged and vessels remain 'always afloat'. In some ports it is impossible for the vessel to remain always afloat and here the term NAABSA, as mentioned earlier, may be negotiated.

6.15   WEATHER AND NAVIGATION

6.15.1 Ocean currents

Ocean currents may be divided into:

(a)   Those caused by the wind

(b)   Those due to the distribution of water masses of varying temperatures, salinity and density and

(c)   Tidal currents.

Currents flow at all depths in all the oceans, but mariners and shipbrokers are usually only interested in surface currents and the effect they have on ships. The main cause of currents in the open ocean is the direction of winds blowing on the sea surface.

Warm currents flowing from the tropics, such as the Gulf Stream, not only ensure a temperate climate for the British Isles but even keep ports as far north as Narvik in Norway ice-free all the year round. Conversely, currents from the poles such as the one sweeping down to the North of Japan result in severe winters on the island of Hokkaido even though it is several degrees of latitude further south than England.

Sea fogs occur where warm moist winds blow over cold currents, lowering the temperature and causing condensation. A famous areas for sea fog is off the coast of Newfoundland, where the warm North Atlantic drift meets the cold Labrador Current (maximum frequency of the phenomena is May to September). Similarly this phenomenon occurs off the coast of California (generally between June and December), in the Bering Sea (June and August), the Baltic regions (November and January) and the Hudson Bay (June and September).

Cold currents from the Polar regions also carry one great hazard to shipping during the summer thaw, *icebergs* that have broken away from ice caps and glaciers and are then carried into shipping lanes by currents. Icebergs carried by the Labrador Current are found in the Newfoundland area before they break up on meeting warmer seas. Also a combination of sea fog and icebergs, as found off the coast of Newfoundland, makes navigation extremely difficult and only relatively recently has new technology helped masters of vessels to detect such risks.

6.15.2 Cyclones

These are regions of low atmospheric pressure and fall into two types. The first is a depression characteristic of temperate latitudes and the second is a much more violent phenomenon, though generally covering a smaller area and typical of the tropics, usually called a tropical cyclone. The two types are similar in that the winds in the Northern Hemisphere circulate in an anti-clockwise direction around its centre (or eye) while in the Southern Hemisphere, they revolve in a clockwise direction. Over north-west Australia, in late summer, the tropical cyclones experienced are called 'Willy-Willies' (January to April). They then recurve to the south-east, cross the coast and bring heavy rain moving overland to the Great Australian Bight, initiallt affecting ports such as Darwin, Port Hedland.

In the China Seas a tropical cyclone is referred to as a typhoon and is generally experienced between May and December but with maximum frequency between July and October. The Philippine islands are directly affected, as is southern China. Like all tropical cyclones, typhoons have winds of tremendous strength and torrential rain and also possible tidal waves affecting ports such as Shanghai, Hong Kong and Manila.

The term 'monsoon' is generally applied to a wind system where there is a complete, or almost complete, reversal of prevailing direction from season to season. It is especially prominent within the tropics on the eastern side of the great landmasses, although it does occur outside the tropics. For eastern Asia it reaches as far north as about 60°N. South-east Asia is pre-eminently a monsoon region. Monsoon gales in the Arabian Sea occur generally from June to August, although tropical storms in the same area may last from May to November. Extremely heavy rains are experienced and also strong winds and heavy seas. Ports affected include Bombay and Bedi on the west coast of India.

The tropical cyclones or revolving storms of the West Indies and Gulf of Mexico are known as hurricanes. They usually originate east of the islands, occasionally as far east as the Cape Verde Islands and take a westwards course, sometimes causing extensive destruction on one island after another before generally recurving to the north-east. Besides the West Indies, the Gulf coasts of the United States and the eastern side of Central America, as far as the Mosquito Coast of Nicaragua, are affected by hurricanes. Costa Rica, Panama and the northern coast of South America, however, lie outside the hurricane region. The hurricane season is between June and November, with a maximum frequency August to October. The name hurricane is also given to tropical cyclones experienced off the coast of Queensland, Australia. As an example of the strength of winds, they can have a mean velocity of over 75 miles per hour or equivalent to a wind force 12 on the Beaufort Scale. Havana (Cuba) and Miami (Florida) are among ports affected.

The **Beaufort Scale** is the series of numbers devised by Admiral Beaufort at the beginning of the 19th century to differentiate between various wind strengths. For example '0' on the Beaufort Scale represents calm, the air being practically motionless, wheras the upper end of the scale, 12, represents a hurricane, the surface wind speed being greater than 75 miles per hour. Between these two extremes, the numbers indicate the intervening wind speeds. The various wind velocities to which numbers on the Beaufort Scale are equivalent have been internationally agreed (see **Appendix 15**).

Often, within the terms of a time charter, the speed of a vessel will be related to a certain number on the Beaufort scale, usually 3 or 4, and the object of this is that the vessel should perform at the prescribed speed with prevailing winds up to a maximum of 3 or 4. Should it not perform at this speed, then the charterer may well make a speed claim against the owners for non-performance.

Another scale used for reporting conditions at sea and sometimes used in vessel performance descriptions and therefore also in any subsequent disputes is the Douglas Sea State Scale. As the name implies, it deals with the state of the sea in terms of the height of the waves. It is a fact that the surface of the sea can often be sufficiently rough to affect the speed of the vessel without the wind in the immediate vicinity being particularly high, due to stormy weather several miles away.

Yet another climatic condition that affects shipping occurs in the Southern Hemisphere between latitudes 40°S and 60°S where there are very few land masses, consequently the winds in this region are very strong and are often referred to as the 'Roaring Forties'.

6.15.3 Ice

Another very important climatic condition affecting shipping in particular is ice. Certain ports freeze for varying periods of time during winter and it is important to be aware of where ice conditions are found and the time of year the condition is prevalent.

Apart from Arctic and Antarctic regions, the main areas where ice affects shipping are:

(a) The Baltic Sea between November and 31 March, including St Petersburg, Helsinki, Luleå, and Stockholm

(b) The St Lawrence River between 31 December and 31 March, including Montreal, Baie Comeau, Port Cartier

(c)   The St Lawrence Seaway between 15 December and 1 April (the opening and closing dates for vessels transiting the Seaway vary from year to year depending upon the severity of the winter), the St Lawrence Seaway Authority, to avoid vessels being trapped in the Great Lakes, publishes the proposed closing date well in advance. While it may still allow vessels to pass through the Seaway after the official closing date, subject to weather conditions, a heavy fine for each day the vessel delays may also be imposed on an escalating basis. (The term FOW – first open water – means the first date at which vessels can enter an area of ice in relative safety although additional insurance premiums would still have to be paid over and above normal rates.)

Additional to these main areas, ice conditions are prevalent in Albany, on the Hudson River. Churchill, situated in remote Hudson Bay, is open only for navigation between the end of July and October.

Ice conditions also affect the west coast of British Columbia, the east coast of Russia, northern China and North Korea between October and May and the Black Sea ports of Russia and Romania.

Advances in ship design have developed ice breakers that endeavour to keep ice-restricted ports open throughout the winter (especially in the Baltic and the Gulf of St Lawrence). During severe winter conditions even those specialist vessels are unable to operate totally successfully. Finland and Russia lead the world in the development of icebreakers, including the use of nuclear-powered vessels.

Reports and forecasts about ice conditions in the Northern Hemisphere are available every winter. BIMCO publish these for north-west Europe and Scandinavia and the Canadian government does the same for its waters.

Merchants whose usual ports and routes are closed by ice must use alternative means of transport (such as rail) to or from ports not affected by ice, such as Narvik (see above) or the Atlantic seaboard ports of Canada.

It must be remembered that severe weather conditions do not merely interfere with safe navigation. Cargo handling operations in ports and interior transport routes may also face difficulties. In severe cold, for example, steel becomes more brittle and machinery can fail as a result. Diesel oil becomes waxy or freezes, and of course human beings cannot function properly for long in extremes of temperature. Monsoon rain is bound to disrupt cargo handling and may well cause delays to inland transport. Tropical storms can similarly wreak havoc by causing damage to port installations, warehouses, road and rail transport as well as ships in port.

6.15.4 Weather routeing

Today's sophisticated systems of weather reporting and forecasting have enabled specialist companies to offer a service to ship's masters. On contracting with a weather routeing company, the master is given information about the weather likely to prevail on the voyage with advice on the course to take to avoid the worst conditions. During the voyage the ship keeps in touch with the routeing service both to report on the weather the ship is actually experiencing and to receive any amendments to the suggested route as a result of the updated forecast. Not only does this service make for safer and quicker passages, but also the data recorded by the routeing company can provide expert evidence when a dispute arises about the effect of weather on a voyage.

Even without actual weather routeing advice, satellite communication systems now enable ships to receive up-to-the-minute weather information including forecasts, charts and satellite images. Nevertheless, casualty reports still contain references to ships sunk without trace, presumable as a result of extreme weather.

The insurance world also takes account of the increased risks caused by climatic conditions and requires shipowners to pay increased premiums if they intend to trade outside the Institute warranty limits.

6.15.5 Salinity of the oceans

The area of oceans (70.8% of the Earth's surface) is far greater than the land area (29.2%). All the world's oceans are saline (saltwater), but the concentration of salt, which affects the density of the water, is not uniform. The variations in salinity are caused by:

(a) changes from mixing and circulation

(b) water evaporation rates

(c) supplies of fresh water.

Highest salinity is found near the tropics because of the high evaporation. It is lower at the Equator as a result of the heavy rain and lower evaporation. Towards the poles, melting ice supplies fresh water and therefore causes lower salinity levels.

6.16 NAVIGATIONAL AND SEASONAL ZONES

Inevitably climatic conditions will affect even the highly sophisticated ships of today. As a result of the campaigning of the social reformer Samuel Plimsoll at the end of the 19th century, a system of marking the position of the minimum freeboard (the distance from the waterline to the main deck) on all British ships was introduced. In the early 1930s a refinement of this system became an international convention. The 'Plimsoll Mark' takes into account the difference in density as well as prescribing a greater freeboard in areas where severe weather is more prevalent. Some such load-line zones are permanent while others are seasonal. **Appendix 5** shows the internationally agreed load-line zones of the world.

The depth to which a ship is allowed to load will determine the weight of cargo it can carry, and this in turn will affect the freight payable. It is clearly important therefore that this factor is taken into account when calculating voyage estimates. During a voyage, a ship may cross from one load-line zone to another more than once, and its draught must not exceed the maximum limits for each zone. This is complicated by the changing seasonal limits in some zones, so the dates of crossing such zones must also be taken into account.

Chapter 7

· ·

International trade practice

7.1 INTRODUCTION

Those of us involved in the shipping business should be concerned with those aspects of international trade that are directly related to the transportation of goods. However, to carry out this service effectively it is necessary to also understand the needs and problems that may be faced by the shippers, merchants and traders whom they service.

International seaborne trade is composed of thousands of voyages whereby goods are carried from one country to another. Each of these voyages comprises many different legal relationships. There are charter parties, contracts of affreightment, contracts of agency, contracts of employment and contracts for the sale of goods. This last is the essence of international trade. It is the reason why the other essential relationships have come into being, and the reason why goods are being shipped abroad. As a buyer in one country has bought goods from a seller in another, it is essential that we appreciate the legal implications of this transaction since these affect many of the practical aspects of international trade.

First, it is necessary to identify the basic elements in a contract for the sale of goods and then to consider the implications that these legal concepts have for the responsibility for insurance coverage and the payment of goods. Concepts such as the passing of risk and property are of fundamental importance in international trade and should be fully understood.

7.2 THE BASIC CONTRACT

The four elements of the basic contract are:

(i)   **the offer**

(ii) **the acceptance** – this must be in identical terms to the offer, otherwise it is a counter-offer, and it must be given in a reasonable manner and within a reasonable time

(iii) **consideration** – this is the 'price' of the two sides of the bargain – what each person will receive 'in consideration for' performing their part of the contract

(iv) **an intention to create legal relations** – the parties must intend legal consequences to attach to their agreement.

In a contract for the sale of goods, therefore, there are three important points that have to be considered. The time or circumstances under which the ownership of the goods passes from the seller to the buyer, when payment is due and at what stage the risk of damage to or loss of the goods moves from seller to buyer.

Note: In international sales it is common for one party to make an offer on its standard terms, and another party to accept that offer on its own standard terms. If these terms are different, there is no acceptance in identical terms to the offer. This may well lead to the conclusion that there was no valid contract. The adoption of an internationally recognised set of standard terms governing international sales prevents this by ensuring that both parties are in agreement as to the terms contained in their contract, there is a valid contract and both parties are aware of their rights and obligations. A widely used form of such terms is the Incoterms form produced by the International Chamber of Commerce, which will be considered later in the chapter.

Under English law a sale of goods is defined as a contract to pass the property in goods for a money consideration, the price.

We shall come back to look at the word 'property', but basically it means 'the ownership'. So the ownership of the goods will be transferred in exchange for a payment of money.

7.3 GOODS

We need to consider two types of 'goods' – specific goods and unascertained goods. Specific goods are those goods, that are readily identifiable at the time the contract is made, for example, the 1,000 New Zealand lamb carcasses numbered Y20,001 to Y21,000.

Unascertained goods, on the other hand, are goods that have yet to be produced by the seller or are part of a larger bulk and have not yet been set aside for a specific contract. For example, if I offer to sell you 50 tonnes of wheat from a stock of 200 tonnes in my warehouse, these are unascertained goods. We do not know which of the 200 tonnes will be the 50 that you receive.

7.4 PROPERTY

The next element in the sale of goods is the passing of property. By 'property' we mean the ownership, so when the 'property passes' the right of ownership is transferred to the buyer. Be careful to distinguish property from possession. The latter signifies mere physical control. Thus I may have in my warehouse goods that I have sold to you and for which you have paid. I have the possession, but you have the property. In summary, when the property passes to the buyer they become the owner of the goods.

The passing of the property has the following specific consequences:

(i) The buyer must then pay the price to the seller (the passing of property and payment of the price are concurrent conditions)

(ii) The risk passes to the buyer (see below)

(iii) Certain specific remedies become available to the seller if the buyer breaches the contract by refusing to take the goods.

The important question must therefore be – when does property pass?

The English Sale of Goods Act provides that "property passes when the parties intend it to." However, there are more helpful specific rules than this which depend upon the distinction between specific and unascertained goods that was noted earlier.

(i) Specific goods – property in specific goods will usually pass at the time the contract is made, even if the goods are not delivered straight away.

(ii) Unascertained goods – property cannot pass at the same stage for unascertained goods. For property to pass there must be what is known as 'appropriation', that is, out of the unascertained goods a parcel of goods must be specified for the particular buyer. The goods thereby become specific and at that moment the property will pass. Thus if I have a warehouse full of grain and I sell you 50 tonnes, property will not pass until I irrevocably earmark and set aside the 50 tonnes that will be delivered to you.

Generally, therefore, property (ownership) passes when the contract is made or, in the case of unascertained goods, when the particular parcel to be delivered is set aside. However, it is always possible for the passing of property to be delayed by the parties. This is frequently the case in international sales, as we shall see below.

7.5 RISK

We saw above that when the property passed, so did the risk and in this case the risk is the danger of damage to the goods. Whoever bears the risk will bear the burden of such damage.

Example: A sells goods to B, and the property and risk pass to B. The goods remain for the time being in A's warehouse. A fire, for which A is not to blame, destroys the warehouse and its contents – B, who is responsible for the risk, has to bear the loss.

Alternatively, A sells goods to B, who takes them away, but because B has not yet paid for them and due to a prior agreement, property and risk remain with A. While the goods are in B's possession, they are damaged. It is A who must bear the loss.

The passing of property and risk is of great importance, so you must ensure that you understand the significance of both concepts and are confident about how they operate.

Important note

We noted above that risk passes at the same time as property. However, this is not always the case. We shall see below that in the case of some contracts for international sale, risk passes before property.

7.6 INTERNATIONAL CONTRACTS OF SALE – INCOTERMS

Having examined and understood the simple model of a contract for the sale of goods, we now look at various contracts that are used for international sales to see how they vary from the basic model. Many standard terms of sale are in everyday use, so to ensure these terms are universally understood the International Chamber of Commerce (ICC) publishes an agreed set of definitions called Incoterms. The current, 2010, edition became effective from 1 January 2011. The outline of the Incoterms, which are set out below, is only a guide to the buyers' and sellers' responsibilities under the individual contracts. Where possible, students should refer to the ICC publication *Incoterms 2010*.

What is new?

Incoterms are divided into two, instead of the previous four, as below:

(i)   Terms for any mode or modes of transport

and

(ii)   Terms for sea and inland waterway transport.

These changes are intended to assist Incoterms users to identify the correct term for their particular requirement.

The former 13 Incoterms have been reduced to 11.

Other features included in *Incoterms 2010* include:

- extensive guidance and illustrative graphics to help users choose the correct rule for each transaction

- new classification to help identify the most suitable rule in relation to the mode of transport

- advice for the use of electronic procedures

- information on security-related clearances for shipments

- advice relating to the use of *Incoterms 2010* in domestic (intra-EU) trade.

Note: It is important to understand that if the parties to a contract intend to be bound by the definitions in Incoterms, they must state this explicitly. Unless they do, there is no certainty that the clarity of the definitions afforded by Incoterms will apply.

Incoterms are designed to cover a wide range of terms, from sales at the point of origin (for example, the seller's factory) such as **EXW** through to delivered at the buyer's door (**DDP**). These terms are not merely inventions of the International Chamber of Commerce, but reflect the terms on which international traders prefer to do business. As we will see, there are many reasons why the parties to the deal will decide on the most appropriate term to be used, including the type of goods, the forms of transport to be used, the method of payment and the state of the market at the time.

International trade is a dynamic business and its customs and practice change with the advent of new modes of transport, improved communications, changes in demand and supply, banking arrangements, national and international laws and hundreds of other factors.

As a result, the terms on which traders do business evolve to suit the changing times. To cope with this, the International Chamber of Commerce regularly reviews and revises Incoterms in accordance with changes in practice, after consultation with trade bodies and other organisations.

Many of the recent amendments, for example, have been made to facilitate the increased use of electronic data interchange.

In 2000, Incoterms encompassed the following terms.

EXW   ex-works

FCA   free carrier

FAS   free alongside ship*

FOB   free on board*

CFR   cost and freight*

CIF   cost, insurance and freight*

CP   carriage paid to

CIP   carriage and insurance paid to

DAF   delivered at frontier

DES   delivered ex-ship*

DEQ   delivered ex-quay*

DDU   delivered duty unpaid

DDP   delivered duty paid

* Denotes maritime Incoterms.

In *Incoterms 2010* DAF, DES, DEQ and DDU terms, which contained significant areas of overlap, have been replaced by two new terms, DAT (delivered at terminal) and DAP (delivered at place).

It should be noted that the terms fall neatly into groups. The 'E' term (ex-works) is used where the seller makes the goods available at their factory or premises. The 'F' terms indicate that the seller must deliver the goods to a carrier named by the buyer. The 'C' terms apply to situations where the seller has to arrange the carriage, but without bearing the risk for loss or damage after shipment and dispatch. The 'D' terms refer to cases where the seller bears all the costs and risks needed to deliver the goods to the country of destination.

Under each of these the Incoterms define the duties of both the buyer and the seller in respect of every stage in the transport chain, establish the division of costs and the stage at which payment must be made, property passes and risk is transferred from one to the other.

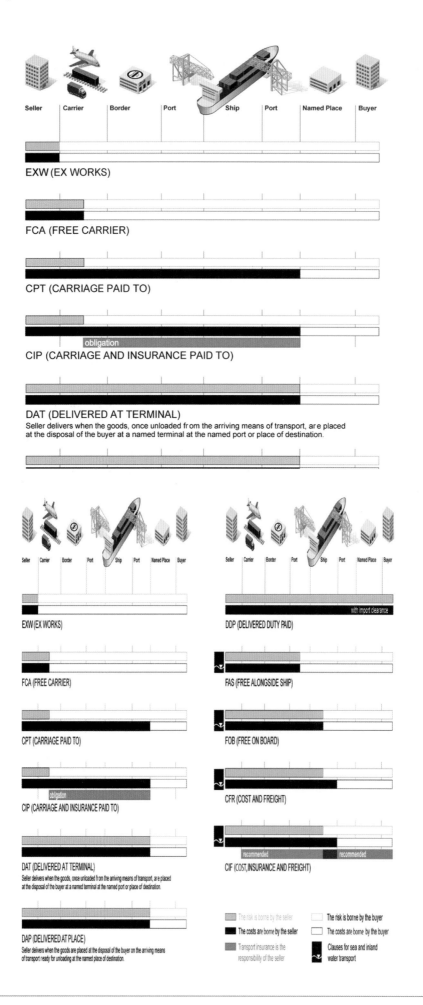

EXW (EX WORKS)

FCA (FREE CARRIER)

CPT (CARRIAGE PAID TO)

CIP (CARRIAGE AND INSURANCE PAID TO)

DAT (DELIVERED AT TERMINAL)
Seller delivers when the goods, once unloaded from the arriving means of transport, are placed at the disposal of the buyer at a named terminal at the named port or place of destination.

EXW (EX WORKS)

FCA (FREE CARRIER)

CPT (CARRIAGE PAID TO)

CIP (CARRIAGE AND INSURANCE PAID TO)

DAT (DELIVERED AT TERMINAL)
Seller delivers when the goods, once unloaded from the arriving means of transport, are placed at the disposal of the buyer at a named terminal at the named port or place of destination.

DAP (DELIVERED AT PLACE)
Seller delivers when the goods are placed at the disposal of the buyer on the arriving means of transport ready for unloading at the named place of destination.

DDP (DELIVERED DUTY PAID)

FAS (FREE ALONGSIDE SHIP)

FOB (FREE ON BOARD)

CFR (COST AND FREIGHT)

CIF (COST, INSURANCE AND FREIGHT)

The risk is borne by the seller

The costs are borne by the seller

Transport insurance is the responsibility of the seller

The risk is borne by the buyer

The costs are borne by the buyer

Clauses for sea and inland water transport

It shows the points in the transport chain where the **costs** transfer from the seller to the buyer for each of these terms. It must be understood, however, that the **risk** may not pass at the same time, and we will examine this discrepancy under each of the most important terms.

Students should be familiar with the basic implications of each of the 13 terms, but the **maritime Incoterms** are the most important for this subject. The full details of the terms can be found in *Incoterms 2010*, but the following explanations illustrate the important points:

7.6.1 FAS – free alongside

Under this term, which also names the loading port (such as "FAS Rotterdam"), the buyer nominates the port, and possibly the berth within that port, to which the goods have to be delivered, and the date(s) of delivery. The seller's obligations cease when the goods are alongside the vessel at the required time. Property and risk pass at this point and the obligation to pay arises.

7.6.2 FOB – free on board

One of the most popular international sales contracts is the FOB form. The seller has responsibility for bringing the goods to the named port and loading them over the ship's rail. They then become the buyer's property and the buyer is also responsible for freight and insurance.

The buyer has a duty to name the ship and port (or more properly a port should be agreed in advance). Indeed, if the seller is not aware of the port during the negotiation of the price, it is extremely difficult for them to calculate the cost of delivering and loading the goods past the ship's rail. For this reason, FOB sales will always be expressed as, for example, "FOB Mombasa" or "FOB Durban". The ship must be nominated within the time specified in the contract. If the nomination is ineffective for some reason, the buyer may renominate provided always that the contract time period has not expired. The buyer usually books the space on, or charters, the vessel they have nominated.

Once a valid nomination has been made, it is the seller's duty to deliver the goods over the ship's rail. Risk will pass at the same time, and the price will become payable. Sometimes the passing of property will be delayed. For example, if the transfer of the bill of lading is delayed, for it is that document which signifies the transfer of ownership.

It is for the buyer to arrange their own insurance, although the seller must give the buyer sufficient information to enable them to effect the insurance. If the seller fails to give the information, the risk will remain with the seller.

7.6.3 Variants on the FOB contract

There are often modifications to the simple FOB format, though it is important to understand that these must be agreed in advance and clearly stated in the contract, as they are not provided for within the standard Incoterms. Under modified FOB contracts it is quite possible for the passing of property to be delayed.

7.6.4 FOB stowed

The cost of stowage rests with the seller, so risk and property will pass on stowage, and not when the goods are simply lifted over the ship's rail.

7.6.5 FOB stowed and trimmed

This only applicable only to bulk cargoes – the seller will need to arrange and pay for the cost of trimming (ie spreading the surface of the cargo in the hold to fill available spaces and/or to reduce the risk of cargo shifting).

7.6.6 FOB with services

The seller may have to arrange additional features for the buyer, such as the shipping space.

7.6.7 CIF (named port of destination) – cost, insurance and freight

This is the most widely used form of international sales contract. As its name implies, it involves the seller not only supplying the goods but also arranging carriage and insurance. The price of goods sold CIF will be considerably higher than for the same goods sold FOB, as the additional freight and insurance elements have to be included in the selling price. The contract is based on the discharge port rather than the load port. This enables the seller to buy goods afloat, if necessary, to fulfill their contract with the buyer.

The seller has an obligation to ship goods as described in the contract and in accordance with any further stipulations in the contract of sale such as time and place,. The seller must arrange a contract of carriage on the usual conditions for the trade in question and must arrange an assignable insurance for reasonable value on the usual terms for the trade in question. The seller must also prepare an invoice for the goods in accordance with the stipulations of the contract of sale.

Finally, the seller must tender all the relevant documents to the buyer (or their agent, or their bank). The relevant documents are the invoice, the bill of lading and the policy of insurance.

The buyer must accept the documents and pay the price. The buyer may of course refuse to accept the seller's documents if they are not in accordance with the contract, though they may be re-tendered by the seller in a satisfactory condition within the contract period. Property passes when the documents are transferred. Risk, however, and this should be specifically noted, is deemed to have passed at the moment of shipment. If anything has happened to the goods during the voyage, the buyer will be protected, as they will receive the insurance policy when the documents are transferred.

It should be noted that the transfer of the documents is, in law, the transfer of the goods, so even if the goods are lost, the transfer of the documents can still complete the sale. The CIF contract has been aptly described as a "contract for the sale of goods performed by the sale of documents".

7.6.8 CFR – cost and freight

It will be self-evident that in this variation of the CIF contract it is the buyer who arranges the insurance. This form is popular in those countries that like to ensure that importing buyers place insurance on all consignments using their own national insurers. Once again, as in the CIF contract, property passes and the price becomes payable upon transfer of the documents, and risk is deemed to pass as from shipment.

7.6.9 DAT – delivered at terminal

Delivered at terminal means that the seller delivers the goods, once they have been unloaded from the arriving means of transport and are placed at the disposal of the buyer at a named terminal at the port or place of destination. 'Terminal' includes any place, whether covered or not, such as a quay, warehouse, container yard or road, rail or air cargo terminal. The seller bears the risks involved in bringing the goods to and unloading them at the destination terminal.

The parties should clearly specify the terminal and, if possible, a specific point within the terminal at the agreed port or place of destination, as the risks up to delivery are for the account of the seller. The seller is advised to negotiate a contract of carriage that precisely matches the exact point of delivery.

If the parties intend the seller to bear the risks and costs involved in transporting and handling the goods from the terminal to another place, then the DAP or DDP rules should be used.

DAT requires the seller to clear the goods for export, where applicable. However, the seller has no obligation to clear the goods for import, pay any import duty or carry out any import customs formalities.

7.6.10 DAP – delivered at place

Delivered at place means that the seller delivers when the goods are placed at the disposal of the buyer on the arriving means of transport ready for unloading at the named place of destination. The seller bears all risks in bringing the goods to the named place.

The parties should clearly specify the point within the agreed place of destination, as the risks to that point are for the account of the seller. The seller is advised to procure contracts of carriage that match this choice precisely.

If the seller incurs costs under its contract of carriage relating to unloading at the place of destination, the seller is not entitled to recover such costs from the buyer unless otherwise agreed between the parties.

DAP requires the seller to clear the goods for export, where applicable. However, the seller has no obligation to clear the goods for import, pay any import duty or carry out any import formalities. If the parties require the seller to clear the goods for import, pay import duty and carry out any import customs formalities, the DDP term should be used.

7.6.11 Non-maritime Incoterms

In addition to the above-mentioned maritime international contracts of sale, you need to understand those international contracts that involve other forms of transport. A brief outline of these is set out below with particular reference to the passing of risk.

7.6.12 EXW – ex-works

The buyer has all the risk and cost from the seller's factory or premises, and usually this will even include loading on to the vehicle. Therefore, the buyer will have all the costs of insurance and carriage and arranging for the export of the goods.

7.6.13 FCA – free carrier named point

In this term of sale the seller has to arrange delivery to the carrier at a named point. The risk then passes to the buyer at this point and they are responsible for the arrangement and payment of insurance and carriage. This term of sale may be used to cover any single mode of transport or multi-modal transport. When using this term it is important to understand the particular responsibilities of buyer and seller in respect of the different types of transport, which may be used. These are set out in detail in *Incoterms 2010*.

7.6.14 CPT – carriage paid to (named place of destination)

In this term the seller is responsible for paying all the freight or carriage to the destination named by the buyer. The risk, however, passes to the buyer once the goods are delivered to the first carrier regardless of the type of transport used and whether it is multi-modal or not.

7.6.15 CIP – carriage and insurance paid

This is very similar to the Incoterm given above except that the seller is responsible for insuring the goods to the final destination, whatever the form of transport.

7.6.16 DDP – delivered duty paid (named place of destination)

Here the seller is responsible for all costs until the goods are delivered to the final destination. This will include the payment of all import duties and taxes that have to be paid on the goods. On occasions goods will be delivered DDP (exclusive of duty and/or taxes) where the buyer will be responsible for meeting any import duties or taxes due.

There are other forms of contract that we have not considered, as they are outside the scope of Incoterms. You will almost certainly come across such expressions as FOT, EX QUAY, C&F and CIFFO. They are all likely to be variations of one or more of the terms defined in *Incoterms 2010*. The FOB contract is particularly suitable for adapting to particular circumstances.

By considering the extreme ends of the range of terms offered under Incoterms, it seems clear that to expect one party or the other to deal with all aspects of international transport must have its drawbacks. If, for example, you are based in Canada and wish to purchase a consignment of washing machines from a manufacturer in Korea, your obligations under an EXW contract would be quite daunting. You would be responsible for arranging and paying for every stage of the transport chain, even the labour and equipment to load the goods at the manufacturer's factory. All the risks involved would be your responsibility, and you would be expected to sort out customs formalities for both exporting and importing countries with a minimum of assistance from the seller.

Given this burden of cost, responsibility and risk, one might assume that all sellers would prefer to sell on EXW terms and that buyers would refuse to accept any terms other than DDP.

The reality is that most goods are sold on terms where both parties have some responsibility for part of the transport. In the previous example, it would almost certainly be easier (and probably cheaper) for the Korean manufacturer to arrange and pay for forklift trucks to load the washing machines on to vehicles and deliver them to the nearest port, than for a non Korean-speaking buyer based in a distant continent and time zone to accomplish the same exercise. At the other end of the journey, the Canadian buyer will be in a much better position to deal with import customs entry, duty payments and to co-ordinate delivery to their depots in Toronto and Vancouver than the seller.

In addition to purely practical considerations, there may well be advantages to one party or the other in controlling the sea transport leg, cargo handling and insurance. An international seller of goods may well find that the buyers regard their arrangements for all aspects of shipment through to a port in their country to be a valuable service, leaving them only with local arrangements to be made. The seller may therefore be able to charge a premium price for this service and hence increase the profitability of the sale.

The exact terms used depend to a large extent on the relative bargaining power of the buyer and seller. Under normal, stable market conditions trading partners may well use either FOB or CIF terms as a matter of course. A sudden swing in the market for those goods may, however, alter the terms under which the goods are sold. In a sellers' market the producer is in a position to dictate the terms upon which they are prepared to sell their goods, which will probably be those which involve the minimum of risk for themselves and ensure the best and fastest payment method. In a buyers' market, a seller will be forced to adapt their terms of sale to the buyer's requirements if they want to enhance their chances of doing business.

Therefore, the terms on which goods are sold in international markets are a compromise, negotiated in the same way as all the other aspects of the business, between the parties who make the deal.

7.7 REMEDIES FOR BREACH OF CONTRACT

No discussion about the international sale of goods is complete without mention of the remedies available for breach of contract. The following is an outline of the most common remedies, using English law as the example.

7.7.1 Remedies of the seller

The buyer will normally be in breach of the contract by refusing to accept the goods, or by refusing to pay for them. The remedies depend upon whether the property has passed or not. As we have seen above, if the property has passed, the price will be due. Thus, if the property has passed, the seller can sue for the price of the goods and their damages will be the entire contract price. This remedy is also available if it is stipulated that the price is to be paid on a certain day and that day has passed.

If the property has not passed, however, the seller will have to sue for damages for non-acceptance of the goods. The disadvantage with this is that the seller will still have the goods and will be obliged to reduce their damages by selling them elsewhere. As a result their recoverable damages will be the difference between the contract price and the price at which they later sold the goods to a third party. This will frequently be negligible.

7.7.2 Stoppage in transit

A further valuable remedy for the seller is the right of stoppage in transit, conferred by the English Sale of Goods Act. This gives the seller the right to stop the goods in the course of carriage and to repossess them when the buyer is insolvent and there is an obvious danger that the seller will not be paid.

There are two important conditions – the insolvency of the buyer, which is paramount, and the goods, which must still be in transit and not have been delivered to the buyer. If the carrier is the buyer's agent (as in a FOB contract), delivery to the carrier will in law be delivery to the buyer and the right of stoppage will not be available. The courts are fairly lenient, however, and in the case of FOB contracts where the seller's duty terminates on delivery to the ship, they have tended to regard the carrier as an independent party and not the buyer's agent – so the right of stoppage may still be exercised. The right is exercised simply by informing the carrier. The seller will be liable for payment of any freight.

7.7.3 Lien

If the seller still has the goods in their possession and the buyer becomes insolvent, the seller may retain the goods in defiance of their duty to deliver by exercising their unpaid seller's lien.

7.7.4 Remedies of the buyer

If the seller is in breach of a condition of the contract, it may arise because of one of the following circumstances:

- late delivery
- short delivery (not delivering a sufficient quantity)
- delivery of damaged goods or goods otherwise in breach of the seller's undertakings
- non-delivery
- tender of defective documents.

The buyer may reject the goods or, at an earlier stage, the documents. Note that acceptance of the documents does not necessarily prevent subsequent rejection of the goods), and sue for damages for non-delivery of the goods. Such damages will be the difference between the contract price and the market price of the goods at the time the goods ought to have been correctly delivered. As with the seller's right to damages for non-acceptance, these may be negligible.

If the buyer decides not to reject the goods, or has lost their right to reject them by having unduly interfered with the goods, they will keep them, and sue for damages for defective delivery. In this case their damages will be calculated according to the difference between the value of their goods as and when delivered and the market value of those goods had they been correctly delivered (ie on time, or undamaged).

Specific performance

The buyer's equivalent of the seller's right to sue for the price is to demand the actual correct delivery of the goods, and thereby the performance of the contract. This is known as asking for an 'order for specific performance'. This is only likely to be granted if it is impossible to obtain the contract goods at any price elsewhere,. Consequently, it is a very rare order for a court to make.

7.8   LAW AND JURISDICTION

This item has as its example the position under English law. Whether a particular contract is, in fact, subject to English law is determined by reference to the contract itself. First and foremost, the contract may actually stipulate that it is to be governed by English law and that disputes are to be referred to an English court or arbitration proceedings. In the absence of such a stipulation, reference must be made to the nationalities of the parties and the countries within which performance of the contract is to take place. If these point overwhelmingly to one country, the law of that country may apply.

Finally, note that there may be a difference between the governing law of a contract and the jurisdiction in which claims may be brought. For example, in the absence of a specific provision in the contract, the High Court in England might consider that it has jurisdiction over a particular dispute, while applying the law of some other country to determine the rights and responsibilities of the parties.

The UK government, along with the governments of other countries, is considering ratification of the UN Convention on Contracts for the International Sale of Goods. If ratified this will fundamentally alter the existing structure of these contracts.

7.9   POSTSCRIPT

It should be noted that this section is concerned only with the legal relationship between the two parties to the contract for the sale of goods. It takes no account of possible relationships between those parties and any third party, such as a carrier, which are beyond the scope of this part of the text.

Vasco da Gama – Portuguese mariner 1469–1524

Chapter 8

· ·

Finance in international trade

8.1 INTRODUCTION

The distance and time scales inherent in international trade present a number of problems for the people working in international business. The buyer wants to make sure that their agreement with the seller ensures the correct delivery of the goods ordered, at the right place, at the right time and with as little adverse effect on their cash flow as possible. On the other hand, the seller wants to make secure their payment within the shortes possible time between producing and/ or shipping the goods and receiving payment. They too are concerned with the maintenance of cash flow.

The concerns of the buyer and seller have implications for those involved in the international transportation of goods, because the method and timing of payment may well be dependent on the correct preparation and presentation of documents, adherence to shipment and delivery dates and any restrictions on transshipment of a consignment.

The emphasis of this chapter is on understanding the role of payments in international trade, the risks involved for the parties and the means by which they can protect themselves or limit their exposure to such risks.

8.2 METHODS OF PAYMENT

In considering methods of payment and the financing of overseas trade, we will focus on two main aspects. First security of payment upon safe and correct delivery of goods and secondl the implications certain methods of payment or financing in international trade have for those in shipping business.

The method of payment in any sales contract is a matter of negotiation between buyer and seller and depends upon the mutual trust that exists as well as the financial standing of the buyer. In a very competitive buyers' market the buyer may be able to negotiate more advantageous payment terms than if it is a sellers' market. It must be remembered that unless cash is handed over directly from buyer to seller without any kind of paperwork every method of payment involves some cost.

There exists a range of methods of payment, some of which are unsuitable for international trade, which provide varying degrees of security and advantage for both buyer and seller. The most advantageous for the seller is **cash with order,** a form of payment in advance. This is also referred to as 'advance payment against pro-forma invoice'. This method is the most secure for the exporter since they receive full payment for the goods ordered before any shipment is made. It is not, however, beneficial to the buyer because, in effect, they are extending credit to the seller and have little redress against delay in shipment or incomplete adherence to the contract.

Open account is the most favourable form of payment for a buyer. In this case the seller dispatches the goods and sends the documents directly to the buyer, and the seller awaits payment by some previously agreed manner. Often the payment terms may be monthly or even longer. While this method of payment is quite normal between companies in the same country that are known to be financially sound, it is a less usual method in international business. However, it is increasingly used between companies that have established trading patterns, particularly in areas like the European Union.

An alternative to the above where there is still mutual trust between buyer and seller is the **bill of exchange**. This document is similar in appearance to a cheque but usually stipulates payment at a future date, for example ninety days from the date of issue. Essentially this extends credit to the buyer, who may be able to sell a significant proportion of the cargo purchased before being required to pay the sum due on the bill. The buyer's cash flow is therefore put under less strain, and they may be able to afford to purchase larger quantities than under a less flexible form of payment. This in turn can benefit the seller, who is able to do more business with their customer as a result. The advantage of bills of exchange from the seller's point of view lies in the difference between the bill of exchange and a cheque. Unlike a cheque, a bill of exchange is negotiable and if the seller does not want to wait the full 90 days to collect payment they can 'discount' (sell) the bill to a bank for slightly less than its face value.

In order to spread the burden of the buyer it may be agreed, for instance, that 25% of the cost of the goods should be paid on receipt (or on transfer of the documents or whatever terms have been agreed for the sale) with the balance payable on three equal bills of exchange maturing at, say, 30, 60 and 90 days respectively.

The buyer signs the bills of exchange and hands them to the seller as part payment (in this case) for the goods. If the seller does not discount the bills at an earlier date, they will then present them on the due date at the buyer's bank (or wherever has been agreed beforehand) for payment. If they choose to discount one or more of the bills, the bank or discount house that buys the debt may sell it on to other institutions or use it as security until the maturity date, when it will be presented for settlement.

Documentary letter of credit

This method of payment, frequently found in international trade, is a very good compromise between the needs of both buyer and seller. It is a fairly flexible form of payment as it gives security to both buyer and seller and is one of the safest methods of payment. It is also a method that requires the carrier or their agent to fulfill their role with the utmost efficiency.

A documentary letter of credit is a document provided by a bank by which it undertakes to pay the seller against presentation of suitable documentary evidence for example, a **bill of exchange** and other documents as specified in the letter of credit, within a specified time period.

The bank providing the documentary letter of credit is known as the issuing bank, and acting on the instruction of the buyer, undertakes to make available a predetermined amount to the seller or *beneficiary*.

The opening of a letter of credit is normally done through the intermediary of another bank in the country of residence of the beneficiary. This is a general rule, but there are exceptions. It is not unusual for a letter of credit to be opened or established in the country of the buyer, and payable there. The applicant or buyer needs to state where the credit is to be paid. If it is not stated then it will be paid in the buyer's country. Some countries may restrict where a letter of credit is established and paid because of foreign exchange restrictions. The intermediary through whom the letter of credit is established is known as the *advising/confirming* or *paying bank*.

There are, therefore, four parties who are involved in documentary credit:

- the buyer – applicant for credit
- the seller – the beneficiary
- the buyer's bank – the issuing bank
- the advising/confirming or paying bank.

It is very important to understand that a bank may not re-interpret the terms of the documentary credit in any way. They must be adhered to exactly. To ensure, as far as is possible, uniformity of interpretation by banks in respect of documentary credits the International chamber of commerce, in conjunction with other interested parties, has produced guidelines entitled *Uniform customs and practice for documentary credits*, usually abbreviated to UCP.

Documentary credits are normally described as irrevocable, meaning that they cannot be revoked once they have been opened, but will lapse if the documents are not presented within the stipulated time. On the buyer's instruction the issuing bank irrevocably commits itself to pay the beneficiary on the correct presentation of the required documents.

If a seller is uncertain of the financial status of the buyer they will require the credit to be confirmed. This means that the bank in the buyer's country notifying the letter of credit gives an undertaking to pay without recourse to the seller (unless it is otherwise stipulated). The seller is certain of receiving payment provided they present the right documents. The correspondent bank may be willing to add their confirmation at the seller's request and expense, if requested and/or authorised by the opening bank to do so.

When the buyer instructs their bank to open a letter of credit they state explicitly the type of credit and the conditions under which the bank will pay the seller. In the example the buyer has elected to pay their **sight draft** provided it is accompanied by certain documents that ensure the delivery of the goods at the correct time and place. Normally, transhipment is allowed and that the documents must be presented for payment within 15 days from the date of shipment. There is usally an expiry date and this would be the latest date for the presentation of documents by the seller.

It is vital that the seller presents the required documents to the bank within the time limit set. It is also essential the documents comply fully with the instructions in the credit and are correctly completed in every detail.

8.3   DOCUMENTS

8.3.1 Invoice

The invoice is evidence of the contract that exists between the buyer and seller. It must specify the quality and quantity of the goods consigned, together with the unit and total price. In some instances the buyer will insist upon the invoice being certified by an independent body such as a chamber of commerce and may even demand that their country's consul confirm this certification. Some countries (because of import restrictions) may require a consular invoice in addition to a commercial invoice.

8.3.2 Insurance

The documentary credit in the example covers a CIF sale and therefore requires a certificate of insurance, an example of which is shown in **Appendix 13**.

8.3.3 Bill of lading (B/L)

It is in this area where a documentary credit is most specific because in its role as a document of title, the bill of lading is the ultimate security for payment. As you see from the bill of lading in **Appendix 14**, the description of the cargo and all the other stipulations in the documentary credit have been complied with. Even the slightest deviation may result in payment being refused or delayed.

Note in the documentary credit the use of the word 'clean' in the description of the bills of lading. The B/L would not be 'clean' if it contained any endorsement relating to the condition of the cargo and such an endorsement would guarantee refusal by the bank to pay.

8.3.4 Other documents

In addition to the documents mentioned in the example, the buyer may demand such things as a certificate of origin, a phytosanitary certificate, a certificate of analysis or other type of independent inspection. The buyer relies on such documentation to provide evidence that the goods covered by the invoice are indeed what they expect them to be, as they pay for the goods at the same moment as they receive the documents.

8.4 CONFIRMING HOUSES

The examples used to explain the financing of international trade, have all involved the seller in one country and the buyer in another. One other method involves confirming houses or, to use their more modern title exporting houses. This method of trading evolved in those European countries such as the UK, the Netherlands, Portugal etc that formerly administered substantial overseas territories, but it is now found in almost all industrialised countries.

The confirming house role is an unusual mixture of agent and principal. The purchase negotiations may take place directly between the overseas buyer and the seller or the buyer may choose to have the confirming house as their agent and locate and order the goods. At the time of shipment, the confirming house earns its title because it 'confirms' responsibility for payment to the seller as and when supplies are shipped. In some contracts the confirming house's commitment goes even further by accepting full liability as a principal vis à vis the seller while still being seen as an agent by the buyer. Regardless of the contract terms relating to the sale, the confirming house will always be a principal in its dealings with the carrier.

8.5 RISKS IN INTERNATIONAL TRADING

To understand the problems of buyers and sellers in international trade it is important to appreciate some of the risks that they face in their normal course of business.

All business carries some element of risk, but international traders have to deal with particular problems and learn to take appropriate actions to limit their exposure if they wish to safeguard their businesses and prosper. These include not only the hazards of handling and transporting goods over long distances to remote locations, but unforeseen fluctuations in transport costs and currencies.

8.6 FOREIGN EXCHANGE FLUCTUATIONS

In any international trade transaction either the buyer or the seller, and sometimes both, will also be involved in a foreign exchange transaction, buying or selling the currency used in payment for the goods or services.

However rates of exchange fluctuate and, therefore, the price set when the sales contract was made may not be directly reflected in the money actually received by the seller or paid by the buyer. To take a simple example, if the price set for a consignment of goods sent to the USA by a UK exporter was $6,000 calculated at an exchange rate of $1.50 to £1, the exporter would expect to receive £4,000 when they changed the dollars at the bank. If, however, by the time payment is actually made and the dollars changed into pounds the rate was $2.00 to £1, the exporter would only receive £3,000, which would quite likely turn the anticipated profit into a loss.

International traders have a number of options they can consider when trying to mitigate the risks of currency fluctuations working against them. After assessing the risks they could decide to do nothing – to take a chance that the fluctuation, if it is unfavourable, will not be so serious as to put the business in peril. In this case they will either buy or sell their currency on the spot market at the time of the transaction. If they are lucky and the exchange rate moves in their favour they can take advantage of an unexpected bonus. Those traders dealing in large amounts of currency or working on small margins may find this to be an unacceptable risk. In this situation, banks can offer various alternatives for hedging against currency losses, such as forward exchange contracts or foreign currency options. Many companies adopt a combination of these methods in order to spread their risk and keep down the costs.

One method of reducing the effect of exchange rate fluctuations and the uncertainty they create is for them to enter into a contract with the bank to buy or sell foreign currency at a future date but at a rate fixed at the time of the contract.

8.6.1 Spot rate

The rate at which currencies are exchanged today is known as the spot rate and these spot rates are quoted in the financial pages of the more 'serious' newspapers. Two rates will, in fact, be quoted: the bank's selling price and the bank's buying price. (Remember that there are two sides to every transaction. If you are buying the bank is selling and if you are selling the bank is buying.)

8.6.2 Forward exchange contracts

A forward rate may be calculated either for a fixed time ahead or for a period of time. For example, a contract made on 1 November that is two months forward fixed becomes due on 1 January.

However, it may be that the exporter is not sure when the buyer will make payment and, therefore, uncertain when they will wish to sell foreign currency to the bank. In this instance they will want to retain some flexibility over the date of the completion of the contract with the bank. They will also want to have what is known as an 'option dated forward contract' so that within certain agreed dates they may choose exactly when they sell the money to the bank. It is important to note that under an option dated forward contract there is no choice about whether to sell (or buy) the money or not. Once the contract is made it is binding and the only choice is over the exact time of completion.

In the example of the two-month fixed contract given above, the currency had to be exchanged on 1 January. If the exporter wanted some flexibility they could choose to have a three-month forward contract with an option over the second and third month.

The various forward rates are calculated by referring to the spot rate (either bank selling or bank buying) and then using the forward rates to calculate the contract price.

The forward rates will be quoted as being at a premium or a discount that reflects the difference in interest rates on the interbank market rather than what the bank regards as the possible exchange rates in the future. For example, currencies with lower interest rates than the pound sterling will be said to stand at a premium while those with higher interest rates will be at a discount.

In the example below we see the US dollar being quoted as a premium.

Spot rate £1 =	$1.5040	—	$1.5120
One month	.10c	—	.05c pm
Two months	.15c	—	.12c pm
Three months	.25c	—	.18c pm

To calculate a forward rate the bank will deduct the appropriate premium from the spot rate. So based on the above figures the forward contract rates would be as follows:

	Bank selling	Bank buying
One month	$1.5030	$1.5115
Two months	$1.5025	$1.5108
Three months	$1.5015	$1.5102

As the dollar becomes more expensive you will get fewer dollars for sterling if you are buying from the bank but more pounds when the bank is buying dollars from you.

Now compare this with an example of the dollar being quoted at a discount:

Spot rate £1 =	$1.5040	—	$1.5120
One month	.03c	—	.08c pm
Two months	.10c	—	.15c pm
Three months	.17c	—	.23c pm

To calculate the forward rate in the case of a currency that is becoming cheaper, the appropriate discount will be added giving the following forward rates.

	Bank selling	Bank buying
One month	$1.5043	$1.5128
Two months	$1.5050	$1.5135
Three months	$1.5057	$1.5143

As the dollar is becoming cheaper when the bank sells you dollars in the future you will get more for your pounds, but if they are buying dollars from you, you will get less in the future than at the spot rate.

If the contract is a forward option then the bank will have the choice of quoting either the rate at the beginning or the end of the option period. For example, if you had the forward option contract mentioned above, three months forward with the option over the second or third months, the rate could either be the one month rate (the rate at the beginning of the period) or the three months rate (the rate at the end of the period). If the currency is at a premium then the bank will sell at the rate at the end of the period and buy at the rate at the beginning of the period. If, on the other hand, the currency is at a discount the bank will sell at the rate at the beginning of the period and buy at the rate at the end of the period.

The bank will always buy or sell at a rate it finds most advantageous. The point is the customer will know exactly what the rate will be when they make the contract and so has certainty about what they will receive in the future, and may well be able to adjust their price to the contract exchange rate.

To sum up, the contract rate is set when the contract is made. The option in the contract is there so that the customer may choose exactly when, during the option period, they will buy or sell the currency concerned. Once the contract is made it must be completed.

The four main rules to remember are:

1. The bank buys high

2. The bank sells low

3. A discount is added to the spot rate

4. A premium is deducted from the spot rate.

Also since the bank is in the business of making a profit, like any other business, it will set the option contract rate that is most advantageous to the bank.

8.6.3 Foreign currency options

These are a more flexible way of obtaining protection against currency rate movements. The key difference between these and the forward currency contract is that the customer is not obliged to declare the option if it is not advantageous to do so. This arrangement with the bank confers a right *but not an obligation* to buy (or sell) currency at an agreed rate. If the currency moves in the trader's favour during the option period, then the option can simply be allowed to lapse. It does, however, provide all-important protection against adverse currency rate fluctuations. If these should occur, the option is available to be exercised.

Foreign currency options are also useful for businesses that may require an amount of a foreign currency at some future date but cannot be sure of this – for example during the negotiation of prices for an international deal which takes into account a known rate of exchange. If the deal goes ahead, the guaranteed rate could be improved upon, but could never be worse than the option rate. If the deal falls through, the option can be allowed to lapse.

There are two basic types of option available from banks. European options, where the exercise date (otherwise known as the 'strike date') is fixed, and is the only date upon which the option can be exercised and American options that can be exercised at any time up to the expiry date, after which it, too, expires. There is a price (known as the premium) that is paid up-front to the bank at the time the option is arranged. This is usually quoted as a percentage of the currency amount, and will be a function of the 'strike' rate agreed, the option period and type, and the bank's assessment of the volatility of the currencies involved and the interest rate differentials between them.

Let us assume that the worst rate an exporter is prepared to accept is \$1.65 when exchanging the proceeds of a sale (in dollars) for pounds sterling. In order to protect themselves against a worse rate, they may decide to buy an American style currency option to sell \$1m at a strike price of \$1.65 for expiry in, say, six months time. If, at any time during this period, the market (spot) rate is worse than \$1.65 the option can be exercised and the dollars sold at \$1.65 through the bank. Alternatively, if the market rate is better than \$1.65 the option can be allowed to lapse and the dollars sold in the market at the spot rate.

Traders regularly working in particular foreign currencies will normally operate foreign currency accounts through their banks so that they can hold sums of one or more currency without being forced to buy or sell at a possible disadvantage at the time they receive or make payments. It should be noted, however, that some countries protect their own currencies by imposing restrictions on the use of foreign currency accounts and permission may have to be sought from government departments to buy or sell currencies.

8.6.4 Transaction costs in international trade

International trade is a complex business, and traders face many more problems than those doing business domestically. The costs involved in trading globally (otherwise known as transaction costs) are many and varied. We have already looked at the risks involved in arranging international payments and those posed by adverse currency movements, but there are others.

Transport costs may also fluctuate according to the state of the market, the costs of bunker fuel and other factors beyond the control of either buyer or seller.

To a limited extent some traders may be able to protect themselves against unforeseen movements in the freight market by trading in freight futures, sometimes known as forward freight agreements (FFAs).

Trading in 'futures' of any type (and if you read the financial press you will see that there are futures markets in most commodities, from crude oil to orange juice) involves forming a view on what the market prices are likely to be at some point in the future.

So long as there are two opposite sides that stand to gain or lose by future price movements (usually the buyer on one hand and the seller on the other) then the conditions exist for a futures market. If I am running a business making instant coffee in Europe, then I have an interest in what the price of the coffee beans will be in the future. My risk is that for some reason beyond my control (such as a world shortage of beans owing to bad weather at harvest time, disease affecting the plantations, political disruptions etc) the price will increase substantially and affect the profitability of my business. If, on the other hand, I grow coffee beans in Kenya, my risk is that when my crop is ready for sale the price will be so low that I cannot cover my costs.

If, as a buyer of coffee, I can find a seller prepared to bet that the price of coffee beans in six months time is going to be no more than 5% above today's price, I can, in effect, lock into this price. If the seller is wrong and the price is substantially higher on the agreed date, they will pay me in proportion to the difference between the price agreed in our futures contract and the actual market price on that date. If the price on the day turns out to be much lower than the price agreed in our futures contract then I would pay them on a similar basis.

As we are both traders in the coffee business we have a lot to lose if the price of coffee moves against us. If the price of coffee in six month's time is higher than the level agreed then I stand to gain financially from the deal. On the other hand, I still have to buy my coffee beans at a higher price, so my gain in the futures deal is offset by having to pay a higher price in the real (physical) market.

On the same basis, a market in freight futures was established, during the 1980s in response to perceived demand from traders. In 1985 the Baltic Exchange inaugurated the Baltic Freight Index, which was designed to reflect as closely as possible the level of freights in the most important sectors of international dry cargo shipping. A list of the component routes that made up the index was developed.

These routes have been revised over the years to reflect changing trends and can be 'weighted' according to their importance in the market at any given time in the real (physical) freight market. A glance at *Lloyd's List* will show how a number of these indices are made up, each reflecting movements in a particular sector of the freight market.

Clearly on any given day it is highly unlikely that there will have been actual fixtures reflecting all of the voyages making up the index. Therefore a panel of the world's leading international ship broking firms submit their informed estimated rates for that day on each of the voyages. The relevant Baltic Exchange committee then discards the highest and lowest figures and averages the remaining figures in order to compute the level of the index for that day.

As well as computing the index on a daily basis, the Baltic Exchange hosted a market for traders dealing in freight futures, known as the Baltic International Freight Futures and Options Exchange (BIFFEX) to allow players to trade in futures contracts in a formal way. Although the market moved from the Baltic Exchange to the London Commodity Exchange in 1991 and then to the London International Financial Futures Exchange, the Baltic Exchange Index is still used as the basis for trading.

Charterers who have sold a commodity to be shipped at some future date are naturally concerned that freight rates might rise, reducing or eroding their trading profits. To protect themselves against this eventuality they can 'buy' freight futures contracts. Therefore, if freight rates rise sharply at the time when they have to fix a ship, the loss they incur on the physical market will be offset to some extent by the profit they make on their futures position.

Shipowners face the exact opposite risk to charterers, as they stand to lose if freight markets plunge. They can protect themselves against falling freight rates by "selling" futures contracts in the same market. If (contrary to their expectations) freight rates actually rise, then they will benefit from higher earnings in the physical market, which will offset the money they lose on their futures trading.

With an index-based futures contract, it is not possible to deliver an actual cargo or a ship in settlement of a position, so all the contracts traded in freight futures are settled in cash, based on the actual level of the index on the date that the position matures.

The FFA market depends on the willingness of shipowners on one hand and charterers on the other to 'buy' and 'sell' contracts. If both parties are involved in the physical markets that are reflected in the index (for example, the charterers may be grain traders active in the US Gulf to northern Europe trade and the shipowners may be operating bulkers of Panamax size in the Atlantic) then they can expect that the index to reflect their actual trading conditions. To this extent, their activity in the futures market can be seen as hedging their prospects in the physical market, if they gain in one, they will lose in the other, thus reducing their exposure to wild fluctuations, which could be disastrous for them.

There is nothing to stop participants who are neither shipowners or charterers from buying or selling contracts in the freight futures markets such trading takes place in virtually all the futures markets and lends liquidity to the market. However, as they have no vested interest in the physical market, they are not involved in hedging operations, but are investing on a purely speculative basis, hoping to make a profit by merely trading the futures market.

It should be clear by now that this is a very specialised form of hedging that requires considerable expertise and knowledge of the market and is not to be undertaken without careful consideration and advice from experts in the field.

8.7   INSURANCE

Insurance is a vital aspect of trade since it provides a secure environment for commerce. International trade has many uncertainties and risks, and therefore insurance assumes a very particular importance. If insurance did not exist, the number of people willing to undertake international trade would undoubtedly diminish. Companies would be forced to 'insure' themselves by retaining large capital sums against the possibilities of loss, which would hamper the management of the business and in turn the opportunities to make profits.

In general, a person may only take out insurance if they have an interest in the goods or property insured. The assured (the person whom the insurance covers) must be in a position to suffer loss if there is a mishap. If that person does not have an insurable interest they will probably not look after the property or goods adequately and would actually benefit if there were a loss. If there is no insurable interest then the claim would be declared void.

The essential features of insurable interest in respect of marine/cargo insurance are:

(a)   There must be a physical object exposed to marine peril.

(b)   The insured must have some legal relationship to that object in consequence of which they benefit by its preservation or are prejudiced by its loss or damage.

In maritime business the insured need not have an insurable interest at the time of placing the insurance, but in order to recover under their policy they must have an interest at **the time of the loss.**

The simplest form of insurable interest is the ownership of the goods being insured, but other kinds of insurable interest do exist.

A buyer will have an insurable interest whether goods are sold FOB or CIF, even though they have the right to reject them if they are contractually incorrect and return them to the seller to whom property will pass.

The seller has an insurable interest while they have the risk or property of the goods or both. If the buyer rejects the goods or there is stoppage in transit, then the rights will revert to the seller. If payment is required before ownership passes, then the goods remain the seller's property until payment is made. Obviously having insurance in place that takes effect at the moment of handover (as risk passes from seller to buyer) is vitally important in ship sale and purchase transactions.

Carriers have an interest because of their liability to cargo owners, as do shippers, to the extent that they wish to cover freight paid in advance.

A charterer has an insurable interest, as they have a liability to the shipowner. For example, if a ship is fixed to load at 'a good and safe berth, always afloat' and, while loading, the ship goes aground as a result of the water being shallower than expected, the owner can justifiably hold the charterer responsible for damage to the hull. Or if the charterer describes the cargo as 'harmless' and it subsequently corrodes the vessel's holds, they will be held responsible for the resulting damage.

Time charterers have additional liabilities to the shipowners in respect of their control over the vessel whilst it is on hire to them, so their insurable interest will be more extensive than that of a voyage charterer. Charterers can take out specific insurance cover in respect of these liabilities.

The insurer has an insurable interest in the risk they have written and therefore the insurer is able to spread the risk they have undertaken through re-insurance.

Commission to agents and **brokerage** fees may also create an insurable interest. Indeed, some shipbroking companies as a matter of routine insure their brokerage under all their time charter fixtures.

A broker can (and should) insure against the risk of making some significant error in the fixture of a ship that might result in a owner or a charterer claiming against them or their principal. This is known as professional indemnity insurance.

8.8   TRADE TERMS IN EXPORT SALES

In any export transaction, the responsibility for arranging insurance will be either with the seller or buyer as agreed in the contract of sale. If the contract includes Incoterms 2010, then the responsibility for the arranging and payment of the insurance will be absolutely clear.

For example, under an FOB sale, the goods are at the risk of the exporter until such time as they have effectively crossed the ship's rail and they will generally arrange their own insurance for that leg of the journey. Once they have crossed the ship's rail, the goods will be at the buyer's risk and it is their responsibility to place the insurance coverage.

If goods are sold CIF then it is the responsibility of the seller to arrange, at their cost and in a form that is transferable, a policy of marine insurance.

The **transferability** of the policy under a CIF sale is vital. While the seller takes out the policy and pays the premium to cover the risk all the time the goods are in transit (i.e. while they are still owned by the seller), the most likely time for damage to be discovered is after discharge when the ownership has passed to the buyer.

8.9   WARRANTIES

In insurance the word 'warranty' has a very specific meaning. It is an undertaking by the insured to observe certain conditions. The rule is embodied in Section 33 of the Marine Insurance Act, which states that:

"A warranty… is a condition which must be exactly complied with, whether it is material to the risk or not. If it be not so complied with, the insurer is discharged from liability."

For example, if there is a condition that the insured goods have a certain type of packaging and this is not adhered to, then in the event of a loss the claim may be disallowed on the grounds that the goods were improperly packed. This is regardless of the fact that the loss may not in any way be due to the packaging.

(a) **Express warranties**

This is an undertaking actually written into the contract to perform a certain act. Failure to carry out the condition may well result in the policy being declared void.

(b) **Implied warranties**

In this case the law regards certain conditions as implied part of the insurance contract, although they may not be specifically stated.

In marine insurance there are two warranties that fall into this category:

1. At the commencement of the risk the venture must be legal to the extent that the insured is in a position to control it.

2. That the vessel is seaworthy, that it is fit for the proposed voyage.

8.10 TYPES OF POLICY FOR CARGO

8.10.1 Facultative insurance

This type of insurance refers to the placing of a specific or named risk and it relates to a particular 'sending' or shipment. As you will have seen from the brief description above, the effecting of this type of insurance may be a relatively complex procedure, therefore most exporters regularly sending goods overseas would find it far too time-consuming for every consignment to be insured in this way.

8.10.2 Open contracts

It is much more advantageous to the exporter if the cost of insurance can be standardised. In this way, when making quotations or agreeing particular terms of sale, the exporter will know approximately what cost to allow for the insurance cover. This has led to the growing use of open contracts in international trade.

There are three types of open contracts: floating policies, open covers and open policies.

8.10.3 Floating policies

This policy provides insurance, that will cover a certain total value of goods. For example, it may cover shipments from London to Vancouver over a period of six months for leather goods to a total value of £1 million. There is an initial general description of the risk but the particulars of the goods and the ship used etc. are declared prior to individual shipments. The shipper declares each of these until the fixed ceiling is reached and the policy is exhausted. Each shipment is declared on special forms and the amount outstanding on the policy is reduced by the amount of that shipment. The assured is bound to declare each shipment and the insurer is bound to accept the shipment providing it complies with the agreed terms. Since the policy is issued when it is first negotiated, policies will not be issued for each individual shipment and certificates of insurance will be issued instead. It is important, therefore, that a seller using CIF terms ensures that the contract allows them to present a certificate of insurance rather than a policy. The disadvantage of this type of policy is that the insurer expects to be paid a premium deposit related to the total value of the policy. An average premium is estimated and is adjusted when the declarations of actual cargo carried are made.

8.10.4 Open covers

Under open covers there is automatic cover available for a period time. This may be for a period of one year or longer or even on a permanent basis unless cancelled by either party. Under this type of agreement, the insurer agrees to cover all consignments and the premium rates are fixed. This gives the greatest flexibility and also stability of pricing to the exporter. Open covers may be arranged on almost any terms and they may be extremely complex. They may contain a limit per consignment (the value of goods to be sent on any one ship) or limit on location (the value of goods to be in one place before shipment). On occasions, floating policies may be issued in conjunction with open cover.

8.10.5 Open policies

These are really a type of open cover that do not relate to a time period but remain in force until cancellation. These policies are usually very individualistic and designed to meet all the demands of modern multi-modal transport. The methods and procedure of declarations against this type of policy are devised to meet the needs of the assured. It is also advantageous to the broker and insurer, since they receive a large volume of business, which can be dealt with in a standardised way.

The open cover or policy has a number of advantages:

● As there is a continuous automatic cover in force, the insured avoids the risk of omitting to effect the necessary insurance cover.

● The cost of obtaining insurance is known in advance, which enables an exporter to include a precise figure for the insurance element when computing the CIF price. It must be remembered that for some commodities the insurance element may be very large.

● Usually insurers are prepared to give better terms to an exporter arranging an annual policy than to one arranging cover on an individual basis.

● It may be, from time to time, that claims will arise which are not strictly speaking recoverable. If the insured has had regular dealings with a particular underwriter, they may well be in a better position to negotiate some form of commercial settlement than for insurance arranged on a facultative basis.

8.11 EFFECTING INSURANCE

Any person involved in international trade would rather have the safe delivery of a consignment than be involved in an insurance claim. However, because of the risks involved in international trade, claims do frequently arise and it is important when this happens that the insurance that has been taken out ensures that the claim will be met.

It is therefore very important that great care is taken when arranging insurance, particularly under an open cover. The failings in any type of cover will probably only become evident when a claim is being made and then it will be too late. Cover should always be as comprehensive as possible and drawn up in such a way that it meets the individual requirements of the company.

In order to understand the considerations an underwriter will weigh up in deciding whether to accept a risk, it is worth examining the type of information they are likely to require:

Cargo and packing

They will require a full description of the goods, together with exact details of the way in which they will be packed. If they are containerised, what type of packing will there be within the container? If they are not containerised will the goods be in cartons, drums, crates or bales, for example?

Method of shipment

They will require full details of the method of shipment, whether it is to be containerised and, if so, will it be door to door, part of a groupage consignment, single or multiple drop etc. If not containerised, will it be a conventional shipment, in a chartered vessel or what special arrangements will be made regarding such things as transhipment?

Voyage

Obviously, in deciding a premium, the length of the voyage and ultimate destination is of major importance, especially if war and strikes rate charges apply. Where there is a high degree of risk, for example, where warlike activities are taking place, the insurance rate will rise. The voyage may also involve an element of storage if the goods are being sent to a distribution centre for onward transmission and the insurer will need to know this as otherwise the cover will cease at the original distribution centre.

Basis of valuation

In export transactions, goods are frequently sold and resold and their value may alter as a result. It is an advantage, therefore, if a value is agreed in advance, not least because this will save a great deal of time and expense in the event of a claim. This is known as a valued policy. The insurer may include expenses and profit and, if no fraud is involved, then the agreed value will be taken as the basis for a claim of total or partial loss. There may be an agreed value of the goods but the insured may decide to take the cover for a lower value. When exporting, for example, the basis of valuation may be CIF invoice value plus 15% and if there were a claim against this policy, then the claimant would receive the CIF value plus 15%. When making a declaration under an open policy it follows the same valuation will be used. The assured may include a percentage to cover anticipated profit/inflation when agreeing a basis of valuation. The principle in marine insurance is to endeavour to place the insured not into the position they were in before the transit began but rather in the position they would have been had the venture been successfully completed. An unvalued policy would require proof of value in the event of a claim.

8.12   CONDITIONS OF INSURANCE

The conditions of insurance, which dictate the level of cover, are of vital importance and merit special consideration. A marine insurance policy is not like a household comprehensive policy or a motor policy where one can presume with some safety that the basic protection is the same with only minor variations. The vast majority of marine policies are specifically drafted to reflect the individual risk. Rather than providing a brief summary of all the various types of policies we examine, in detail the three most popular.

The old-fashioned Institute cargo clauses (all risks, with average and free of particular average) have been redundant since 1 January 1982 and have been superseded by three new clauses, namely Institute cargo clauses (A), (B) and (C). The fundamental change is that, whereas under the old system the SG policy form (which was first adopted in 1779) and the clauses had to be read as one, the new clauses are designed and to be read and interpreted as standalone clauses.

Incidentally, the exact meaning of the letters SG seems to have been lost in the annals of time, but the most popular theory is that they simply refer to 'ship and goods'.

8.12.1 Institute cargo clauses (C)

These clauses cover only fire, explosion, vessels or craft being stranded, grounded, sunk or capsized, overturning or derailment of land conveyances, collision or contact, discharge of cargo at a port of distress, general average sacrifice and jettison.

They exclude deliberate damage by the wrongful act of any person or persons, ie malicious damage, but this cover can be included by the addition of the new Malicious Damage Clause in return for paying an additional premium. This clause protects against the major casualties only.

8.12.2 Institute cargo clauses (B)

These clauses offer, in addition to the cover given by the 'C' clauses, the following additional perils:

Earthquake, volcanic eruption or lightening, washing overboard, entry of sea, lake or river water into a vessel, craft, hold conveyance, lift van or place of storage, plus total loss of packages lost overboard or dropped overboard during loading or unloading.

It should be noted that the 'B' Clause also carries the Deliberate Damage Exclusion and that the additional cover in the terms of new Malicious Damage Clause should be sought.

Important. Neither 'B' nor 'C' clauses cover theft.

8.12.3 Institute cargo clauses (A)

These clauses are without doubt the most widely used clauses when dealing with dry cargoes. The cover afforded is well defined by the paramount clause, which reads: "Against all risks of loss of or damage to the subject matter insured."

Ordinary leakage, ordinary losses in weight or volume, ordinary wear and tear are excluded, as are the risks of inherent dangers and delay.

8.12.4 Conditions common to Institute cargo clauses (A), (B) and (C)

1) Clause 4.3 Packing
   This clause excludes claims "resulting from insufficiency or unsuitability of the packing or preparation of the subject matter"

2) Clause 4.6 Insolvency
   This clause excludes loss or damage arising from insolvency or financial default of the owners, managers, charterers or operators of a vessel being used. Again this is not new as it has never been the intention for a marine cargo policy to guarantee the performance of third parties and to meet their liabilities. This clause should encourage the insured to use only creditworthy and reputable sea carriers.

3) Clause 4.7 and Clause 4.8 Atomic weapons
   In common with the radioactive contamination exclusion clause, which is used in other branches of insurance, this clause, for clarity, excludes the result of a non-warlike use of an atomic weapon. This obviously relates to misuse or accidental misuse.

4) Clause 7.3 Terrorists
   This clause excludes damage caused by any terrorist or person acting from a political motive. It is a clause that has particular relevance to some countries and is a point of particular importance in inland transit cases in those countries. To obtain such cover the Institute war clauses must be incorporated.

Irrespective of the basic conditions of insurance selected, you will normally opt for the inclusion of cover against the risk of "war and strikes." There are some popular misconceptions, even among people employed in the insurance industry as to what is and what is not covered under these clauses. It is important to examine these clauses in a little more detail.

8.12.5 Institute war clauses

In simple terms, this provides for loss or damage to the insured interest caused by hostilities, warlike operations, civil war, revolution, rebellion, insurrection etc. It is not generally appreciated that cover attaches only as the interest insured is loaded on board the overseas vessel and terminates once it has been discharged. In other words, the war risks cover only applies while the goods are at sea and does not attach while the goods are travelling on land. In addition, the cover specifically excludes loss or damage from the use of any atomic or nuclear weaponry.

8.12.6 Institute strikes, riots and civil commotions clauses

Taking the simple case of a dock strike in Liverpool, the following situation will emerge:

- Assuming that your cargo is caught up in a strike, the period of transit will inevitably be prolonged. During this time the normal risks, particularly those of theft and pilferage, will obviously be enhanced. Under the standard cargo policies, provision is made for cover to continue during this extended period.

- The insurance covers physical loss or damage to the property insured directly caused by strikers, locked-out workmen or persons taking part in labour disturbances, riots, civil commotions and by persons acting maliciously,

- What the strike clauses specifically exclude is loss or damage, caused by the passive action of the strikers in withdrawing their labour.

With some commodities it will not make any difference whether the voyage takes one week or one month, but for perishables the situation is quite different. When dealing in perishables, it is possible in some instances to negotiate this additional form of cover, but it is something that is often overlooked.

8.13 PREMIUMS

Each exporter's insurance rate will depend on their individual claims record. An underwriter assessing insurance risk takes many factors into account. They will obviously look at the commodity, the conditions of insurance they are being asked to grant, the adequacy of the packing, the attention given to shipping arrangements, destinations, etc. However, primarily they are guided in their judgement by the exporter's past claims experience.

In this regard there are a number of ways in which an exporter can make a positive contribution towards keeping their insurance costs to a minimum and this will be dealt with in a little more detail when discussing the question of loss prevention.

8.14 CLAIMS PROCEDURE

It is imperative that when claims do arise they are handled efficiently so that settlement can be made without delay and for this reason merchants should become familiar with the steps to take in the event of such a claim.

1. Any news regarding a claim or even a potential claim should be communicated to insurers at the earliest opportunity.

2. If the loss is likely to exceed a minimum amount, underwriters will normally require a survey report. Lloyd's agents, who are available in practically every major port throughout the world and are at the service of all underwriters, conduct surveys. When instructed, they carry out inspections and issue recommendations regarding repairs etc. Where a shipper has sold CIF, for example, and has issued the consignee with an insurance certificate the Lloyd's agent will appear on that certificate. Once the claim has been quantified and documented, underwriters are normally in a position to transfer the insurance money directly to the consignee through the Lloyd's aqgent.

3. A written claim should be made immediately on the carrier/shipowner, as failure to do so can prejudice the insurer's rights of recovery.

What happens in practice is that when the claim has been settled between the underwriter and exporter, it is then at the discretion of the underwriter to decide whether or not there is a claim worth pursuing against the carrier concerned (subrogation applies here).

4. Clean receipts should never be given if there is loss or damage to the cargo. The delivery docket/consignment note should be claused accordingly.

5. Finally, insurers will then require some or all of the following documents:

   (a) Insurance certificate

   (b) Commercial invoice

   (c) Bill of lading or consignment note, whichever is applicable

   (d) Delivery receipt

   (e) Correspondence with carriers/shipowners

   (f) Repair estimates

   (g) Surveyor's report.

Marine insurance claims are settled in the currency expressed on the insurance policy/certificate. If the claims are to be paid in the local currency it is necessary that the insurance certificate is issued and the premium paid in that currency also. The surveyor's fees/expenses form an admissible part of the claim once the claim itself is recoverable.

8.15   THE PRINCIPLE OF AVERAGE

Average is a technical term relating to partial loss. The concept of **partial loss** may be subdivided into **prticular average** or **general average**

8.15.1 Particular average

This term refers to accidental loss of or damage to specific items where only the claimant's cargo (or ship) is involved. A claim under the policy of insurance would naturally follow such an incident.

8.15.2 General average

This is a partial loss where everyone shares the loss of the cargo belonging to an individual because the loss is deemed to have benefited all involved in the venture.

A general average loss may occur for example, when:

(a) part of the cargo is sacrificed to save the entire venture

(b) part of the vessel is sacrificed to save the entire venture

(c) a ship and cargo are saved by unloading and reloading a stranded vessel

(d) water used to extinguish a fire, damages cargo (damage by fire would not be general average)

(e) cargo is lost due to it being used as fuel because no other is available. This may only be applicable if the action is undertaken to save the whole venture.

The foregoing are only examples and the list is by no means exhaustive.

The principle behind general average is that as all the parties benefited from the sacrifice, they should all contribute to the cost of saving the venture in proportion to the value of their property.

To establish each party's contribution, the list of expenses is passed to specialists known as average adjusters. To ensure that all the parties involved pay their share, their cargo is only released in exchange for an average bond plus in some cases an average guarantee. The cargo owner's insurers provide the latter document and if it is not forthcoming the carrying line may demand an actual cash deposit from the consignee.

General average is a highly complex subject and those needing a more extensive knowledge are recommended to study the ICS book *Marine Insurance*.

The practical steps that have to be undertaken by agents attending ships that have declared general average are contained in the ICS publications covering the relevant specialist subjects, such as *Port Agency* and *Ship Operations and Management*.

Post-Panamax container ship *CSCL Africa*, of 8,500teu capacity

Chapter 9

· ·

International shipping organisations

9.1 INTRODUCTION

A great many international organisations are directly or indirectly connected with the business of shipping. Some of them are intergovernmental, but the majority are in the private sector. Some of the more important and influential are included below.

It will be simplest to consider them in the following categories:

- Shipowners' organisations
- Brokers' and agents' organisations
- United Nations organisations
- Other shipping-related bodies.

It must be borne in mind that these are dynamic organisations, working in a fast-moving business and an ever-changing world. The internet is the ideal medium for keeping track of the latest developments in all these bodies, and the following 'thumbnail' descriptions contain details of useful websites.

9.2 SHIPOWNERS' ORGANISATIONS

9.2.1 International Chamber of Shipping

The International Chamber of Shipping (ICS) was established in 1921 and adopted its current title in 1948. Its members are composed of national shipowners' associations and shipping companies that together represent half the world's merchant fleet.

The ICS represents the collective views of the international merchant ship operators from different nations, sectors and trades. It is heavily involved in a wide variety of areas including technical, legal and operational matters affecting merchant shipping. It has consultative status with a number of intergovernmental bodies including the IMO, the World Customs Organization, the International Telecommunications Union and UNCTAD.

The London-based International Chamber of Shipping shares a secretariat with the International Shipping Federation (ISF), the only international employers' organisation dedicated to maritime manpower issues.

ISF is financed wholly by its members annual subscriptions paid by its members and calculated on the basis of the size of the fleet the member represent. It provides a forum for national shipowners' and managers' associations worldwide in the field of human resources, training and welfare as well as the traditional employers' issues

The International Chamber of Shipping and the International Shipping Federation share an informative website at **www.marisec.org.**

This also contains a list of the member organisations that make up the ICS, such as the Hellenic Chamber of Shipping, the Cyprus Shipping Council, the Japanese Shipowner's Association and the UK Chamber of Shipping, with hyperlinks to each of these organisations.

9.2.2 Intercargo

The International Association of Dry Cargo Shipowners, known as Intercargo was the idea of the late Antony Chandris who saw a need for a new international organisation to represent the interests of shipowners in the dry cargo (bulk) sector. Intertanko had shown what such an organisation could do for owners of tanker tonnage.

The first meeting took place in 1980, composed of founding members drawn largely from Greece with a handful from Scandinavia and Hong Kong. In 20 years the membership has grown to more than one hundred companies and groups that between them control some 30 million tons deadweight.

Intercargo is unique as the only international shipowners' group whose sole objective is the promotion and protection of the interests of private, independent owners in the dry bulk sector.

Its concerns are policy issues of a governmental or commercial nature that affect the overall health of the sector and not practical day-to-day questions, which are best dealt with by others. (Intercargo is required under its constitution not to duplicate the work of other bodies but, where appropriate, to work with them.)

Services provided by Intercargo to its members include an information service, advice, guidance and representation, with an active committee structure looking after policy, technical and commercial issues and participation in the work of the IMO, where the organisation has observer status.

For information and news on Intercargo's current activities, have a look at its website at **www.intercargo.org.**

9.2.3 Intertanko

The International Association of Independent Tanker Owners was established in 1970. It defines its three main goals as "safe transport, cleaner seas and free competition".

Independent owners control more than 70% of the world's tanker tonnage, and Intertanko represents over 75% of this sector, acting as a service association gathering intelligence and dispensing advice and information to members. Membership is open to owners and managing operators of tankers which are independent, excluding tonnage owned by oil companies and governmental agencies. It numbers some 235 owners and operators controlling 285 million deadweight tons of tankers, plus 300 associate members. Part of the success of Intertanko is that it has proved its worth as a pressure group.

Not only does Intertanko gather information and provide an intelligence centre for members; it has also always been particularly interested in documentary work and has pioneered and published forms for all types of tanker chartering. In addition it takes a keen interest in all aspects of maritime safety, particularly those affecting tanker operators, their ships, officers and crews.

Intertanko has an informative website at **www.intertanko.com** where the latest news of its activities can be found alongside useful links to other tanker-related sites.

9.2.4 Baltic and International Maritime Council (BIMCO)

The Baltic and International Maritime Council was founded in 1905 by a group of shipowners engaged principally in the Baltic and White Sea trades. At that time it was known as the Baltic and White Sea Conference and concerned itself mainly with regulating and improving the financial rewards of the timber trades.

Later it adopted a far wider outlook (though still predominantly dry cargo bulk trades) and changed its name to the Baltic and International Maritime Conference with the last word being changed to Council relatively recently.

Its membership is now international and consists of shipowners and operators (representing 60% of the world's merchant fleet), shipbrokers and agents, maritime lawyers and P&I clubs.

BIMCO's stated objectives are among others to pursue all issues affecting its members, seeking cooperation rather than confrontation, and providing input of a practical nature to ensure that the economic impact of new regulations on shipowners is fully appraised in the process.

For many years it has issued approved documents including charter parties and bills of lading, sometimes in collaboration with other bodies such as the Chamber of Shipping and FONASBA, and sometimes after agreement with organisations of charterers or shippers. This documentary role is the activity for which BIMCO is best known, although its many other activities are equally important.

An innovation in recent years has been the staging of one-day (sometimes two-day) courses in maritime centres around the world. These have attracted considerable support from local shipping audiences to hear papers delivered by eminent practitioners in the industry.

BIMCO was quick to realise the benefits of computer-based communication and information systems for its membership, and began pioneering work in this field during the late 1980s. Now its members can access much of its vast store of information on line. Though much of this information is restricted to its subscribers, a great deal of useful material can be found at **www.bimco.dk** including drafts of many of BIMCO's approved charter parties and other documents.

Throughout its life BIMCO has had its headquarters in Bagsvaerd, Copenhagen.

9.3   BROKERS' AND AGENTS' ORGANISATIONS

9.3.1 Institute of Chartered Shipbrokers

It all began in 1911. At that time London was, as now, a centre of many shipping activities and it was also a thriving port with busy berths along both banks of the Thames. But London was not the only town where the business of shipping played an important role. At many ports, especially those involved with Britain's extensive coal export trade, there were shipping exchanges for the chartering of tramp vessels and offices acting as agents for them when they called.

None of those provincial centres handled the volume of business transacted on London's Baltic Exchange, but they all shared a common desire to form an organisation devoted to the maintenance of the same ethical standards for which the 'Baltic' was famous. Thus it was that the different local associations of shipbrokers came together in 1911 and the Institute of Shipbrokers was formed.

It soon became apparent that the maintenance of standards needed more than simply the mutual desire and agreement to act in an ethical manner so a programme of education and training was devised.

Having formed itself into an organisation with the dual aims of education and the discipline involved in the maintenance of standards, the Institute was able to approach the Privy Council which granted its first Royal Charter in 1920.

The Privy Council's origins go back to the 16th century and it is a uniquely British body. It is the highest-ranking committee in the country presided over by the reigning sovereign, and granting royal charters is a small, but nonetheless important, aspect of its work.

As the bye-laws state, the charter enables the Institute "To devise and impose means for testing the qualifications of candidates for admission to professional membership by examination in theory and practice" and to "exercise professional supervision over the Members of the Institute and secure for them such definite professional standing as may assist them in the discharge of their duties".

The professional standing which the Institute is able to confer comprises membership (MICS) for those who pass the qualifying examinations and satisfy the Council that they are "fit and proper persons". Those who attain positions of influence in the profession may apply for promotion to fellowship (FICS) and may then call themselves chartered shipbrokers.

Since 1920, shipping has become more complex to the extent that the name 'shipbroker' which at one time was thought to apply only to those engaged in chartering dry cargo tramp ships, now embraces separate specialisations in tanker chartering, ship management, sale and purchase, port agency and liner trades. Each of these 'disciplines' is now examined separately in the qualifying examinations.

In 1984, the Institute succeeded in obtaining an amendment to its royal charter, which permitted several changes in the byelaws, one of which was the formation of an additional class of membership for companies, which enables the Institute to represent the interests of firms and corporations.

The most important amendment was, however, the removal of the limitation that restricted membership only to UK and the Commonwealth citizens. Today anyone in the world may be granted admission provided they fulfill the membership qualifications. This has enabled the Institute of Chartered Shipbrokers to become truly international.

Further information can, of course, be obtained from **www.ics.org.uk.**

9.3.2 Baltic Exchange

The Baltic Exchange is a limited company owned by its shareholders that comprise member companies, their principals and representatives on the Exchange and individual members.

The members of the Exchange, both corporations and individuals, are engaged in numerous trading spheres.

The largest activity conducted by members of the Exchange is in the international freight market, with chartering of vessels of all flags by charterers of all trading countries. Other activities carried out by member companies include the sale and purchase of ships, and the chartering and sale and purchase of aircraft. All these activities are international in scope.

The majority of members of the Exchange are brokers acting in the various markets as intermediaries between the principals. All the international trading activities concerned produce foreign exchange and members of the Baltic are major invisible export earners for the UK.

Commodity trading of various types was formerly carried out on the Exchange, including futures markets trading in agricultural commodities, specifically wheat, barley, potatoes, soya and meat, and the first freight futures market conducted through BIFFEX, which was launched in 1985.

The Exchange traces its origins to a club established in 1823 representing the users of the Baltic Coffee House which, in turn, started as a coffee house called the Virginia and Maryland until 1744, when it became the Virginia and Baltic.

The Baltic merged in 1900 with the London Shipping Exchange, and the main Exchange building was subsequently purpose-built and completed in 1903. The site of 14/20 St Mary Axe was acquired in 1947 and the building linked to the Exchange was built there in 1955/56. Sir Winston Churchill laid the foundation stone on 2 March 1955, and HM The Queen opened the building on 21 November 1956.

Membership of the Exchange is open to corporations registered in the UK, which have to be represented by principals resident in the UK for three years prior to election. It is also open to individuals in their own name or operating in partnerships.

The Exchange is governed by a board of 15 directors, 12 of whom are elected by shareholders and three by members. It has disciplinary powers of censure, suspension and expulsion over members and is responsible for sustaining proper ethical standards in trading. The Exchange derives its income from membership subscriptions and from rents of the offices, which it owns.

Members of the Baltic who carry on business as 'brokers only' will have signed the Brokers Letter by which they undertake not to trade as principals.

Members are required to operate separate bank accounts for clients and must take out appropriate insurance cover against errors and omissions, and breach of warranty of authority.

Information is posted on the official notice board for the guidance of members who are expected to conform with directions made from time to time in the interests of the market as a whole.

The secretary of the Exchange acts as chief executive of the organisation, carrying out policy determined by the directors and being responsible for the administration and organisation of the Exchange and its staff

Ethics

The motto of the Exchange – Our Word Our Bond – symbolises the importance of ethics in trading. Members need to rely on each other and, in turn, on their principals for many contracts verbally expressed and only subsequently confirmed in writing. The Baltic Exchange trading community has long been regarded the principle of treating others as one would wish to be treated oneself as the basis for ethical trading.

The directors have highlighted, from time to time practices, that they consider do not accord with Baltic ethics. These include:

1. Organisations operating as freight contractors/freight speculators offering named tonnage against tenders without the authority of owners/disponent owners.

2. Withholding payment of commissions when due in respect of hire/freight earned and paid.

3. Using information obtained through members in order to effect business direct with overseas principals or their local brokers and thus bypassing the Exchange.

The Baltic Exchange generates a number of freight indices, and these, along with real-time market information and a substantial database of shipping information, can be accessed by members through the Exchange's internet portal.

The Exchange building was destroyed by a terrorist bomb in 1992, which effectively put paid to the daily trading activity of the organisation. However, the spirit and character of the Baltic lives on. In its new home, a short distance along St Mary Axe from its former site, trading on 'the floor' is now restricted to a token session weekly. It is nonetheless still a powerful force in shipping circles and in the City of London. Those interested can see the full detail of the Baltic Code and much else besides on the Exchange's site at **www.balticexchange.com.**

9.3.3 Federation of National Associations of Shipbrokers and Agents (FONASBA)

The Federation of National Associations of Ship Brokers and Agents was formed in 1969 from national European shipbroker and agent associations to represent the interests of the liner agent, the tramp port agent, and the shipbroker engaged in the chartering of ships. Some 26 countries worldwide are now represented through their national members' associations.

FONASBA may be consulted and itself speaks with authority on all relevant matters concerning the shipping profession insofar as they affect shipbrokers and agents. It consults with national and international bodies, authorities and organisations on matters of concern to the shipping profession. It encourages fair and equitable practice of the profession of shipbrokers and agents and to that effect:

1. Supports its members when the basis and general interests of their profession are in question.

2. Co-ordinates common efforts to improve, simplify and standardise shipping contracts and documents.

3. Ensures an efficient exchange of information of general or particular interest.

The Federation aims particularly to co-operate with organisations of shipowners, merchants, and charterers on an international level, believing that the special relationship between its members and cargo and owner interests will enable FONASBA to bring to international discussions experience and expertise co-ordinated on a worldwide basis and thus make its contribution to international trade.

FONASBA's Chartering and Documentary Committee has actively participated in the revision of charter parties and other shipping documents. It has, for example, issued forms of liner and general agency agreements, an International Brokers' Commission Contract, a Time Charter Interpretation Code and a Guide to Standard Port Agency Conditions as well as devising the Multiform charter party (1982) as an alternative to the old General Voyage Charter Party (GENCON).

The Chartering and Documentary Committee also played a leading role in the revision of charter parties such as NORGRAIN 89, NYPE 93 and AMWELSH 93 issued by the American Agents' and Brokers' Association (ASBA). The guiding policy in all charter revisions is to remain objective and adopt an evenhanded position between charterer and owners irrespective of the current state of the market. The Federation advocates terms that are equitable to both sides, that are clear, comprehensive and reflect current conditions.

FONASBA's secretariat is based in London. It has consultative status with UNCTAD and attends the meetings in Geneva when shipping documentation is discussed and it speaks there as the voice of shipbrokers and agents internationally.

It now incorporates a daughter organisation, ECASBA (the European Community Association of Shipbrokers and Agents), which works in similar fields for the benefit of members within the European Union.

Further details of FONASBA's activities can be found on its website at **www.fonasba.com.**

9.3.4 International Federation of Forwarding Agents' Associations (FIATA)

FIATA's initials stem from its French title, as the Federation Internationale des Associations de Transitaires et Assimiles. The organisation was founded in Vienna in 1926. It is a non-governmental organisation representing an industry closely allied to the shipbroking sector, which incorporates more than 40,000 freight-forwarding firms in 150 countries worldwide.

FIATA is active in the fields of airfreight, customs and multi-modal transport as well as shipping and has working groups and committees that examine developments in sea, rail and air transport. These groups and committees have been active in producing recommended forms of documentation such as non-negotiable waybills, shippers' dangerous goods declarations, multimodal transport bills of lading, warehouse receipts and so on. Many readers will have seen the FIATA logo appearing on such documents.

FIATA's membership consists of national associations, such as the British International Freight Association (BIFA), groups and individual members.

More information about the federation, together with a full membership list, can be found on its website, **www.fiata.com.**

9.4   UNITED NATIONS ORGANISATIONS

9.4.1 International Maritime Organization (IMO)

The focus of the International Maritime Organization is safety at sea. A United Nations conference in 1948 adopted a convention that established the Inter-Governmental Maritime Consultative Organization (IMCO), which thus became the first international body devoted exclusively to maritime matters. The convention came into force in 1958, with the new body meeting for the first time the following year. It adopted its current name in 1982

IMCO took over the responsibility for upholding the International Convention for the Prevention of Pollution of the Sea by Oil (Oilpol), which had been passed in 1954. So, from the start, "the improvement of maritime safety and the prevention of marine pollution have been IMO's most important objectives".

In 1960 IMCO updated the existing International Convention for the Safety of Life at Sea (SOLAS), which had its origins in the *Titanic* disaster of 1912. SOLAS was further updated in 1974 and 2004. Its measures include machinery and electrical installations, the safety of navigation, the development of dangerous goods and nuclear ships.

The organisation is the only United Nations specialised agency to have its headquarters in the United Kingdom. It is based at 4 Albert Embankment, London.

The governing body of IMO is the Assembly, which meets once every two years. It consists of all 132 member states and one associate member.

IMO's Council comprises 32 member governments elected by the Assembly and acts as the organisation's governing body between Assembly sessions.

IMO is a technical organisation, and most of its work is conducted by committees and sub-committees, such as the Maritime Safety Committee (MSC) and the Marine Environment Protection Committee (MEPC). Such committees have contributed to promoting the adoption of some 30 conventions and protocols, and issued well over 600 codes and recommendations concerning maritime safety, the prevention of pollution and related matters.

Evidence shows that IMO measures have already proved beneficial in many areas. For example, the number of collisions between ships has been greatly reduced in areas where IMO-approved traffic separation schemes have been introduced.

More recently the IMO has been responsible for implementing the International Safety Management (ISM) Code for ships, imposing mandatory standards on safety procedures for all types of seagoing vessels and their operating companies.

The International Ship and Port Facilities Security (ISPS) Code is a part of the SOLAS Convention that IMO devised in response to concerns over security and terrorism, particularly after the terrorist attacks on New York in September 2001. ISPS includes elements of two other problems, piracy and stowaways, that have been of concern for many years. It came into force on 1 July 2004.

As the full name suggests, the ISPS Code works on two levels: ships and ports. Governments and maritime administrations must appoint **recognised security organisations (RSOs)** to certify the security arrangements that have been made in ports, on ships and in the shore offices of shipping companies. Exactly what sort of organisation can become an RSO is entirely at the discretion of national governments. Within the UK, only the Maritime and Coastguard Agency (MCA) has the power to vet ships, but many flag states have delegated the work to classification societies.

To comply with the code, ships and ports have to be subjected to a risk assessment, after which a security plan is drawn up. The plan is then reviewed by the RSO and, after a successful inspection and audit of the port or ship, a certificate is issued. After the coming into force of the code, countries with ports can deny entry to any ship that does not have a certificate, as well as ships coming from ports, that have not been certified as complying with the code.

On a practical level, both ports and ships operate on a three-stage security alert, with the precautions taken dependent on the security threat assessed. This means that for the most part both operate at the lowest level until some intelligence received makes a higher level desirable.

Updated information on the IMO's conventions, codes, rules and publications can be found on the organisation's formidable website: **www.imo.org.**

The IMO itself has no direct power to enforce its conventions. When they have been adopted, it is required that they be incorporated into the laws of flag countries, which are then responsible for ensuring conformity. The actual work of surveying vessels and the issuing of certificates of compliance is usually dealt with by classification societies. Inspection and enforcement is normally undertaken by port state control organisations operating under the direction of flag states and maritime countries.

9.4.2 United Nations Council for Trade and Development (UNCTAD)

Unlike the IMO, which is a technical body, UNCTAD is more of a political organisation. As its name suggests, UNCTAD is that arm of the United Nations dedicated to trade and development.

UNCTAD, based in Geneva, has a shipping division staffed by a dedicated team whose efforts have met with a mixed degree of success. Their non-mandatory minimum standards for shipping agents, which were promulgated in March 1988, were endorsed enthusiastically by almost all countries represented. Similarly, their maritime training programmes, tailor-made for developing nations, are held in high regard.

Less successful have been UNCTAD's attempts to regulate liner trading with the Code of Practice for Liner Conferences (usually remembered for one clause often referred to as the 40-40-20 rule). This international convention was overtaken by commercial evolution and attempts to modify it have been unsuccessful.

UNCTAD also launched the Hamburg Rules, which seek to regulate shipowners' liabilities on more favourable terms towards merchants than the more universally adopted Hague or Hague-Visby Rules. To date, insufficient countries have ratified the Hamburg Rules for it to have made any significant impact.

Two attempts to standardise the basic clauses in charter parties have so far failed to make progress. This, however, may not be surprising in view of the large volume of chartering that is controlled by groups that are quite happy with existing charter parties.

It would be quite unfair to judge UNCTAD by these few well-publicised failures; its successes often go unnoticed. That there are successes at all is often surprising when one considers that the officials have to endeavour to achieve a consensus among members with very different outlooks and objectives, aligned in groups of developed and developing countries.

UNCTAD's proceedings and other current topics can be found at **www.unctad.org**.

9.5 OTHER SHIPPING-RELATED BODIES

9.5.1 International Chamber of Commerce

Chambers of commerce exist in a wide variety of shapes and sizes. From one end of the spectrum there are small associations of traders in a single shopping area to chambers, which represent the commerce and industry of a town, city or region up to national chambers, that speak for an entire country.

As the name implies, they are groupings of traders, manufacturers and merchants some of whom may be in direct competition one with another but who come together to deal with problems affecting all of them.

Many of their activities have no discernible impact upon shipping, but others most certainly do. An example is that their independence and integrity are sufficient for their validation of, say a certificate of origin to be an acceptable document either in its own right or as a prerequisite before such a document receiving consulate approval.

In some countries, businesses must, by law, register with their local or regional chamber of commerce. Others are given the responsibility for conducting commercial auctions and other market activities, thus making them into influential and powerful bodies. They may also be involved in commercial arbitrations or provide references for local companies and trade contacts for national or international purposes.

The chambers influence international trade through the **International Chamber of Commerce (ICC).** In the same way as national shipping associations have benefited from the formation of an international body, the International Chamber of Commerce has more than made its mark by its publication of such handbooks as *Incoterms 2010*, an internationally agreed glossary of terms used in international trade.

Similarly ICC's Uniform Customs and Practice for Documentary Credits (commonly known as UCP) has proved to be of great benefit in this vital aspect of international trade. These are only examples of the many areas where the ICC has proved of immense value.

In the field of shipping business, the International Chamber of Commerce sponsored both the International Maritime Bureau (see below), which is concerned principally with maritime fraud, and the Centre for Maritime Co-operation (also based in London) to encourage an open market approach to maritime developments and to foster maritime joint ventures.

All students of the shipping business should have access to *Incoterms 2010*, which can be ordered from the ICC's headquarters in Paris or through national chambers of commerce. Alternatively, all its publications may be seen on the ICC website at **www.iccwbo.org.**

9.5.2 International Maritime Bureau (IMB)

ICC International Maritime Bureau

The International Maritime Bureau was formed under the auspices of the International Chamber of Commerce in an endeavour to reduce maritime fraud.

The guiding hand from the beginning was Eric Ellen, who witnessed maritime fraud at first hand when he was Chief Constable of the Port of London.

The problem he saw was twofold. First, that maritime fraud by its very nature took place in several jurisdictions so that even when it was discovered it was extremely difficult to prosecute the perpetrators.

The second problem was that the victims of maritime fraud, knowing that restitution was unlikely, were often too embarrassed to tell the world that they had been deceived.

The IMB has made great strides in overcoming merchants' reticence, which has in turn alerted the commercial world to the different types of fraudulent activity.

There is still some way to go before the problem of jurisdiction is overcome. Most countries' laws only permit them to prosecute criminals for acts taking place within their own territory.

Among its activities, the IMB aims to authenticate suspect bills of lading and other documents, to disseminate information on maritime crime, to offer advice and assistance in avoiding the risk of fraud, to raise awareness of the dangers of maritime crime and provide help and training with counter-measures.

In 1992, in response to violent criminal activity in the Malacca Strait and elsewhere in the Far East, the IMB established the Piracy Reporting Centre in Kuala Lumpur. As a result much has been done to heighten awareness of this dangerous crime and led to the prosecution and conviction of many criminals.

An interesting recent development has been the inauguration of a simple and relatively inexpensive satellite tracking system known as SHIPLOC that allows merchants and shipping companies to monitor the exact location of their ships using a personal computer with internet access. Information about SHIPLOC and other activities of the IMB can be found through the ICC website, **www.iccwbo.org**.

9.5.3 The Corporation of Lloyd's ('Lloyd's of London')

Lloyd's is an insurance market of a kind to be found nowhere else in the world. Almost anything can be insured there – ships, aircraft, civil engineering projects, factories, oil rigs and refineries to name but a few of the thousands of risks that are placed at Lloyd's each year.

Lloyd's is not a company. It has no shareholders and accepts no corporate liability for risks insured there. Lloyd's is a society of underwriters, all of whom accept insurance risks for their personal profit or loss and are liable to the full extent of their private fortunes to meet their insurance commitments. In 1871 the UK Parliament passed the Lloyd's Act , which created the Corporation of Lloyd's.

The principle of individual and unlimited liability remains as valid today as it was three centuries ago. The Corporation, through the Council of Lloyd's, nevertheless lays down stringent regulations governing the financial requirements both for Lloyd's membership and the audit of underwriting accounts. The most recent Act of Parliament covering the activities of Lloyd's is the Lloyd's Act 1982, which resulted from an inquiry into the society's constitution and the effectiveness of its powers of self-regulation.

The Corporation of Lloyd's also provides its members with their premises and a variety of centralised supporting services. Details of these can be seen at **www.lloydsoflondon.co.uk.**

As was the case three centuries ago, private individuals subscribe a policy at Lloyd's today with unlimited liability. Today, however, more than 20,000 members of Lloyd's are grouped into some 40 syndicates varying in size from a few to more than 1,000 names. The affairs of each syndicate are managed by an underwriting agent who is responsible for appointing a professional underwriter for each main class of business. Underwriting membership is open to men and women of any nationality provided that they meet the stringent financial requirements of the Council of Lloyd's.

9.5.4 Lloyd's agents

Lloyd's has always been closely connected with the sea and accordingly developed a worldwide shipping intelligence system. An important aspect of this system is the network of agents throughout the world, one of whose functions is to send to Lloyd's shipping, aviation and other news relating to the ports and areas in which they operate.

Lloyd's agents are also called upon to appoint surveyors to report on damage or loss and it is the practice for marine policies of Lloyd's underwriters and insurance companies to state that claims settlement will be assisted if Lloyd's agents are called in to conduct a survey. Lloyd's agents in certain circumstances deal with non-marine surveys and claims and they also work in conjunction with Lloyd's Aviation Department in arranging surveys on damaged aircraft. The first Lloyd's agent appointed abroad was in Madeira in 1811 and by the end of that year 150 firms had been appointed. Today there are some 500 agents, many of whom have held the post for 100 years or more.

Arrangements for collecting, processing and publishing the enormous volume of information received from Lloyd's agents throughout the world was the responsibility of Lloyd's of London Press Limited, now T&F Informa, publisher of *Lloyd's List* and formerly a subsidiary of the Corporation of Lloyd's, but now an independent organisation. This information, together with details of maritime and aviation casualties, market reports and articles of interest to the insurance and shipping businesses, are published daily in *Lloyd's List*, reputed to be the world's oldest daily newspaper.

9.6 CLASSIFICATION SOCIETIES

9.6.1 Lloyd's Register of Shipping

Confusion often arises over Lloyd's Register of Shipping and the Corporation of Lloyd's. They are in fact two quite different and independent organisations though sharing the same origin and name. In the days of Lloyd's coffee house, underwriters collected and catalogued information concerning the characteristics and construction of individual vessels to help them in their insurance activities. This register of ships, known as the underwriters' register or green book, was first published in 1760. In 1797 a dispute over classification methods prompted shipowners to publish their own book, which appeared in 1799 and remained a rival register until 1834 when a common problem of finance brought about a reconciliation that resulted in the formation of Lloyd's Register of Shipping. Since then it has remained an independent classification society.

Lloyd's Register of Shipping is a non-profit-making concern that obtains its funds from fees charged for the services of its surveyors and from subscriptions to the register book. The society is run by the General Committee, composed of underwriters, shipowners, shipbuilders, marine engineers, steel makers and representatives of shipping organisations. All these serve voluntarily.

The Register is independent of any official control but its authority is such that all maritime governments accept classification by Lloyd's Register as indicating that statutory requirements in respect of structural strength have been met.

The research and technical advisory services department is constantly engaged in the study of new developments and projects providing valuable technical advice to the industry as a whole. The society has a research laboratory for the investigation of technical problems wherever they may arise. A special technical investigation department deals quickly with problems involving failures in ships' machinery all over the world as well as providing special services.

The technical records department houses records of all kinds of damage or failure occurring in ships and it is these records which owners will inspect before offering for a ship in the secondhand sale and purchase market.

The volumes of Lloyd's Register are published jointly with *Fairplay*, annually in bound form and on CD-Rom, and subscribers through the Lloyd's Register website can access updated information. They include details of all merchant ships over 100 tons regardless of whether or not they are classified by Lloyd's.

The classification of vessels requires that they undergo a special survey every four years when the hull and machinery are inspected. In times of high inflation and increasing technology the four-year survey cycle became difficult to operate and now most vessels are on a continuous hull and machinery survey cycle. The surveys are carried out by a staff of about 1,500 qualified surveyors based worldwide, which includes specialists up to date in all the technical fields.

Almost all the maritime countries of the world have developed classification societies, some of the best known include:

France	Bureau Veritas (BV)	Founded 1828
Germany	Germanischer Lloyd (GL)	Founded 1867
Italy	Registro Italiano Navale (RINA)	Founded 1861
Japan	Nippon Kaiji Kyokai (NKK)	Founded 1899
Norway	Det Norske Veritas (DNV)	Founded 1864
USA	American Bureau of Shipping (ABS)	Founded 1862

The independent status of classification societies, their integrity and the nature of their work have led many of these organisations to widen their sphere of activities.

Lloyd's Register, for example, offers many specialist services from its wide range of expertise, from approval of naval architects' plans and computer testing of hull designs to advice on marine engine lubricants and the auditing of ISO 9000 systems.

For full information about these and other classification societies, please refer to their websites as follows:

Lloyd's Register – **www.lr.org**

American Bureau of Shipping – **www.eagle.org**

Bureau Veritas – **www.veristar.com**

China Classification Society – **www.ccs.org.cn**

Det Norske Veritas – **www.dnv.com**

Germanischer Lloyd – **www.GermanLloyd.org**

Korean Register of Shipping – **www.krs.co.kr**

Nippon Kaiji Kyokai (ClassNK) – **www.classnk.or.jp**

Registro Italiano Navale – **www.rina.org**

Russian Maritime Register of Shipping – **www.rs-head.spb.ru**

9.6.2 International Association of Classification Societies (IACS)

IACS

The world's principal classification societies make up the membership of IACS, along with one associate member. Around 90% of the world's cargo-carrying tonnage is covered by the classification, design, construction and through-life compliance rules and standards set by the association's members.

IACS devotes a great deal of its energy to establishing and upholding standards for the classification of ships. It has promoted a code of ethics to which it expects its members to adhere, and promotes transparency within the system of classification.

To obtain membership of IACS, a classification society must satisfy demanding criteria on quality systems and procedures. Individual classification societies have been suspended from membership for failing to uphold the standards required.

IACS has had to deal with much criticism of the system of classification following a series of serious maritime accidents where certification issued by one or more of its members has been called into question in the public domain. It has attempted to address the difficulty perceived by the public of the commercial aspects of classification society work influencing the standards applied to members' tonnage.

Those wishing to know more about IACS's latest activities are recommended to look at its website, **www.iacs.org.uk.**

9.6.3 International Transport Workers' Federation (ITF)

The ITF formed during the closing years of the 19th century as an international secretariat of transport unions all over the world. It now has a membership of more than 400 trade unions from nearly 100 countries and claims to represent more than four million transport workers.

At the time of its formation there was no such thing as an open registry – dubbed by some a 'flag of convenience'. When that phenomenon emerged, the ITF saw it as an attempt to undermine trade unionism in general and the standards of seafarers' working and safety conditions in particular. In 1950, at its Stuttgart Congress, the ITF adopted a plan of action, which in principle required all owners to adhere to certain defined minimum conditions. Failure to do so would result in a boycott to bring such owners to the negotiating table.

Much of that resolution remains in place to this day. However, a somewhat ambitious part of the plan was to force owners away from flags of convenience by an international blockade. In the event, this did not go beyond a four-day boycott in 1958.

A more practical resolution was passed at its 1971 congress in Vienna when a standard agreement was drawn up for use by all ships whose crews were not covered by an agreement properly negotiated between union and employer.

Such agreements also included provision for contributions to an ITF fund set up to sustain the campaign and to provide, in addition, charitable support to seamen's missions and other forms of welfare in port and on board.

The strength of the ITF lies in the fact that almost all transport unions are affiliated to it. This means that immobilising a ship by arranging for the withdrawal of services such as tug crews and lock keepers to the offending ship is relatively straightforward. So many of the ITF's ideals are praiseworthy that affiliated unions are quick to support any boycott.

The ITF now provides for permanent officials in many major ports and makes available valuable facilities for Mission to Seafarers branches and other welfare organisations worldwide. They have taken the lead in many difficult situations where crews have been in danger or stranded without funds and its intelligence network is first class.

Cruise ship *Eurodam*, which has accommodation for 2,104 passengers and 929 crew.

Chapter 10

• •

Communications in business

10.1   INTRODUCTION

Communication is the successful exchange of information between at least two parties. It therefore deals with the transmitting and receiving of information in various formats.

Shipping is a communication-intensive industry and communication skills are a vital element.

Communication is an essential part of human interaction. The benefits of effective communication are many and obvious as they enhance all aspects of our personal and professional lives. Ineffective or misunderstood communications in our personal lives may give rise to problems or embarrassment, but in our professional lives the results of misunderstandings may have much more serious results.

10.2   BASIC PRINCIPLES OF BUSINESS COMMUNICATION

Shipping, like many other industries, is full of jargon and abbreviations and it is most important to be sure that the other person is thoroughly familiar with the terms you are using, particularly as the customary language of shipping is English, which may not be the native language of either of the parties who are communicating.

The international nature of the shipping industry means that it is important to remember that the recipient of your message may be located in another time zone and, although the wide use of modern mobile communication devices allows people to be contactable without limit, they may not be readily available to receive your message or respond to its contents.

10.3   METHODS OF BUSINESS COMMUNICATION

Modern communication culture has changed immeasurably in recent years. Even relatively recently communication with colleagues, principals, agents, cargo receivers and other parties was completed by three primary methods; the landline telephone, the telex and the written or typed letter. These formats have been largely superseded by mobile telephones, email, instant messaging, the internet and PDA technology.

10.3.1 Letter/report/memorandum

The written letter is still regarded as an excellent communicative tool, especially for contractual and complex communications. In some instances hard copy paper documents are required in business to meet legal and/or audit requirements.

10.3.2 Face to face

Even in times where there is an abundance of communication tools available, for some, face-to-face meetings are an essential way to establish a sound business relationship. Quite often, the technicalities of contractual negotiations are more easily overcome during face-to-face meetings.

10.3.3 Landline telephone

This is a reliable and cost-efficient method of communication. Although it is still personal, it has the disadvantage that the nuances conveyed by facial expression and body language are not accessible.

10.3.4 Mobile telephone

The mobile telephone is more than just a convenience and is now regarded as a vital business tool. The technology associated with mobile telephones over the past few years allows those involved in the shipping industry, which sometimes relies on quick decisions, to be readily available from almost any location worldwide.

10.3.5 Tele/video conferencing

This type of communication allows for some of the benefits of meeting in person without the inconvenience and cost of travel.

Video conferencing uses phone lines to transmit video, as well as sound, between two or more locations. Due to the fact that cameras, microphones, audio playback, special software and high-bandwidth networks are required, video conferencing is generally only available from appropriately equipped facilities. However, as networks become more powerful and the hardware components less expensive, a lower-quality version of this function is available on many personal computers.

10.3.6 Short message service (SMS)/multimedia messaging Service (MMS)

SMS is a communication that allows the interchange of short text messages between mobile telephones. It is estimated that, globally, there are 2.5 billion active SMS users, accounting for75% of all mobile telephones subscribers.

MMS is a telecommunications standard, again by mobile telephones or PDA, for sending messages that includes multimedia objects such as images, audio and video.

10.3.7 Electronic mail (email)

Email is a standard form of business communication offering a cost-effective, efficient and almost instantaneous service. It allows the same message to be sent to a number of addresses simultaneously and the recipient can forward the message to other contacts. Attachments, such as documents, spreadsheets, digital photographs and scanned images can be sent with the message and arrive in a form that can be manipulated by the receiver without any further processing. Email is commonly used for internal communications in large organisations and between those who maintain their own secure networks. The use of email has made the telex system largely redundant.

A side effect of the general adoption of email by the business community as a means of communication has been the acceptance of a relatively informal style of written communication that did not exist in the media formerly used. Emails are generally written in casual style, reflecting the informality that has become acceptable in the business world.

10.3.8 Facsimile

The facsimile (or fax) is a convenient and universally accepted method of transmitting a document via a standard telephone connection. Along with scanned email documents, this has immediate advantages of permitting, for example, a copy of a charter party complete with alterations and additions, to be sent to the recipient. Diagrams, handwritten messages etc. can also be transmitted over this system.

10.3.9 Electronic data interchange

Many large organisations and government departments now make use of electronic means of transmitting data between computers to remove the need for slow and labour intensive paper documentation or re-entering data. This saves time, money and resources in the routine submission of statistical data, customs entries and other information.

In the shipping business most multi-modal transport systems now rely on electronic methods of document transmission. In recent years the introduction of new technology has allowed the standardisation of these systems and the ongoing improvement in information technology techniques will make this practice increasingly standard.

10.3.10 Data storage and retrieval

A vital advantage of business computer systems is the ability to store and retrieve large volumes of information rapidly, and to collate and sort data at speeds unachievable by any other means.

This facility enables, for example, a sale and purchase broker to interrogate a database applying the criteria of a range of ships required by a potential buyer and to select only those that may be of interest. This information can then be transmitted instantly to the client without further need for processing.

Similarly, subscribers to organisations whose role is to provide information can use their own computer terminals to access real-time online data stored by the organisation itself. So, for example, subscribers to Lloyd's Register of Ships can (using their own confidential log-in details) access up-to-date information on new additions or alterations to the Register instantaneously. This facility is extremely valuable for a business that depends on fast access to accurate data.

10.3.11 Internet and e-commerce

While the internet provides a medium for the transmission of email and remote access to the databases of large organisations, as well as the means of electronic banking and data interchange, it also provides, through the worldwide web, a massive resource for business in terms of access to information.

Few organisations, do not maintain their own website, which can act as a showcase for their business, a valuable source of information to their customers and potential customers and a means of conducting business electronically.

Internet purchasing is now an established and accepted aspect of commercial life and a website, properly maintained, can display information and illustrations of articles or services for sale.

However, chartering a ship or booking cargo space is not quite such a simple transaction, although it is now possible, through a number of organisations, to carry out such business transactions using the internet.

10.3.12 Intranet

An intranet uses the same technology as the internet but operates within the confines of a single organisation. The principal constraint is the bandwidth (capacity) of the organisation's network, but information is much less expensive to distribute and maintain with an intranet than with paper equivalents.

10.4 CONCLUSION

It is evident that modern communication methods have transformed the way in which business is conducted and that, arguably, without the advances in technology international trade would not have advanced to where it is today.

While technological advances in communication methods have facilitated the efficient flow of information, it must be remembered that e-commerce is vulnerable to risk and all organisations must ensure that they adopt rigorous risk management procedures to ensure the integrity and security of their systems.

Appendices

GENCON

1. Shipbroker	**RECOMMENDED** **THE BALTIC AND INTERNATIONAL MARITIME COUNCIL** **UNIFORM GENERAL CHARTER (AS REVISED 1922,1976 and 1994)** (To be used for trades for which no specially approved form is in force) **CODE NAME: "GENCON"** Part I
	2. Place and date
3. Owners/Place of business (Cl. 1)	4. Charterers/Place of business (Cl. 1)
5. Vessel's name (Cl. 1)	6. GT/NT(Cl. 1)
7. DWT all told on summer load line in metric tons (abt.) (Cl. 1)	8. Present position (Cl. 1)
9. Expected ready to load (abt.) (Cl. 1)	
10. Loading port or place (Cl. 1)	11 Discharging port or place (Cl. 1)
12. Cargo (also state quantity and margin in Owners' option, if agreed; if full and complete cargo not agreed state "part cargo" (Cl. 1)	
13. Freight rate (also state whether freight prepaid or payable on delivery) (Cl. 4)	14. Freight payment (state currency and method of payment; also beneficiary and bank account) (Cl. 4)
15. State if vessel's cargo handling gear shall not be used (Cl. 5)	16. Laytime (if separate laytime for load, and disch. is agreed, fill in a) and b). If total laytime for load, and disch., fill in c) only) (Cl. 6)
17. Shippers/Place of business (Cl. 6)	a) Laytime for loading
18. Agents (loading) (Cl. 6)	(b) Laytime for discharging
19. Agents (discharging) (Cl. 6)	c) Total laytime for loading and discharging
20. Demurrage rate and manner payable (loading and discharging) (Cl. 7)	21. Cancelling date (Cl. 9)
	22. General Average to be adjusted at (Cl. 12)
23. Freight Tax (state if for the Owners' account (Cl.13 (c))	24. Brokerage commission and to whom payable (Cl. 15)
25. Law and Arbitration (state 19 (a), 19 (b) or 19 (c) of Cl. 19; if 19 (c) agreed also state Place of Arbitration) (if not filled in 19 (a) shall apply) (Cl. 19)	
(a) State maximum amount for small claims/shortened arbitration (Cl. 19)	26. Additional clauses covering special provisions, if agreed

It is mutually agreed that this Contract shall be performed subject to the conditions contained in this Charter Party which shall include Part I as well as Part II. In the event of a conflict of conditions, the provisions of Part I shall prevail over those of Part II to the extent of such conflict.

Signature (Owners)	Signature (Charterers)

GENCON (continued)

1. It is agreed between the party mentioned in Box 3 as the Owners of the Vessel named in Box 5, of the GT/NT indicated in Box 6 and carrying about the number of metric tons of deadweight capacity all told on summer loadline stated in Box 7, now in position as stated in Box 8 and expected ready to load under this Charter Party about the date indicated in Box 9, and the party mentioned as the Charterers in Box 4 that:

The said Vessel shall, as soon as her prior commitments have been completed, proceed to the loading port(a) or place(s) stated in Box 10 or so near thereto as she may safely get and lie always afloat, and there load a full and complete cargo (if shipment of deck cargo agreed same to be at the Charterers' risk and responsibility) as stated in Box 12, which the Charterers bind themselves to ship, and being so loaded the Vessel shall proceed to the discharging port(s) or place(s) stated in Box 11 as ordered on signing Bills of Lading, or so near thereto as she may safely get and lie always afloat, and there deliver the cargo.

2. **Owners' Responsibility Clause**

The Owners are to be responsible for loss of or damage to the goods or for delay in delivery of the goods only in case the loss, damage or delay has been caused by personal want of due diligence on the part of the Owners or their Manager to make the Vessel in all respects seaworthy and to secure that she is properly manned, equipped and supplied, or by the personal act or default of the Owners or their Manager.

And the Owners are not responsible for loss, damage or delay arising from any other cause whatsoever, even from the neglect or default of the Master or crew or some other person employed by the Owners on board or ashore for whose acts they would, but for this Clause, be responsible, or from unseaworthiness of the Vessel on loading or commencement of the voyage or at any time whatsoever.

3. **Deviation Clause**

The Vessel has liberty to call at any port or ports in any order, for any purpose, to sail without pilots, to tow and/or assist Vessels in all situations, and also to deviate for the purpose of saving life and/or property.

4. **Payment of Freight**

(a) The freight at the rate stated in Box 13 shall be paid in cash calculated on the intaken quantity of cargo.

(b) _Prepaid._ If according to Box 13 freight is to be paid on shipment, it shall be deemed earned and non-returnable, Vessel and/or cargo lost or not lost.

Neither the Owners nor their agents shall be required to sign or endorse bills of lading showing freight prepaid unless the freight due to the Owners has actually been paid.

(c) _On delivery._ If according to Box 13 freight, or part thereof, is payable at destination it shall not be deemed earned until the cargo is thus delivered. Notwithstanding the provisions under (a), if freight or part thereof is payable on delivery of the cargo the Charterers shall have the option of paying the freight on delivered weight/quantity provided such option is declared before breaking bulk and the weight/quantity can be ascertained by official weighing machine, joint draft survey or tally.

Cash for Vessel's ordinary disbursements at the port of loading to be advanced by the Charterers, if required, at highest current rate of exchange, subject to two (2) per cent to cover insurance and other expenses.

5. **Loading/Discharging**

(a) Costs/Risks

The cargo shall be brought into the holds, loaded, stowed and/or trimmed, tallied, lashed and/or secured and taken from the holds and discharged by the Charterers, free of any risk, liability and expense whatsoever to the Owners. The Charterers shall provide and lay all dunnage material as required for the proper stowage and protection of the cargo on board, the Owners allowing the use of all dunnage available on board. The Charterers shall be responsible for and pay the cost of removing their dunnage after discharge of the cargo under this Charter Party and time to count until dunnage has been removed.

(b) Cargo Handling Gear

Unless the Vessel Is gearless or unless it has been agreed between the parties that the Vessel's gear shall not be used and stated as such in Box 15, the Owners shall throughout the duration of loading/discharging give free use of the Vessel's cargo handling gear and of sufficient motive power to operate all such cargo handling gear. All such equipment to be in good working order. Unless caused by negligence of the stevedores, time lost by breakdown of the Vessel's cargo handling gear or motive power - pro rata the total number of cranes/winches required at that time for the loading/discharging of cargo under this Charter Party - shall not count as laytime or time on demurrage. On request the Owners shall provide free of charge cranemen/winchmen from the crew to operate the Vessel's cargo handling gear, unless local regulations prohibit this, in which latter event shore labourers shall be for the account of the Charterers. Cranemen/winchmen shall be under the Charterers' risk and responsibility and as stevedores to be deemed as their servants but shall always work under the supervision of the Master.

(c) Stevedore Damage

The Charterers shall be responsible for damage (beyond ordinary wear and tear) to any part of the Vessel caused by Stevedores. Such damage shall be notified as soon as reasonably possible by the Master to the Charterers or their agents and to their Stevedores, failing which the Charterers shall not be held responsible. The Master shall endeavour to obtain the Stevedores' written acknowledgement of liability.

The Charterers are obliged to repair any stevedore damage prior to completion of the voyage, but must repair stevedore damage affecting the Vessel's seaworthiness or class before the Vessel sails from the port where such damage was caused or found. All additional expenses Incurred shall be for the account of the Charterers and any time lost shall be for the account of and shall be paid to the Owners by the Charterers at the demurrage rate.

6. **Laytime**

* _(a) Separate laytime for loading and discharging_

The cargo shall be loaded within the number of running days/hours as indicated in Box 16, weather permitting, Sundays and holidays excepted, unless used, in which event time used shall count.

The cargo shall be discharged within the number of running days/hours as indicated in Box 16, weather permitting, Sundays and holidays excepted, unless used, in which event time used shall count.

* _(b) Total laytime for loading and discharging_

The cargo shall be loaded and discharged within the number of total running days/hours as indicated, in Box 16, weather permitting, Sundays and holidays excepted, unless used, in which event time used shall count.

(c) Commencement of laytime (loading and discharging)

Laytime for loading and discharging shall commence at 13.00 hours, if notice of readiness is given up to and including 12.00 hours, and at 06.00 hours next working day if notice given during office hours after 12.00 hours. Notice of readiness at loading port to be given to the Shippers named in Box 17 or if not named, to the Charterers or their agents named in Box 18. Notice of readiness at the discharging port to be given to the Receivers or. If not known, to the Charterers or their agents named in Box 19.

If the loading/discharging berth is not available on the Vessel's arrival at or off the port of loading/discharging, the Vessel shall be entitled to give notice of readiness within ordinary office hours on arrival there, whether in free pratique or not, whether customs cleared or not. Laytime or time on demurrage shall then count as if she were In berth and in all respects ready for loading/discharging provided that the Master warrants that she is in fact ready In all respects. Time used in moving from the place of waiting to the loading/discharging berth shall not count as laytime.

If, after inspection, the Vessel Is found not to be ready in all respects to load/discharge time lost after the discovery thereof until the Vessel is again ready to load/discharge shall not count as laytime.

Time used before commencement of laytime shall count.

* _Indicate alternative (a) or (b) as agreed, in Box 16._

7. **Demurrage**

Demurrage at the loading and discharging port is payable by the Charterers at the rate stated in Box 20 in the manner stated in Box 20 per day or pro rata for any part of a day. Demurrage shall fall due day by day and shall be payable upon receipt of the Owners' invoice.

In the event the demurrage is not paid in accordance with the above, the Owners shall give the Charterers 96 running hours written notice to rectify the failure. If the demurrage is not paid at the expiration of this time limit and if the vessel is in or at the loading port, the Owners are entitled at any time to terminate the Charter Party and claim damages for any losses caused thereby.

8. **Lien Clause**

The Owners shall have a lien on the cargo and on all sub-freights payable in respect of the cargo, for freight, deadweight, demurrage, claims for damages and for all other amounts due under this Charter Party including costs of recovering same.

9. **Cancelling Clause**

(a) Should the Vessel not be ready to load (whether in berth or not) on the cancelling date indicated in Box 21, the Charterers shall have the option of cancelling this Charter Party.

(b) Should the Owners anticipate that, despite the exercise of due diligence, the Vessel will not be ready to load by the cancelling date, they shall notify the Charterers thereof without delay stating the expected date of the Vessel's readiness to load and asking whether the Charterers will exercise their option of cancelling the Charter Party, or agree to a new cancelling date.

Such option must be declared by the Charterers within 48 running hours after the receipt of the Owners' notice. If the Charterers do not exercise their option of cancelling, then this Charter Party shall be deemed to be amended such that the seventh day after the new readiness date stated in the Owners' notification to the Charterers shall be the new cancelling date.

The provisions of sub-clause (b) of this Clause shall operate only once, and In case of the Vessel's further delay, the Charterers shall have the option of cancelling the Charter Party as per sub-clause (a) of this Clause.

10. **Bills of Lading**

Bills of Lading shall be presented and signed by the Master as per the "Cangenbill" Bill of Lading form, Edition 1994, without prejudice to this Charter Party, or by the Owners' agents provided written authority has been given by Owners to the agents, a copy of which is to be furnished to the Charterers. The Charterers shall indemnify the Owners against all consequences or liabilities that may arise from the signing of bills of lading as presented to the extent that the terms or contents of such bills of lading impose or result In the imposition of more onerous liabilities upon the Owners than those assumed by the Owners under this Charter Party.

11. **Both-to-Blame Collision Clause**

If the Vessel comes into collision with another vessel as a result of the negligence of the other vessel and any act, neglect or default of the Master. Mariner, Pilot or the servants of the Owners In the navigation or in the management of the Vessel, the owners of the cargo carried hereunder will indemnify the Owners against all loss or liability to the other or non-carrying vessel or her owners in so far as such loss or liability represents loss of, or damage to, or any claim whatsoever of the owners of said cargo, paid or payable by the other or non-carrying vessel or her owners to the owners of said cargo and set-off, recouped or recovered by the other or non-carrying vessel or her owners as part of their claim against the carrying Vessel or the Owners. The foregoing provisions shall also apply where the owners, operators or those in charge of any vessel or vessels or objects other than, or in addition to, the colliding vessels or objects are at fault in respect of a collision or contact.

12. **General Average and New Jason Clause**

General Average shall be adjusted In London unless otherwise agreed in Box 22 according to York-Antwerp Rules 1994 and any subsequent modification thereof. Proprietors of cargo to pay the cargo's share in the general expenses even if same have been necessitated through neglect or default of the Owners' servants (see Clause 2).

If General Average is to be adjusted in accordance with the law and practice of the United States of America, the following Clause shall apply: "In the event of accident, danger, damage or disaster before or after the commencement of the voyage, resulting from any cause whatsoever, whether due to negligence or not, for which, or for the consequence of which, the Owners are not responsible, by statute, contract or otherwise, the cargo shippers, consignees or the owners of the cargo shall contribute with the Owners In General Average to the payment of any sacrifices, losses or expenses of a General Average nature that may be made or incurred and shall pay salvage and special charges incurred in respect of the cargo. If a salving vessel is owned or operated by the Owners, salvage shall be paid for as fully as if the said salving vessel or vessels belonged to strangers. Such deposit as the Owners, or their agents, may deem sufficient to cover the estimated contribution of the goods and any salvage and special charges thereon shall, if required, be made by the cargo, shippers, consignees or owners of the goods to the Owners before delivery".

13. **Taxes and Dues Clause**

(a) _On Vessel_ -The Owners shall pay all dues, charges and taxes customarily levied on the Vessel, howsoever the amount thereof may be assessed.

(b) _On cargo_ -The Charterers shall pay all dues, charges, duties and taxes customarily levied on the cargo, howsoever the amount thereof may be assessed.

(c) _On freight_ -Unless otherwise agreed In Box 23, taxes levied on the freight shall be for the Charterers' account.

GENCON (continued)

PART II

"Gencon" Charter (As Revised 1922, 1976 and 1994)

14. **Agency**

In every case the Owners shall appoint their own Agent both at the port of loading and the port of discharge.

15. **Brokerage**

A brokerage commission at the rate stated In Box 24 on the freight, dead-freight and demurrage earned is due to the party mentioned In Box 24.

In case of non-execution 1/3 of the brokerage on the estimated amount of freight to be paid by the party responsible for such non-execution to the Brokers as indemnity for the tatter's expenses and work. In case of more voyages the amount of indemnity to be agreed.

16. **General Strike Clause**

(a) If there is a strike or lock-out affecting or preventing the actual loading of the cargo, or any part of it, when the Vessel is ready to proceed from her last port or at any time during the voyage to the port or ports of loading or after her arrival there, the Master or the Owners may ask the Charterers to declare, that they agree to reckon the laydays as if there were no strike or lock-out. Unless the Charterers have given such declaration in writing (by telegram, if necessary) within 24 hours, the Owners shall have the option of cancelling this Charter Party. If part cargo has already been loaded, the Owners must proceed with same, (freight payable on loaded quantity only) having liberty to complete with other cargo on the way for their own account.

(b) If there is a strike or lock-out affecting or preventing the actual discharging of the cargo on or after the Vessel's arrival at or off port of discharge and same has not been settled within 46 hours, the Charterers shall have the option of keeping the Vessel waiting until such strike or lock-out is at an end against paying half demurrage after expiration of the time provided for discharging until the strike or lock-out terminates and thereafter full demurrage shall be payable until the completion of discharging, or of ordering the Vessel to a safe port where she can safely discharge without risk of being detained by strike or lock-out. Such orders to be given within 48 hours after the Master or the Owners have given notice to the Charterers of the strike or lock-out affecting the discharge. On delivery of the cargo at such port, all conditions of this Charter Party and of the Bill of Lading shall apply and the Vessel shall receive the same freight as if she had discharged at the original port of destination, except that if the distance to the substituted port exceeds 100 nautical miles, the freight on the cargo delivered at the substituted port to be increased in proportion.

(c) Except for the obligations described above, neither the Charterers nor the Owners shall be responsible for the consequences of any strikes or lock-outs preventing or affecting the actual loading or discharging of the cargo.

17. **War Risks ("Voywar 1993")**

(1) For the purpose of this Clause, the words:

(a) The "Owners" shall include the shipowners, bareboat charterers, disponent owners, managers or other operators who are charged with the management of the Vessel, and the Master; and

(b) "War Risks" shall Include any war (whether actual or threatened), act of war, civil war, hostilities, revolution, rebellion, civil commotion, warlike operations, the laying of mines (whether actual or reported), acts of piracy, acts of terrorists, acts of hostility or malicious damage, blockades (whether imposed against all Vessels or imposed selectively against Vessels of certain flags or ownership, or against certain cargoes or crews or otherwise howsoever), by any person, body, terrorist or political group, or the Government of any state whatsoever, which, in the reasonable Judgement of the Master and/or the Owners, may be dangerous or are likely to be or to become dangerous to the Vessel, her cargo, crew or other persons on board the Vessel.

(2) If at any time before the Vessel commences loading, it appears that, in the reasonable judgement of the Master and/or the Owners, performance of the Contract of Carriage, or any part of it, may expose, or is likely to expose, the Vessel, her cargo, crew or other persons on board the Vessel to War Risks, the Owners may give notice to the Charterers cancelling this Contract of Carriage, or may refuse to perform such part of it as may expose, or may be likely to expose, the Vessel, her cargo, crew or other persons on board the Vessel to War Risks; provided always that if this Contract of Carriage provides that loading or discharging is to take place within a range of ports, and at the port or ports nominated by the Charterers the Vessel, her cargo, crew, or other persons onboard the Vessel may be exposed, or may be likely to be exposed, to War Risks, the Owners shall first require the Charterers to nominate any other safe port which lies within the range for loading or discharging, and may only cancel this Contract of Carriage It the Charterers shall not have nominated such safe port or ports within 48 hours of receipt of notice of such requirement.

(3) The Owners shall not be required to continue to load cargo for any voyage, or to sign Bills of Lading for any port or place, or to proceed or continue on any voyage, or on any part thereof, or to proceed through any canal or waterway, or to proceed to or remain at any port or place whatsoever, where it appears, either after the loading of the cargo commences, or at any stage of the voyage thereafter before the discharge of the cargo is completed, that. In the reasonable judgement of the Master and/or the Owners, the Vessel, her cargo (or any part thereof), crew or other persons on board the Vessel (or any one or more of them) may be, or are likely to be, exposed to War Risks, if it should so appear, the Owners may by notice request the Charterers to nominate a safe port for the discharge of the cargo or any part thereof, and if within 48 hours of the receipt of such notice, the Charterers shall not have nominated such a port, the Owners may discharge the cargo at any safe port of their choice (including the port of loading) in complete fulfilment of the Contract of Carriage. The Owners shall be entitled to recover from the Charterers the extra expenses of such discharge and, if the discharge takes place at any port other than the loading port to receive the full freight as though the cargo had been carried to the discharging port and if the extra distance exceeds 100 miles, to additional freight which shall be the same percentage of the freight contracted for as the percentage which the extra distance represents to the distance of the normal and customary route, the Owners having a lien on the cargo for such expenses and freight.

(4) If at any stage of the voyage after the loading of the cargo commences, it appears that, in the reasonable judgement of the Master and/or the Owners, the Vessel, her cargo, crew or other persons on board the Vessel may be, or are likely to be, exposed to War Risks on any part of the route (including any canal or waterway) which is normally and customarily used in a voyage of the nature contracted for, and there is another longer route to the discharging port, the Owners shall give notice to the Charterers that this route will be taken, in this event the Owners shall be entitled, if the total extra distance exceeds 100 miles, to additional freight which shall be the same percentage of the freight contracted for as the percentage which the extra distance represents to the distance of the normal and customary route.

(5) The Vessel shall have liberty:-

(a) to comply with all orders, directions, recommendations or advice as to departure, arrival, routes, sailing in convoy, ports of call, stoppages, destinations, discharge of cargo, delivery or in any way whatsoever which are given by the Government of the Nation under whose flag the Vessel sails, or other Government to whose laws the Owners are subject, or any other Government which so requires, or any body or group acting with the power to compel compliance with their orders or directions;

(b) to comply with the orders, directions or recommendations of any war risks underwriters who have the authority to give the same under the terms of the war risks insurance;

(c) to comply with the terms of any resolution of the Security Council of the United Nations, any directives of the European Community, the effective orders of any other Supranational body which has the right to issue and give the same, and with national laws aimed at enforcing the same to which the Owners are subject, and to obey the orders and directions of those who are charged with their enforcement;

(d) to discharge at any other port any cargo or part thereof which may render the Vessel liable to confiscation as a contraband carrier;

(e) to call at any other port to change the crew or any part thereof or other persons on board the Vessel when there is reason to believe that they may be subject to internment, imprisonment or other sanctions;

(f) where cargo has not been loaded or has been discharged by the Owners under any provisions of this Clause, to load other cargo for the Owners' own benefit and carry it to any other port or ports whatsoever, whether backwards or forwards or in a contrary direction to the ordinary or customary route.

(6) If in compliance with any of the provisions of sub-clauses (2) to (5) of this Clause anything is done or not done, such shall not be deemed to be a deviation, but shall be considered as due fulfilment of the Contract of Carriage.

18. **General Ice Clause**

Port of loading

(a) In the event of the loading port being inaccessible by reason of ice when the Vessel is ready to proceed from her last port or at any time during the voyage or on the Vessel's arrival or in case frost sets In after the Vessel's arrival, the Master for fear of being frozen in is at liberty to leave without cargo, and this Charter Party shall be null and void.

(b) If during loading the Master, for fear of the Vessel being frozen In, deems it advisable to leave, he has liberty to do so with what cargo he has on board and to proceed to any other port or ports with option of completing cargo for the Owners' benefit for any port or ports including port of discharge. Any part cargo thus loaded under this Charter Party to be forwarded to destination at the Vessel's expense but against payment of freight, provided that no extra expenses be thereby caused to the Charterers, freight being paid on quantity delivered (in proportion if lumpsum), all other conditions as per this Charter Party.

(c) In case of more than one loading port, and if one or more of the ports are closed by ice, the Master or the Owners to be at liberty either to load the part cargo at the open port and fill up elsewhere for their own account as under section (b) or to declare the Charter Party null and void unless the Charterers agree to load full cargo at the open port.

Port of discharge

(a) Should ice prevent the Vessel from reaching port of discharge the Charterers shall have the option of keeping the Vessel waiting until there opening of navigation and paying demurrage or of ordering the Vessel to a safe and immediately accessible port where she can safely discharge without risk of detention by ice. Such orders to be given within 48 hours after the Master or the Owners have given notice to the Charterers of the Impossibility of reaching port of destination.

(b) If during discharging the Master for fear of the Vessel being frozen in deems it advisable to leave, he has liberty to do so with what cargo he has on board and to proceed to the nearest accessible port where she can safely discharge.

(c) On delivery of the cargo at such port, all conditions of the Bill of Lading shall apply and the Vessel shall receive the same freight as if she had discharged at the original port of destination, except that if the distance of the substituted port exceeds 100 nautical miles, the freight on the cargo delivered at the substituted port to be increased in proportion.

19. **Law and Arbitration**

* (a) This Charter Party shall be governed by and construed in accordance with English law and any dispute arising out of this Charter Party shall be referred to arbitration in London in accordance with the Arbitration Acts 1950 and 1979 or any statutory modification or re-enactment thereof for the time being in force. Unless the parties agree upon a sole arbitrator, one arbitrator shall be appointed by each party and the arbitrators so appointed shall appoint a third arbitrator, the decision of the three-man tribunal thus constituted or any two of them, shall be final. On the receipt by one party of the nomination in writing of the other party's arbitrator, that party shall appoint their arbitrator within fourteen days, failing which the decision of the single arbitrator appointed shall be final.

For disputes where the total amount claimed by either party does not exceed the amount stated in Box 25** the arbitration shall be conducted in accordance with the Small Claims Procedure of the London Maritime Arbitrators Association.

* (b) This Charter Party shall be governed by and construed In accordance with Title 9 of the United States Code and the Maritime Law of the United States and should any dispute arise out of this Charter Party, the matter in dispute shall be referred to three persons at New York, one to be appointed by each of the parties hereto, and the third by the two so chosen; their decision or that of any two of them shall be final, and for purpose of enforcing any award, this agreement may be made a rule of the Court. The proceedings shall be conducted in accordance with the rules of the Society of Maritime Arbitrators, Inc..

For disputes where the total amount claimed by either party does not exceed the amount stated in Box 25** the arbitration shall be conducted In accordance with the Shortened Arbitration Procedure of the Society of Maritime Arbitrators, Inc..

* (c) Any dispute arising out of this Charter Party shall be referred to arbitration at the place indicated In Box 25, subject to the procedures applicable there. The laws of the place indicated in Box 25 shall govern this Charter Party.

(d) If Box 25 in Part I is not filled in, sub-clause (a) of this Clause shall apply.

** (a),(b) and (c) are alternatives; indicate alternative agreed in Box 25.*

*** Where no figure is supplied in Box 25 in Part I, this provision only shall be void but the other provisions of this Clause shall have full force and remain in effect.*

Institute of Chartered Shipbrokers

TIME CHARTER
New York Produce Exchange Form

November 6th, 1913 - Amended October 20th, 1921; August 6th, 1931; October 3rd, 1946; June 12th, 1981

	THIS CHARTER PARTY, made and concluded in 1
	.... day of 19 2
Owners	between 3
	.... Owners of 4
	the good .... Steamship/Motorship 5
Description	of .... of .... tons gross register, and 6
of	.... tons net register, having engines of 7
Vessel	horsepower and with hull, machinery and equipment in a throughly efficient 8

THIS CHARTER PARTY, made and concluded in   1
.... day of 19   2

Owners between   3
.... Owners of   4

Description
of
Vessel
the good .... Steamship/Motorship   5
of .... of .... tons gross register, and   6
.... tons net register, having engines of   7
horsepower and with hull, machinery and equipment in a throughly efficient   8
state, and classed .... of about   9
.... cubic feet grain/bale capacity   10
...., and about   11
.... long/metric tons deadweight capacity (cargo and   12
bunkers, including fresh water and stores not exceeding   13
long/metric tons) on a salt water draft of .... on summer   14
freeboard, inclusive of permanent bunkers, which are of the capacity of about   15
.... long/metric tons of   16
.... fuel oil and   17
long/metric tons of ...., and   18
capable of steaming, fully laden, under good weather conditions about   19
.... knots on a consumption of about   20
long/metric tons of   21
....   22
now   23
.... and   24

Charterers   25
.... Charterers of the City of   26

The Owners agree to let and the Charterers agree to hire the vessel from the   27

Duration time of delivery for about   28
....   29
.... within below mentioned trading limits.   30

Sublet Charterers shall have liberty to sublet the vessel for all or any part of the   31
time covered by this Charter, but Charterers shall remain responsible for the   32
fulfillment of this Charter.   33

Delivery Vessel shall be placed at the disposal of the Charterers.................................   34
....   35
....   36
....   37
in such dock or at such berth or place (where she may safely lie, always afloat,   38
at all times of tide, except as otherwise provided in Clause 6) as the Charterers   39
may direct. If such dock, berth or place be not available, time shall count as   40
provided in Clause 5. Vessel on her delivery shall be ready to receive cargo with   41
clean-swept holds and tight, staunch, strong and in every way fitted for ordi-   42
nary cargo service, having water ballast and with sufficient power to operate all   43
cargo-handling gear simultaneously (and with full complement of officers and   44
crew for a vessel of her tonnage), to be employed in carrying lawful merchan-   45

Dangerous dise excluding any goods of a dangerous, injurious, flammable or corrosive   46
Cargo nature unless carried in accordance with the requirements or recom-   47
mendations of the proper authorities of the state of the vessel's registry and of   48
the states of ports of shipment and discharge and of any intermediate states or   49
ports through whose waters the vessel must pass. Without prejudice to the   50

Cargo generality of the foregoing, in addition the following are specifically excluded: 51
Exclusions livestock of any description, arms, ammunition, explosives............................   52
....   53
....   54
....   55
....   56

124

Code word for this Charter Party
"SHELLVOY 6"

Issued March 2005

VOYAGE CHARTER PARTY
LONDON,

PREAMBLE	1

IT IS THIS DAY AGREED between | 2

of   (hereinafter referred to as "Owners"), being owners /disponent owners of the____ | 3

motor/steam tank vessel called   with an IMO number of | 4

(hereinafter referred to as "the vessel") | 5

and | 6

(hereinafter referred to as "Charterers"): | 7

that the service for which provision is herein made shall be subject to the terms and conditions of this Charter which includes Part I, | 8
Part II and Part III. In the event of any conflict between the provisions of Part I, Part II and Part III hereof, the provisions of Part I shall prevail. | 9

PART I 10

(A) Description of vessel	(I) Vessel	Owners warrant that at the date hereof, and from the time when the obligation to proceed to the loadport(s) attaches, the	11 12
	(i)	Is classed	13
	(ii) (a)	Has a deadweight of .... (1000 kg) on a salt-water draft on assigned summer freeboard of ....m. and if applicable,	14 15
	(b)	Has on board documentation showing the following additional drafts and deadweights	16
	(iii)	Has capacity for cargo of .... m³,	17
	(iv)	Is fully fitted with heating systems for all cargo tanks capable of maintaining cargo at a temperature of up to degrees Celsius and can accept a cargo temperature on loading of up to a maximum of degrees Celsius.	18 19
	(v)	Has tanks coated as follows:	20
	(vi)	Is equipped with cranes/derricks capable of lifting to and supporting at the vessel's port and starboard manifolds submarine hoses of up to tonnes (1000 kg) in weight.	21 22
	(vii)	Can discharge a full cargo (whether homogenous or multi grade) either within 24 hours, or can maintain a back pressure of 100 PSI at the vessel's manifold and Owners warrant such minimum performance provided receiving facilities permit and subject always to the obligation of utmost despatch set out in Part II, clause 3 (1). The discharge warranty shall only be applicable provided the kinematic viscosity does not exceed 600 centistokes at the discharge temperature required by Charterers. If the kinematic viscosity only exceeds 600 centistokes on part of the cargo or particular grade(s) then the discharge warranty shall continue to apply to all other cargo/grades.	23 24 25 26 27 28
	(viii)	Has or will have carried, for the named Charterers, the following three cargoes (all grades to be identified) immediately prior to loading under this Charter:- Last Cargo/Charterer 2ⁿᵈ Last Cargo/Charterer 3ʳᵈ Last Cargo/Charterer	29 30 31 32 33
	(ix)	Has a crude oil washing system complying with the requirements of the International Convention for the Prevention of Pollution from Ships 1973 as modified by the Protocol of 1978 ("MARPOL 73/78").	34 35
	(x)	Has an operational inert gas system and is equipped for and able to carry out closed sampling/ullaging/loading and discharging operations in full compliance with the International Safety Guide for Oil Tankers and Terminals ("ISGOTT") guidelines current at the date of this Charter.	36 37 38
	(xi)	Has on board all papers and certificates required by any applicable law, in force as at the date of this Charter, to enable the vessel to perform the charter service without any delay.	39 40

Issued March 2005 **"SHELLVOY 6"**

(xii)	Is entered in the	P&I Club, being a member of the International Group of P&I Clubs.	41

(xiii) Has in full force and effect Hull and Machinery insurance placed through reputable Brokers on Institute Time   42
Clauses-Hull dated   for the value of   43

(xiv) Complies with the latest edition of the Oil Companies International Marine Forum ("OCIMF") standards for oil tankers'   44
manifolds and associated equipment applicable to its size for cargo manifolds and vapour recovery systems.   45

(xv) Is equipped to comply with, and is operated in accordance with, and has on board, the latest edition of the International   46
Chamber of Shipping ("ICS") and/or OCIMF guidelines / publications covering: 47

        (a) Ship to Ship Operations   48
        (b) ISGOTT   49
        (c) Clean Seas Guide for Oil Tankers   50
        (d) Bridge Procedure Guide   51

(II)   Throughout the charter service, Owners shall ensure that the vessel shall be maintained, or that they take all steps   52
necessary to promptly restore vessel to be, within the description in Part I clause (A)(I) and any questionnaires requested by   53
Charterers or within information provided by Owners.   54

(III)   Owners warrant that any information provided on any Questionnaire(s) requested by Charterers or any other vessel   55
information/details provided by Owners to Charterers is always complete and correct as at the date hereof, and from the time when   56
the obligation to proceed to the loadport attaches and throughout the charter service. This information is an integral part of this   57
Charter but if there is any conflict between the contents of the Questionnaire(s), or information provided by Owners, and any other   58
provisions of this Charter then such other provisions shall govern.   59

(B) Position/ Readiness   Now   Expected ready to load   60

In addition to the above details on the position of the vessel Owners will advise Charterers of the known programme, including any   61
contractual options available to the Charterers in Part I clause (A)(I) (viii) above between current position up to expected ready to   62
load date at Charterers nominated or indicated first load port/area. Owners will not, unless with Charterers' prior consent, negotiate   63
or enter into any business or give current Charterers any further options that may affect or alter the programme of the vessel as given   64
in this clause.   65

(C) Laydays   Commencing Noon Local Time on   (Commencement Date)   66

          Terminating Noon Local Time on   (Termination Date)   67

(D) Loading port(s)/ Range   68

(E) Discharging port(s)/ Range   69

(F) Cargo description   Charterers' option   70

Owners warrant that where different grades of cargo are carried pursuant to this Part I clause (F), they will be kept in complete   71
segregation from each other during loading, transit, and discharge, to include the use of different pumps/lines for each grade. If,   72
however, Charterers so require it, the vessel may be required to: 73

(a) co-mingle different grades of cargo providing such grades fall within the cargo description set out in this Part I clause (F);   74
(b) otherwise breach the vessel's natural segregation;   75
(c) add dye to the cargo after loading, and/or   76
(d) carry out such other cargo operations as Charterers may reasonably require as long as the vessel is capable of such operations   77

provided that the Charterers will indemnify Owners for any loss damage delay or expense caused by following Charterers'   78
instructions, except to the extent that such loss damage delay or expense could have been avoided by the exercise of due diligence   79
by Owners.   80

(G) Freight rate   At   % of the rate for the voyage as provided for in the New Worldwide Tanker Nominal Freight Scale current at the date   81
    of
commencement of loading (hereinafter referred to as "Worldscale") per ton (2240 lbs)/tonne (1000 Kg) or, if agreed, the following   82
lumpsum amount(s)/or freight per tonne for named load and discharge area(s)/port(s) combinations   83

Printed by BIMCO's idea

Issued March 2005 **"SHELLVOY 6"**

(H) Freight payable to			84
(I) Laytime	running hours		85
(J) Demurrage per day (or pro rata)			86
(K) ETAs	All radio/telex/e-mail messages sent by the master to Charterers shall be addressed to		87
	All telexes must begin with the vessel name at the start of the subject line (no inverted commas, or use of MT / SS preceding the		88
	vessel name)		89

(L) Speed — The vessel shall perform the ballast passage with utmost despatch and the laden passage at knots weather and safe navigation 90

permitting at a consumption of tonnes of Fuel oil (state grade) per day. 91

Charterers shall have the option to instruct the vessel to increase speed with Charterers reimbursing Owners for the additional 92
bunkers consumed, at replacement cost. 93
Charterers shall also have the option to instruct the vessel to reduce speed on laden passage. Additional voyage time caused by such 94
instructions shall count against laytime or demurrage, if on demurrage, and the value of any bunkers saved shall be deducted from 95
any demurrage claim Owners may have under this Charter with the value being calculated at original purchase price. 96
Owners shall provide documentation to fully support the claims and calculations under this clause. 97

(M) Worldscale — Worldscale Terms and Conditions apply / do not apply to this Charter. [delete as applicable] 98

(N) Casualty/ Accident contacts — In the event of an accident / marine casualty involving the vessel, Owners' technical managers can be contacted on a 24 hour basis 99
as follows: 100
Company Full Name: 101
Contact Person: 102
Full Address: 103
Telephone Number: 104
Fax Number: 105
Telex Number: 106
Email Address: 107
24 Hour Emergency Telephone number: 108

(O) Special provisions 109

Signatures — IN WITNESS WHEREOF, the parties have caused this Charter consisting of the Preamble, Parts I, II and III to be executed as of the 110
day and year first above written. 111

By 112

By 113

Issued March 2005   **"SHELLVOY 6"**

PART II

Condition of vessel	1. Owners shall exercise due diligence to ensure that from the time when the obligation to proceed to the loading port(s) attaches and throughout the charter service -	1 2
	(a) the vessel and her hull, machinery, boilers, tanks, equipment and facilities are in good order and condition and in every way equipped and fit for the service required; and	3 4
	(b) the vessel has a full and efficient complement of master, officers and crew and the senior officers shall be fully conversant in spoken and written English language	5 6

and to ensure that before and at the commencement of any laden voyage the vessel is in all respects fit to carry the   7
cargo specified in Part I clause (F). For the avoidance of doubt, references to equipment in this Charter shall include   8
but not be limited to computers and computer systems, and such equipment shall (inter alia) be required to continue   9
to function, and not suffer a loss of functionality and accuracy (whether logical or mathematical) as a result of the   10
run date or dates being processed.   11

Cleanliness of tanks

2. Whilst loading, carrying and discharging the cargo the master shall at all times keep the tanks, lines and   12
pumps of the vessel always clean for the cargo. Unless otherwise agreed between Owners and Charterers the vessel   13
shall present for loading with cargo tanks ready and, subject to the following paragraphs, if vessel is fitted with Inert   14
Gas System ("IGS"), fully inerted.   15

Charterers shall have the right to inspect vessel's tanks prior to loading and the vessel shall abide by   16
Charterers' instructions with regard to tank or tanks which the vessel is required to present ready for entry and   17
inspection. If Charterer's inspector is not satisfied with the cleanliness of the vessel's tanks, Owners shall clean   18
them in their time and at their expense to the satisfaction of Charterers' inspector, provided that nothing herein shall   19
affect the responsibilities and obligations of the master and Owners in respect of the loading, carriage and care of   20
cargo under this Charter nor prejudice the rights of Charterers, should any contamination or damage subsequently be   21
found, to contend that the same was caused by inadequate cleaning and/or some breach of this or any other clause   22
of this Charter.   23

Notwithstanding that the vessel, if equipped with IGS, shall present for loading with all cargo tanks fully   24
inerted, any time used for de-inerting (provided that such de-inerting takes place after laytime or demurrage time has   25
commenced or would, but for this clause, have commenced) and/or re-inerting those tanks that at Charterers'   26
specific request were gas freed for inspection, shall count as laytime or if on demurrage as demurrage, provided the   27
tank or tanks inspected are found to be suitable. In such case Charterers will reimburse Owners for bunkers   28
consumed for de-inerting/re-inerting, at replacement cost.   29

If the vessel's tanks are inspected and rejected, time used for de-inerting shall not count towards laytime or   30
demurrage, and laytime or demurrage time shall not commence or recommence, as the case may be, until the tanks   31
have been re-inspected, approved by Charterers' inspector, and re-inerted.   32

Voyage

3. (1) Subject to the provisions of this Charter the vessel shall perform her service with utmost despatch and   33
shall proceed to such berths as Charterers may specify, in any port or ports within Part I clause (D) nominated by   34
Charterers, or so near thereunto as she may safely get and there, always safely afloat, load the cargo specified in   35
Part I clause (F) of this Charter, but not in excess of the maximum quantity consistent with the International Load   36
Line Convention for the time being in force and, being so loaded, proceed as ordered on signing bills of lading to   37
such berths as Charterers may specify, in any port or ports within Part I clause (E) nominated by Charterers, or so   38
near thereunto as she may safely get and there, always safely afloat, discharge the cargo.   39

Charterers shall nominate loading and discharging ports, and shall specify loading and discharging berths   40
and, where loading or discharging is interrupted, shall provide fresh orders in relation thereto.   41
In addition Charterers shall have the option at any time of ordering the vessel to safe areas at sea for wireless orders.   42
Any delay or deviation arising as a result of the exercise of such option shall be compensated by Charterers in   43
accordance with the terms of Part II clause 26 (1).   44

(2) Owners shall be responsible for and indemnify Charterers for any *direct* time, costs, delays or loss including but   45
not limited to use of laytime, demurrage, deviation expenses, replacement tonnage, lightening costs and associated   46
fees and expenses due to any failure whatsoever to comply fully with Charterers' voyage instructions and clauses in   47
this Charter which specify requirements concerning Voyage Instructions and/ or Owners'/masters' duties including,   48
without limitation to the generality of the foregoing, loading more cargo than permitted under the International Load   49
Line Convention, for the time being in force, or for not leaving sufficient space for expansion of cargo or loading   50
more or less cargo than Charterers specified or for not loading/discharging in accordance with Charterers'   51
instructions regarding the cargo quantity or draft requirements.   52
This clause 3(2) shall have effect notwithstanding the provision of Part II clause 32 (a) of this Charter or Owners'   53
defences under the Hague-Visby Rules.   54

(3) Owners shall always employ pilots for berthing and unberthing of vessels at all ports and/or berths under   55
this Charter unless prior exemption is given by correct and authorised personnel. Owners to confirm in writing if   56
they have been exempt from using a pilot and provide Charterers with the details, including but not limited to, the   57
authorising organisation with person's name.   58

(4) Without prejudice to the provisions of sub-clause (2) of this clause, and unless a specific prior agreement   59
exists, if a conflict arises between terminal orders and Charterers' voyage instructions, the master shall stop cargo   60
operations, and/or other operations under dispute, and contact Charterers immediately. Terminal orders shall never   61

PART II

supersede Charterers' voyage instructions and any conflict shall be resolved prior to resumption of cargo, or other,	62
operations in dispute. Where such a conflict arises the vessel shall not sail from the port or resume cargo operations,	63
and/or other operations under dispute, until Charterers have directed the vessel to do so.	64
Time spent resolving the vessel/terminal conflict will count as laytime or demurrage except that failure of	65
Owners/master to comply with the procedure set forth above shall result in the deduction from laytime or	66
demurrage time of the time used in resolving the vessel/terminal instruction conflict	67

(5) In this Charter, "berth" means any berth, wharf, dock, anchorage, submarine line, a position alongside 〔68〕
any vessel or lighter or any other loading or discharging point whatsoever to which Charterers are entitled to order 〔69〕
the vessel hereunder, and "port" means any port or location at sea to which the vessel may proceed in accordance 〔70〕
with the terms of this Charter. 〔71〕

Safe berth   4. Charterers shall exercise due diligence to order the vessel only to ports and berths which are safe for 〔72〕
the vessel and to ensure that transhipment operations conform to standards not less than those set out in the latest 〔73〕
edition of ICS/OCIMF Ship-to-Ship Transfer Guide (Petroleum). Notwithstanding anything contained in this 〔74〕
Charter, Charterers do not warrant the safety of any port, berth or transhipment operation and Charterers shall 〔75〕
not be liable for loss or damage arising from any unsafety if they can prove that due diligence was exercised in the 〔76〕
giving of the order or if such loss or damage was caused by an act of war or civil commotion within the trading 〔77〕
areas defined in Part I clauses (D/E). 〔78〕

Freight   5. (1) Freight shall be earned concurrently with delivery of cargo at the nominated discharging port or ports 〔79〕
and shall be paid by Charterers to Owners without any deductions, except as may be required in the Singapore 〔80〕
Income Tax Act and/or under Part II clause 48 and/or under clause 55 and/or under Part III clause 4(a), in United 〔81〕
States Dollars at the rate(s) specified in Part I clause (G) on the gross bill of lading quantity as furnished by the 〔82〕
shipper (subject to Part II clauses 8 and 40), upon receipt by Charterers of notice of completion of final discharge of 〔83〕
cargo, provided that no freight shall be payable on any quantity in excess of the maximum quantity consistent with 〔84〕
the International Load Line Convention for the time being in force. 〔85〕

If the vessel is ordered to proceed on a voyage for which a fixed differential is provided in Worldscale, such 〔86〕
fixed differential shall be payable without applying the percentage referred to in Part I clause (G). 〔87〕

If cargo is carried between ports and/or by an agreed route for which no freight rate is expressly quoted in 〔88〕
Worldscale, then the parties shall, in the absence of agreement as to the appropriate freight rate, apply to 〔89〕
Worldscale Association (London) Ltd., or Worldscale Association (NYC) Inc., for the determination of an 〔90〕
appropriate Worldscale freight rate. If Owners or master unilaterally elect to proceed by a route that is different to 〔91〕
that specified in Worldscale, or different to a route agreed between Owners and Charterers, freight shall always be 〔92〕
paid in accordance with the Worldscale rate as published or in accordance with any special rate applicable for the 〔93〕
agreed route. 〔94〕

Save in respect of the time when freight is earned, the location of any transhipment at sea pursuant to Part II 〔95〕
clause 26(2) shall not be an additional nominated port, unless otherwise agreed, for the purposes of this Charter 〔96〕
(including this clause 5) and the freight rate for the voyage shall be the same as if such transhipment had not taken 〔97〕
place. 〔98〕

(2) If the freight in Part I clause (G) is a lumpsum amount and such lumpsum freight is connected with a 〔99〕
specific number of load and discharge ports given in Part I clause (L) and Owners agree that Charterers may order 〔100〕
the vessel to additional load and/or discharge ports not covered by the agreed lumpsum freight, the following shall 〔101〕
apply: 〔102〕

    (a) the first load port and the final discharge port shall be deemed to be the port(s) that form the voyage and 〔103〕
        on which the lumpsum freight included in Part I clause (G) refers to; 〔104〕

    (b) freight for such additional ports shall be calculated on basis of deviation. Deviation shall be calculated 〔105〕
        on the difference in distance between the specified voyage (for which freight is agreed) and the voyage 〔106〕
        actually performed. 〔107〕

BP Shipping Marine Distance Tables (2004), produced by AtoBriac shall be used in both cases. 〔108〕
Deviation time/bunker consumption shall be calculated using the charter speed and bunker consumption as per the 〔109〕
speed and consumptions given in Part I clause (L) of this Charter. 〔110〕
Deviation time and time spent in port shall be charged at the demurrage rate in Part I clause (J) of this Charter 〔111〕
except that time used in port which would otherwise qualify for half rate laytime and/or demurrage under Part II 〔112〕
clause (15) (2) of this Charter will be charged at half rate. 〔113〕
Additional bunkers consumed shall be paid at replacement cost, and actual port costs shall be paid as incurred. 〔114〕
Such deviation costs shall be paid against Owners' fully documented claim. 〔115〕

Claims, dues   6. (1) Dues and other charges upon the vessel, including those assessed by reference to the quantity of cargo 〔116〕
and other loaded or discharged, and any taxes on freight whatsoever shall be paid by Owners, and dues and other charges 〔117〕
charges upon the cargo shall be paid by Charterers. However, notwithstanding the foregoing, where under a provision of 〔118〕
Worldscale a due or charge is expressly for the account of Owners or Charterers then such due or charge shall be 〔119〕
payable in accordance with such provision. 〔120〕

(2) Any costs including those itemised under applicable "Worldscale" as being for Charterers' account shall, 〔121〕

PART II

unless otherwise instructed by Charterers, be paid by Owners and reimbursed by Charterers against Owners' fully	122
documented claim.	123

       (3) Charterers shall be discharged and released from all liability in respect of any charges/claims (other than | 124
demurrage and Worldscale charges/dues and indemnity claims) including but not limited to additional bunkers, | 125
detention, deviation, shifting, heating, deadfreight, speed up, slow down, drifting, port costs, additional freight, | 126
insurance, Owner may send to Charterers under this Charter unless any such charges/claims have been received by | 127
Charterer in writing, fully and correctly documented, within ninety (90) days from completion of discharge of the | 128
cargo concerned under this Charter. Part II clause 15 (3) of this Charter covers the notification and fully documented | 129
claim procedure for demurrage. | 130

       (4) If, after disconnection of hoses, the vessel remains at berth for vessel's purposes, Owners shall be | 131
responsible for all direct and indirect costs whether advised to Owners in advance or not, and including charges by | 132
Terminal/Suppliers/Receivers. | 133

Loading and discharging cargo   7. The cargo shall be loaded into the vessel at the expense of Charterers and, up to the vessel's permanent | 134
hose connections, at Charterers' risk. The cargo shall be discharged from the vessel at the expense of Owners | 135
and, up to the vessel's permanent hose connections, at Owners' risk. Owners shall, unless otherwise notified by | 136
Charterers or their agents, supply at Owners' expense all hands, equipment and facilities required on board for | 137
mooring and unmooring and connecting and disconnecting hoses for loading and discharging. | 138

Deadfreight   8. Charterers need not supply a full cargo, but if they do not freight shall nevertheless be paid as if the | 139
vessel had been loaded with a full cargo. | 140

       The term "full cargo" as used throughout this Charter means a cargo which, together with any collected | 141
washings (as defined in Part II clause 40) retained on board pursuant to the requirements of MARPOL 73/78, fills | 142
the vessel to either her applicable deadweight or her capacity stated in Part I clause (A) (I) (iii), whichever is less, | 143
while leaving sufficient space in the tanks for the expansion of cargo. If under Part I clause (F) vessel is chartered | 144
for a minimum quantity and the vessel is unable to load such quantity due to having reached her capacity as stated in | 145
Part I clause (A) (I) (iii), always leaving sufficient space for expansion of cargo, then without prejudice to any | 146
claims which Charterers may have against Owners, no deadfreight between the quantity loaded and the quantity | 147
shown in Part I clause (F) shall be due. | 148

Shifting   9. Charterers shall have the right to require the vessel to shift at ports of loading and/or discharging from a | 149
loading or discharging berth within port limits and/or to a waiting place inside or outside port limits and back to the | 150
same or to another such berth/place once or more often on payment of all additional expenses incurred. For the | 151
purposes of and shifting the places grouped in Port and Terminal Combinations in Worldscale are | 152
to be considered as berths within a single port. If at any time before cargo operations are completed it becomes | 153
dangerous for the vessel to remain at the specified berth as a result of wind or water conditions, Charterers shall pay | 154
all additional expenses of shifting from any such berth and back to that or any other specified berth within port | 155
limits (except to the extent that any fault of the vessel contributed to such danger). | 156

       Subject to Part II clause 14(a) and (c) time spent shifting shall count against laytime or if the vessel is on | 157
demurrage for demurrage. | 158

Charterers' failure to give orders   10. If the vessel is delayed due to Charterers' breach of Part II clause 3 Charterers shall, subject to the terms | 159
hereof, compensate Owners in accordance with Part II clause 15(1) and (2) as if such delay were time exceeding the | 160
laytime. Such compensation shall be Owners' sole remedy in respect of such delay. | 161

       The period of such delay shall be calculated: | 162
    (i)   from 6 hours after Owners notify Charterers that the vessel is delayed awaiting nomination of loading or | 163
        discharging port until such nomination has been received by Owners, or | 164
    (ii) from 6 hours after the vessel gives notice of readiness at the loading or discharging port until | 165
        commencement of loading or discharging, | 166
as the case may be, subject always to the same exceptions as those set out in Part II clause 14. Any period of | 167
delay in respect of which Charterers pay compensation pursuant to this clause 10 shall be excluded from any | 168
calculation of time for laytime or demurrage made under any other clause of this Charter. | 169

       Periods of delay hereunder shall be cumulative for each port, and Owners may demand compensation after | 170
the vessel has been delayed for a total of 20 running days, and thereafter after each succeeding 5 running days of | 171
delay and at the end of any delay. Each such demand shall show the period in respect of which compensation is | 172
claimed and the amount due. Charterers shall pay the full amount due within 14 days after receipt of Owners' | 173
demand. Should Charterers fail to make any such payments Owners shall have the right to terminate this Charter | 174
by giving written notice to Charterers or their agents, without prejudice to any claims which Charterers or | 175
Owners may have against each other under this Charter or otherwise. | 176

Laydays/ Termination   11. Should the vessel not be ready to load by noon local time on the termination date set out in Part I clause | 177
(C) Charterers shall have the option of terminating this Charter unless the vessel has been delayed due to Charterers' | 178
change of orders pursuant to Part II clause 26, in which case the laydays shall be extended by the period of | 179
such delay. | 180

PART II

As soon as Owners become aware that the vessel will not be ready to load by noon on the termination date,	181
Owners will give notice to Charterers declaring a new readiness date and ask Charterers to elect whether or not to	182
terminate this Charter.	183
Within 4 days after such notice, Charterers shall either:	184

(i)   declare this Charter terminated or 185
(ii)   confirm a revised set of laydays which shall be amended such that the new readiness date stated shall 186
       be the commencement date and the second day thereafter shall be the termination date or, 187
(iii) agree a new set of laydays or an extension to the laydays mutually acceptable to Owners and Charterers 188

    The provisions of this clause and the exercise or non-exercise by Charterers of their option to terminate 189
shall not prejudice any claims which Charterers or Owners may have against each other. 190

Laytime   12. (1) The laytime for loading, discharging and all other Charterers' purposes whatsoever shall be the 191
number of running hours specified in Part I clause (I). Charterers shall have the right to load and discharge at all 192
times, including night, provided that they shall pay for all extra expenses incurred ashore. 193

        (2) If vessel is able to, and Charterers so instruct, the vessel shall load earlier than the commencement of 194
of laydays and Charterers shall have the benefit of such time saved by way of offset from any demurrage incurred. 195
Such benefit shall be the time between commencement of loading until the commencement of the original laydays. 196

Notice of   13. (1) Subject to the provisions of Part II clauses 13(3) and 14, 197
readiness/   (a)   Time at each loading or discharging port shall commence to run 6 hours after the vessel is in 198
Running   all respects ready to load or discharge and written notice thereof has been tendered by the 199
time   master or Owners' agents to Charterers or their agents and the vessel is securely moored at 200
                           the specified loading or discharging berth. However, if the vessel does not proceed 201
                           immediately to such berth time shall commence to run 6 hours after (i) the vessel is lying in 202
                           the area where she was ordered to wait or, in the absence of any such specific order, in a 203
                           usual waiting area and (ii) written notice of readiness has been tendered and (iii) the 204
                           specified berth is accessible. A loading or discharging berth shall be deemed inaccessible 205
                           only for so long as the vessel is or would be prevented from proceeding to it by bad weather, 206
                           tidal conditions, ice, awaiting daylight, pilot or tugs, or port traffic control requirements 207
                           (except those requirements resulting from the unavailability of such berth or of the cargo). 208
                           If Charterers fail to specify a berth at any port, the first berth at which the vessel loads or 209
                           discharges the cargo or any part thereof shall be deemed to be the specified berth at such 210
                           port for the purposes of this clause. 211
                           Notice shall not be tendered before commencement of laydays and notice tendered by radio 212
                           shall qualify as written notice provided it is confirmed in writing as soon as reasonably 213
                           possible. 214
                           Time shall never commence before six hours after commencement of laydays unless loading 215
                           commences prior to this time as provided in clause 13 (3). 216
                           If Owners fail; 217
                     (i)   to obtain Customs clearance; and/or 218
                     (ii)   to obtain free pratique unless this is not customary prior to berthing; and/or 219
                     (iii) to have on board all papers/certificates required to perform this Charter, either within 220
                            the 6 hours after notice of readiness originally tendered or when time would otherwise 221
                            normally commence under this Charter, then the original notice of readiness shall not 222
                            be valid. A new notice of readiness may only be tendered when Customs clearance and/or 223
                            free pratique has been granted and/or all papers/certificates required are in order in accordance 224
                            with relevant authorities' requirements. Laytime or demurrage, if on demurrage, would then 225
                            commence in accordance with the terms of this Charter. All time, costs and expenses as a 226
                            result of delays due to any of the foregoing shall be for Owners' account. 227
            (b)   Time shall: 228
                     (i)   continue to run until the cargo hoses have been disconnected. 229
                     (ii)   recommence two hours after disconnection of hoses if the vessel is delayed for Charterers' 230
                            purposes and shall continue until the termination of such delay provided that if the vessel waits 231
                            at any place other than the berth, any time or part of the time on passage to such other place that 232
                            occurs after two hours from disconnection of hoses shall not count. 233

        (2) If the vessel loads or discharges cargo by transhipment at sea time shall commence in accordance with 234
Part II clause 13 (I) (a), and run until transhipment has been completed and the vessels have separated, always 235
subject to Part II clause 14. 236

        (3) Notwithstanding anything else in this clause 13, if Charterers start loading or discharging the 237
vessel before time would otherwise start to run under this Charter, time shall run from commencement of such 238
loading or discharging. 239

        (4) For the purposes of this clause 13 and of Part II clause 14 and Part II clause 15 "time" shall mean laytime 240

PART II

	or time counting for demurrage, as the case may be.	241

Suspension of time	14.	Time shall not count when:	242
	(a)	spent on inward passage from the vessel's waiting area to the loading or discharging berth	243
		specified by Charterers, even if lightening occurred at such waiting area; or	244
	(b)	spent in carrying out vessel operations, including but not limited to bunkering, discharging	245
		slops and tank washings, and handling ballast, except to the extent that cargo operations are	246
		carried on concurrently and are not delayed thereby; or	247
	(c)	lost as a result of:	248
		(i) breach of this Charter by Owners; or	249
		(ii) any cause attributable to the vessel, (including but not limited to the warranties in Part I	250
		(A) of this Charter) including breakdown or inefficiency of the vessel; or	251
		(iii) strike, lock-out, stoppage or restraint of labour of master, officers or crew of the vessel or	252
		tug boats or pilot.	253

Demurrage	

15. (1) Charterers shall pay demurrage at the rate specified in Part I clause (J). 254

If the demurrage rate specified in Part I clause (J) is expressed as a percentage of Worldscale such percentage 255
shall be applied to the demurrage rate applicable to vessels of a similar size to the vessel as provided in Worldscale 256
or, for the purpose of clause 10 and/or if this Charter is terminated prior to the commencement of loading, in 257
Worldscale current at the termination date specified in Part I clause (C). 258

Demurrage shall be paid per running day or pro rata for part thereof for all time which, under the provisions 259
of this Charter, counts against laytime or for demurrage and which exceeds the laytime specified in Part I clause (I). 260
Charterers' liability for exceeding the laytime shall be absolute and shall not in any case be subject to the 261
provisions of Part II clause 32. 262

(2) If, however, all or part of such demurrage arises out of or results from fire or explosion or strike or 263
failure/breakdown of plant and/or machinery at ports of loading and/or discharging in or about the plant of 264
Charterers, shippers or consignees of the cargo (not being a fire or explosion caused by the negligence or wilful act 265
or omission of Charterers, shippers or consignees of the cargo or their respective servants or agents), act of God, act 266
of war, riot, civil commotion, or arrest or restraint of princes, rulers or peoples, the laytime used and/or the rate of 267
demurrage shall be reduced by half for such laytime used and/or for such demurrage or such parts thereof. 268

(3) Owners shall notify Charterers within 60 days after completion of discharge if demurrage has 269
been incurred and any demurrage claim shall be fully and correctly documented, and received by Charterers, within 270
90 days after completion of discharge . If Owners fail to give notice of or to submit any such claim with 271
documentation, as required herein, within the limits aforesaid, Charterers' liability for such demurrage shall be 272
extinguished. 273

(4) If any part cargo for other Charterers, shippers or consignees (as the case may be) is loaded or discharged 274
at the same berth, then any time used by the vessel waiting at or for such berth and in loading or discharging which 275
would otherwise count as laytime or if the vessel is on demurrage for demurrage, shall be pro-rated in the proportion 276
that Charterers' cargo bears to the total cargo to be loaded or discharged at such berth. If however, the running of 277
laytime or demurrage, if on demurrage, is solely attributable to other parties' cargo operations then such time shall 278
not count in calculating laytime or demurrage, if on demurrage, against Charterers under this Charter. 279

Vessel inspection	

16. Charterers shall have the right, but no duty, to have a representative attend on board the vessel at any 280
loading and/or discharging ports and the master and Owners shall co-operate to facilitate his inspection 281
of the vessel and observation of cargo operations. However, such right, and the exercise or non-exercise 282
thereof, shall in no way reduce the master's or Owners' authority over, or responsibility to 283
Charterers and third parties for, the vessel and every aspect of her operation, nor increase Charterers' 284
responsibilities to Owners or third parties for the same. 285

Cargo inspection	

17. This clause 17 is without prejudice to Part II clause 2 hereof. Charterers shall have the right to require 286
inspection of the vessel's tanks at loading and/or discharging ports to ascertain the quantity and quality of the cargo, 287
water and residues on board. Depressurisation of the tanks to permit inspection and/or ullaging shall be carried out 288
in accordance with the recommendations in the latest edition of the ISGOTT guidelines. Charterers shall also have 289
the right to inspect and take samples from the bunker tanks and other non-cargo spaces. Any delay to the vessel 290
caused by such inspection and measurement or associated depressurising/repressurising of tanks shall count against 291
laytime, or if the vessel is on demurrage, for demurrage. 292

Cargo measure-ment	

18. The master shall ascertain the contents of all tanks before and after loading and before and after 293
discharging, and shall prepare tank-by-tank ullage reports of the cargo, water and residues on board which shall 294
be promptly made available to Charterers or their representative if requested. Each such ullage report shall show 295
actual ullage/dips, and densities at observed and standard temperature (15° Celsius). All quantities shall be 296
expressed in cubic metres at both observed and standard temperature. 297

Inert gas	

19. The vessel's inert gas system (if any) shall comply with Regulation 62, Chapter II-2 of the 1974 Safety of 298

PART II

Life at Sea Convention as modified by the Protocol of 1978, and any subsequent amendments, and Owners warrant | 299
that such system shall be operated (subject to the provisions of Part II clause 2), during loading, throughout the | 300
voyage and during discharge, and in accordance with the guidance given in the IMO publication "Inert Gas System | 301
(1983)". Should the inert gas system fail, Section 8 (Emergency Procedures) of the said IMO publication shall be | 302
strictly adhered to and time lost as a consequence of such failure shall not count against laytime or, if the vessel is | 303
on demurrage, for demurrage. | 304

Crude oil washing

20. If the vessel is equipped for crude oil washing Charterers shall have the right to require the vessel to | 305
crude oil wash, concurrently with discharge, those tanks in which Charterers' cargo is carried. If crude oil washing | 306
is required by Charterers any additional discharge time thereby incurred, always subject to the next succeeding | 307
sentences, shall count against laytime or, if the vessel is on demurrage, for demurrage. The number of hours | 308
specified in Part I clause (A) (I) (vii) shall be increased by 0.6 hours per cargo tank washed, always subject | 309
to a maximum increase of 8 hours. If vessel fails to maintain 100 PSI throughout the discharge then any time over | 310
24 hours, plus the additional discharge performance allowance under this clause, shall not count as laytime or | 311
demurrage, if on demurrage. This clause 20 does not reduce Owners' liability for the vessel to perform her service | 312
with utmost despatch as setout in Part II, Clause 3(1). The master shall provide Charterers with a crude oil washing log | 313
identifying each tank washed, and stating whether such tank has been washed to the MARPOL minimum standard | 314
or has been the subject of additional crude oil washing and whether requested by Charterers or otherwise. | 315

Overage insurance

21. Any additional insurance on the cargo required because of the age of the vessel shall be for Owners' | 316
account. | 317

Ice

22. The vessel shall not be required to force ice or to follow icebreakers. If the master finds that a | 318
nominated port is inaccessible due to ice, the master shall immediately notify Charterers requesting revised | 319
orders and shall remain outside the ice-bound area; and if after arrival at a nominated port there is danger of the | 320
vessel being frozen in, the vessel shall proceed to the nearest safe and ice free position and at the same time | 321
request Charterers to give revised orders. | 322

In either case if the affected port is: | 323

(i)   the first or only loading port and no cargo has been loaded, Charterers shall either nominate | 324
another port,or give notice cancelling this Charter in which case they shall pay at the demurrage | 325
rate in Part I clause (J)for the time from the master's notification aforesaid or from notice | 326
of readiness on arrival, as the case may be,until the time such cancellation notice is given; | 327

(ii)   a loading port and part of the cargo has been loaded, Charterers shall either nominate another | 328
port, or order the vessel to proceed on the voyage without completing loading in which case | 329
Charterers shall pay for any deadfreight arising therefrom; | 330

(iii) a discharging port, Charterers shall either nominate another port or order the vessel to proceed to or | 331
return to and discharge at the nominated port. If the vessel is ordered to proceed to or return to a | 332
nominated port, Charterers shall bear the risk of the vessel being damaged whilst proceeding to or | 333
returning to or at such port, and the whole period from the time when the master's request for revised | 334
orders is received by Charterers until the vessel can safely depart after completion of discharge shall | 335
count against laytime or, if the vessel is on demurrage, for demurrage. | 336

If, as a consequence of Charterers revising orders pursuant to this clause, the nominated port(s) or the | 337
number or rotation of ports is changed, freight shall nevertheless be paid for the voyage which the vessel would | 338
otherwise have performed had the orders not been so revised, such freight to be increased or reduced by the | 339
amount by which, as a result of such revision of orders, | 340

(a)   the time used including any time awaiting revised orders (which shall be valued at the demurrage rate | 341
in Part I clause (J)), and | 342

(b)   the bunkers consumed, at replacement cost and | 343

(c)   the port charges | 344
for the voyage actually performed are greater or less than those that would have been incurred on the | 345
voyage which, but for the revised orders under this clause, the vessel would have performed. | 346

Quarantine

23. Time lost due to quarantine shall not count against laytime or for demurrage unless such quarantine | 347
was in force at the time when the affected port was nominated by Charterers. | 348

Agency

24. The vessel's agents shall be nominated by Charterers at nominated ports of loading and discharging. | 349
Such agents, although nominated by Charterers, shall be employed and paid by Owners. | 350

Charterers' obligation at shallow draft port/ Lightening in port

25.(1) If the vessel, with the quantity of cargo then on board, is unable due to inadequate depth of | 351
water in the port safely to reach any specified discharging berth and discharge the cargo there always safely afloat, | 352
Charterers shall specify a location within port limits where the vessel can discharge sufficient cargo into vessels or | 353
lighters to enable the vessel safely to reach and discharge cargo at such discharging berth, and the vessel shall | 354
lighten at such location. | 355

(2) If the vessel is lightened pursuant to clause 25(1) then, for the purposes of the calculation | 356

Issued March 2005   **"SHELLVOY 6"**

PART II

of laytime and demurrage, the lightening place shall be treated as the first discharging berth within the port where   357
such lightening occurs.   358

Charterers'
orders/
Change of
orders/ Part
cargo
transhipment

26. (1) If, after loading and/or discharging ports have been nominated, Charterers wish to vary such   359
nominations or their rotation, Charterers may give revised orders subject to Part I clause (D) and/or (E), as the case   360
may be. Charterers shall reimburse Owners at the demurrage rate provided in Part I clause (J) for any deviation or   361
delay which may result therefrom and shall pay at replacement cost for any extra bunkers consumed.   362
Charterers shall not be liable for any other loss or expense which is caused by such variation.   363

(2) Subject to Part II clause 33(6), Charterers may order the vessel to load and/or discharge any part of the   364
cargo by transhipment at sea in the vicinity of any nominated port or en route between two nominated ports, in   365
which case unless Charterers elect, (which they may do at any time) to treat the place of such transhipment as a load   366
or discharge port (subject to the number of ports and ranges in Part I clauses (D) and (E) of this Charter), Charterers   367
shall reimburse Owners at the demurrage rate specified in Part I clause (J) for any additional steaming time and/or   368
delay which may be incurred as a consequence of proceeding to and from the location at sea of such transhipment   369
and, in addition, Charterers shall pay at replacement cost for any extra bunkers consumed.   370

(3) Owners warrant that the vessel, master, officers and crew are, and shall remain during this Charter,   371
capable of safely carrying out all the procedures in the current edition of the ICS/ OCIMF Ship to Ship Transfer   372
Guide (Petroleum). Owners further warrant that when instructed to perform a ship to ship transfer the master   373
Officers and crew shall, at all times, comply with such procedures. Charterers shall provide, and pay for,   374
the necessary equipment and, if necessary, mooring master, for such ship to ship operation.   375

Heating of
cargo

27. If Charterers require cargo heating the vessel shall, on passage to and whilst at discharging port(s),   376
Maintain the cargo at the loaded temperature or at the temperature stated in Part I clause (A) (I) (iv), whichever is   377
the lower. Charterers may request that the temperature of the cargo be raised above or lowered below that at which   378
it was loaded, in which event Owners shall use their best endeavours to comply with such request and Charterers   379
shall pay at replacement cost for any additional bunkers consumed and any consequential delay to the vessel   380
shall count against laytime or, if the vessel is on demurrage, for demurrage.   381

ETA

28. (1) Owners shall give Charterers a time and date of expected arrival at the first load port or if the loading   382
range is in the Arabian Gulf, the time of her expected arrival off Quoin Island (hereinafter called "load port"   383
in this clause) at the date of this Charter. Owners shall further advise Charterers at any time between the   384
Charter date and arrival at load port of any variation of 6 hours or more in vessel's expected arrival   385
time/date at the load port.   386
(2) Owners undertake that, unless Charterers require otherwise, the master shall: 387
(a)   advise Charterers immediately on leaving the final port of call on the previous voyage   388
of the time and date of the vessel's expected arrival at the first loading port and shall further   389
advise Charterers 72, 48, 36, and 24 hours before the expected arrival time/date.   390
(b)   advise Charterers immediately after departure from the final loading port, of the vessel's   391
expected time of arrival at the first discharging port or the area at sea to which the vessel has been   392
instructed to proceed for wireless orders, and confirm or amend such advice not later than 72, 48, 36   393
and 24 hours before the vessel is due at such port or area;   394
(c)   advise Charterers immediately of any variation of more than six hours from expected times of arrival   395
at loading or discharging ports, Quoin Island or such area at sea to Charterers;   396
(d)   address all messages as specified in Part I clause (K).   397
Owners shall be responsible for any consequences or additional expenses arising as a result of non-compliance   398
with this clause.   399
(3) If at any time prior to the tender of notice of readiness at the first load port, the vessel ceases to comply   400
with the description set out in Part I clause (A) and in any questionnaire(s), the Owners shall immediately notify   401
Charterers of the same, providing full particulars, and explaining what steps Owners are taking to ensure that the   402
vessel will so comply. Any silence or failure on the part of Charterers to respond to or any inaction taken in respect   403
of any such notice shall not amount to a waiver of any rights or remedies which Charterers may have in respect of   404
the matters notified by Owners.   405

Packed
cargo

29. Charterers have the option of shipping products and/or general cargo in available dry cargo space, the   406
Quantity being subject to the master's discretion. Freight shall be payable at the bulk rate in accordance with   407
Part II clause 5 and Charterers shall pay in addition all expenses incurred solely as a result of the packed cargo being   408
carried. Delay occasioned to the vessel by the exercise of such option shall count against laytime or, if the vessel is   409
on demurrage, for demurrage.   410

Subletting/
Assignment

30. Charterers shall have the option of sub-chartering the vessel and/or of assigning this Charter to any   411
person or persons, but Charterers shall always remain responsible for the due fulfilment of all the terms and   412
conditions of this Charter. Additionally Charterers may Novato this charter to any company of the Royal Dutch/   413
Shell Group of Companies.   414

PART II

Liberty

31. The vessel shall be at liberty to tow or be towed, to assist vessels in all positions of distress and to deviate   415
for the purpose of saving life or property. On the laden voyage the vessel shall not take on bunkers or deviate or   416
stop, except as allowed in this clause 31, without prior permission of Charterers , Cargo Insurers, and Owners' P&I   417
Club.   418

Exceptions

32. (1) The vessel, her master and Owners shall not, unless otherwise in this Charter expressly provided,   419
be liable for any loss or damage or delay or failure arising or resulting from any act, neglect or default of the   420
master, pilots, mariners or other servants of Owners in the navigation or management of the vessel; fire, unless   421
caused by the actual fault or privity of Owners; collision or stranding; dangers and accidents of the sea; explosion,   422
Bursting of boilers, breakage of shafts or any latent defect in hull, equipment or machinery; provided, however,   423
that Part I clause (A) and Part II clauses 1 and 2 hereof shall be unaffected by the foregoing. Further, neither the   424
vessel, her master or Owners, nor Charterers shall, unless otherwise in this Charter expressly provided, be liable for   425
any loss or damage or delay or failure in performance hereunder arising or resulting from act of God, act of war, act   426
of public enemies, seizure under legal process, quarantine restrictions, strikes, lock-outs, restraints of labour, riots,   427
civil commotions or arrest or restraint of princes, rulers or people.   428

(2) Nothing in this Charter shall be construed as in any way restricting, excluding or waiving the right   429
of Owners or of any other relevant persons to limit their liability under any available legislation or law.   430

(3) Clause 32(1) shall not apply to or affect any liability of Owners or the vessel or any other relevant   431
person in respect of   432

    (a)   loss or damage caused to any berth, jetty, dock, dolphin, buoy, mooring line, pipe or   433
            crane or other works or equipment whatsoever at or near any port to which the vessels   434
            may proceed under this Charter, whether or not such works or equipment belong to Charterers,   435
            or   436

    (b)   any claim (whether brought by Charterers or any other person) arising out of any loss of or   437
            damage to or in connection with the cargo. Any such claim shall be subject to the   438
            Hague-Visby Rules or the Hague Rules, or the Hamburg Rules as the case may be, which   439
            ought pursuant to Part II clause 37 hereof to have been incorporated in the relevant bill of lading   440
            (whether or not such Rules were so incorporated) or, if no such bill of lading is issued, to the   441
            Hague-Visby rules unless the Hamburg Rules compulsory apply in which case to the Hamburg   442
            Rules.   443

Bills of
lading

33. (1) Subject to the provisions of this clause Charterers may require the master to sign lawful bills of   444
lading for any cargo in such form as Charterers direct.   445

(2) The signing of bills of lading shall be without prejudice to this Charter and Charterers hereby   446
indemnify Owners against all liabilities that may arise from signing bills of lading to the extent that the same   447
impose liabilities upon Owners in excess of or beyond those imposed by this Charter.   448

(3) All bills of lading presented to the master for signature, in addition to complying with the   449
Requirements of Part II clauses 35, 36 and 37, shall include or effectively incorporate clauses substantially similar to   450
the terms of Part II clauses 22, 33(7) and 34.   451

(4) All bills of lading presented for signature hereunder shall show a named port of discharge. If   452
when bills of lading are presented for signature discharging port(s) have been nominated hereunder, the   453
discharging port(s) shown on such bills of lading shall be in conformity with the nominated port(s). If at the time   454
of such presentation no such nomination has been made hereunder, the discharging port(s) shown on such bills of   455
lading must be within Part I clause (E) and shall be deemed to have been nominated hereunder by virtue of such   456
presentation.   457

(5) Article III Rules 3 and 5 of the Hague-Visby Rules shall apply to the particulars included in the   458
bills of lading as if Charterers were the shippers, and the guarantee and indemnity therein contained shall apply to   459
the description of the cargo furnished by or on behalf of Charterers.   460

(6) Notwithstanding any other provisions of this Charter, Owners shall be obliged to comply with   461
any orders from Charterers to discharge all or part of the cargo provided that they have received from Charterers   462
written confirmation of such orders.   463
If Charterers by telex, facsimile or other form of written communication that specifically refers to this clause request   464
Owners to discharge a quantity of cargo either: 465

    (a)   without bills of lading and/or   466
    (b)   at a discharge place other than that named in a bill of lading and/or   467
    (c)   that is different from the bill of lading quantity   468
then Owners shall discharge such cargo in accordance with Charterers' instructions in consideration of receiving the   469
Following indemnity which shall be deemed to be given by Charterers on each and every such occasion and which is limited   470
in value to 200 per cent of the C.I.F. value of the cargo on board: 471

    (i)   Charterers shall indemnify Owners, and Owners' servants and agents in respect of any liability loss or damage   472
            of whatsoever nature (including legal costs as between attorney or solicitor and client and associated expenses)   473
            which Owners may sustain by reason of delivering such cargo in accordance with Charterers' request.   474
    (ii)   If any proceeding is commenced against Owners or any of Owners' servants or agents in connection with the   475

PART II

		vessel having delivered cargo in accordance with such request, Charterers shall provide Owners or any of	476
		Owners' servants or agents from time to time on demand with sufficient funds to defend the said proceedings.	477
	(iii)	If the vessel or any other vessel or property belonging to Owners should be arrested or detained, or if the arrest	478

(iii) If the vessel or any other vessel or property belonging to Owners should be arrested or detained, or if the arrest or detention thereof should be threatened, by reason of discharge in accordance with Charterers' instruction as aforesaid, Charterers shall provide on demand such bail or other security as may be required to prevent such arrest or detention or to secure the release of such vessel or property and Charterers shall indemnify Owners in respect of any loss, damage or expenses caused by such arrest or detention whether or not the same may be justified.

(iv) Charterers shall, if called upon to do so at any time while such cargo is in Charterers' possession, custody or control, redeliver the same to Owners.

(v) As soon as all original bills of lading for the above cargo which name as discharge port the place where delivery actually occurred shall have arrived and/or come into Charterers' possession, Charterers shall produce and deliver the same to Owners, whereupon Charterers' liability hereunder shall cease.

Provided however, if Charterers have not received all such original bills of lading by 24.00 hours on the day 36 calendar months after the date of discharge, then this indemnity shall terminate at that time unless before that time Charterers have received from Owners written notice that:

(a) some person is making a claim in connection with Owners delivering cargo pursuant to Charterers' request or

(b) legal proceedings have been commenced against Owners and/or carriers and/Charterers and/or any of their respective servants or agents and/or the vessel for the same reason.

When Charterers have received such a notice, then this indemnity shall continue in force until such claim or legal proceedings are settled. Termination of this indemnity shall not prejudice any legal rights a party may have outside this indemnity.

(vi) Owners shall promptly notify Charterers if any person (other than a person to whom Charterers ordered cargo to be delivered) claims to be entitled to such cargo and/or if the vessel or any other property belonging to Owners is arrested by reason of any such discharge of cargo.

(vii) This indemnity shall be governed and construed in accordance with the English law and each and any dispute arising out of or in connection with this indemnity shall be subject to the jurisdiction of the High Court of Justice of England.

(7) The master shall not be required or bound to sign bills of lading for any blockaded port or for any port which the master or Owners in his or their discretion consider dangerous or impossible to enter or reach.

(8) Charterers hereby warrant that on each and every occasion that they issue orders under Part II clauses 22, 26, 34 or 38 they will have the authority of the holders of the bills of lading to give such orders, and that such bills of lading will not be transferred to any person who does not concur therein.

(9) Owners hereby agree that original bill(s) of lading, if available, will be allowed to be placed on board. If original bill(s) of lading are placed on board, Owners agree that vessel will discharge cargo against such bill(s) of lading carried on board, on receipt of receivers' proof of identity.

War risks   34.(1) If

(a) any loading or discharging port to which the vessel may properly be ordered under the provisions of this Charter or bills of lading issued pursuant to this Charter be blockaded, or

(b) owing to any war, hostilities, warlike operation, civil commotions, revolutions, or the operation of international law (i) entry to any such loading or discharging port or the loading or discharging of cargo at any such port be considered by the master or Owners in his or their discretion dangerous or prohibited or (ii) it be considered by the master or Owners in his or their discretion dangerous or impossible or prohibited for the vessel to reach any such loading or discharging port,

Charterers shall have the right to order the cargo or such part of it as may be affected to be loaded or discharged at any other loading or discharging port within the ranges specified in Part I clause (D) or (E) respectively (provided such other port is not blockaded and that entry thereto or loading or discharging of cargo thereat or reaching the same is not in the master's or Owners' opinion dangerous or impossible or prohibited).

(2) If no orders be received from Charterers within 48 hours after they or their agents have received from Owners a request for the nomination of a substitute port, then

(a) if the affected port is the first or only loading port and no cargo has been loaded, this Charter shall terminate forthwith;

(b) if the affected port is a loading port and part of the cargo has already been loaded, the vessel may proceed on passage and Charterers shall pay for any deadfreight so incurred;

(c) if the affected port is a discharging port, Owners shall be at liberty to discharge the cargo at any port which they or the master may in their or his discretion decide on (whether within the range specified in Part I clause (E) or not) and such discharging shall be deemed to be due fulfilment of the Contract or Contracts of Affreightment so far as cargo so discharged is concerned.

(3) If in accordance with clause 34(1) or (2) cargo is loaded or discharged at any such other port, freight shall be paid as for the voyage originally nominated, such freight to be increased or reduced by the amount by which, as a result of loading or discharging at such other port,

(a) the time on voyage including any time awaiting revised orders (which shall be valued at the demurrage rate in Part I clause (J)), and

| | 476–537 |

PART II

(b)	the bunkers consumed, at replacement cost, and	538
(c)	the port charges	539

for the voyage actually performed are greater or less than those which would have been incurred on the voyage originally 540
nominated save as aforesaid, the voyage actually performed shall be treated for the purpose of this Charter as if it were the 541
voyage originally nominated. 542

(4) The vessel shall have liberty to comply with any directions or recommendations as to departure, arrival, routes, ports 543
of call, stoppages, destinations, zones, waters, delivery or in any otherwise whatsoever given by the government of the nation 544
under whose flag the vessel sails or any other government or local authority including any de facto government or local authority 545
or by any person or body acting or purporting to act as or with the authority of any such government or authority or by any 546
committee or person having under the terms of the war risks insurance on the vessel the right to give any such directions 547
or recommendations. If by reason of or in compliance with any such directions or recommendations anything is done or is not 548
done, such shall not be deemed a deviation. 549

If, by reason of or in compliance with any such directions or recommendations as are mentioned in clause 34 (4), the vessel does 550
not proceed to the discharging port or ports originally nominated or to which she may have been properly ordered under the 551
provisions of this Charter or bills of lading issued pursuant to this Charter, the vessel may proceed to any discharging port on 552
which the master or Owners in his or their discretion may decide and there discharge the cargo. Such discharging shall be 553
deemed to be due fulfilment of the contract or contracts of Affreightment and Owners shall be entitled to freight as if discharging 554
had been effected at the port or ports originally nominated or to which the vessel may have been properly ordered under the 555
provisions of this Charter or bills of lading issued pursuant to this Charter. All extra expenses involved in reaching and 556
discharging the cargo at any such other discharging port shall be paid by Charterers and Owners shall have a lien on the cargo for 557
all such extra expenses. 558

(5) Owners shall pay for all additional war risk insurance premiums, both for annual periods and also for the specific 559
performance of this Charter, on the Hull and Machinery value, as per Part I clause (A) (I) (xiii) applicable at the date of this 560
Charter, or the date the vessel was fixed "on subjects" (whichever is the earlier), and all reasonable crew war bonus. The period 561
of voyage additional war risks premium shall commence when the vessel enters a war risk zone as designated by the London 562
insurance market and cease when the vessel leaves such zone. If the vessel is already in such a zone the period shall commence 563
on tendering notice of readiness under this Charter. 564

Any increase or decrease in voyage additional war risk premium and any period in excess of the first fourteen days shall be for 565
Charterers' account and payable against proven documentation. Any discount or rebate refunded to Owners for whatever reason 566
shall be passed on to Charterers. Any premiums, and increase thereto, attributable to closure insurance (i.e. blocking and 567
trapping) shall be for Owners' account. 568

Both to blame clause   35. If the liability for any collision in which the vessel is involved while performing this Charter falls to be determined in 569
accordance with the laws of the United States of America, the following clause, which shall be included in all bills of lading 570
issued pursuant to this Charter shall apply: 571
"If the vessel comes into collision with another vessel as a result of the negligence of the other vessel and any act, neglect or 572
default of the master, mariner, pilot or the servants of the Carrier in the navigation or in the management of the vessel, the 573
owners of the cargo carried hereunder will indemnify the Carrier against all loss or liability to the other or non-carrying vessel 574
or her owners in so far as such loss or liability represents loss of, or damage to, or any claim whatsoever of the owners of the said 575
cargo, paid or payable by the other or non-carrying vessel or her owners to the owners of the said cargo and set off, recouped or 576
recovered by the other or non-carrying vessel or her owners as part of their claim against the carrying vessel or the Carrier. 577

The foregoing provisions shall also apply where the owners, operators or those in charge of any vessel or vessels or objects 578
other than, or in addition to, the colliding vessels or objects are at fault in respect of a collision or contact." 579

General average/ New Jason clause   36. General average shall be payable according to the York/Antwerp Rules 1994, as amended from time to time, and shall 580
be adjusted in London. All disputes relating to General Average shall be resolved in London in accordance with English Law. 581
Without prejudice to the foregoing, should the adjustment be made in accordance with the Law and practice of the United States 582
of America, the following clause, which shall be included in all bills of lading issued pursuant to this Charter, shall apply: 583
"In the event of accident, danger, damage or disaster before or after the commencement of the voyage, resulting from any 584
cause whatsoever, whether due to negligence or not, for which, or for the consequence of which, the Carrier is not responsible, 585
by statute, contract or otherwise, the cargo, shippers, consignees or owners of the cargo shall contribute with the Carrier in 586
general average to the payment of any sacrifices, losses or expenses of a general average nature that may be made or incurred 587
and
shall pay salvage and special charges incurred in respect of the cargo. 588

If a salving vessel is owned or operated by the Carrier, salvage shall be paid for as fully as if the said salving vessel or 589
vessels belonged to strangers. Such deposit as the Carrier or its agents may deem sufficient to cover the estimated contribution of 590
the cargo and any salvage and special charges thereon shall, if required, be made by the cargo, shippers, consignees or owners of 591
the cargo to the Carrier before delivery." 592

Clause Paramount   37. The following clause shall be included in all bills of lading issued pursuant to this Charter: 593
(1) Subject to sub-clauses (2) or (3) hereof, this bill of lading shall be governed by, and have effect subject to the rules 594
contained in the International Convention for the Unification of Certain Rules relating to bills of lading signed at Brussels on 25th 595
August 1924 (hereafter the "Hague Rules") as amended by the Protocol signed at Brussels on 23rd February 1968 (hereafter the 596
"Hague-Visby Rules"). Nothing contained herein shall be deemed to be either a surrender by the carrier of any of his rights or 597

PART II

immunities or any increase of any of his responsibilities or liabilities under the Hague-Visby Rules. 598

(2) If there is governing legislation which applies the Hague Rules compulsorily to this bill of lading, to the exclusion of 599
the Hague-Visby Rules, then this bill of lading shall have effect subject to the Hague Rules. Nothing herein contained shall be 600
deemed to be either a surrender by the carrier of any of his rights or immunities or an increase of any of his responsibilities or 601
liabilities under the Hague Rules. 602

(3) If there is governing legislation which applies the United Nations Convention on the Carriage of Goods By Sea 1978 603
(hereafter the "Hamburg Rules") compulsorily to this bill of lading to the exclusion of the Hague-Visby Rules, then this bill of 604
lading shall have effect subject to the Hamburg Rules. Nothing herein contained shall be deemed to be either a surrender by the 605
carrier of any of his rights or immunities or an increase of any of his responsibilities or liabilities under the Hamburg Rules. 606

(4) If any term of this bill of lading is repugnant to the Hague-Visby Rules, or Hague Rules or Hamburg Rules, if 607
applicable, such term shall be void to that extent but no further. 608

(5) Nothing in this bill of lading shall be construed as in any way restricting, excluding or waiving the right of any 609
relevant party or person to limit his liability under any available legislation and/or law. 610

Back loading 38. Charterers may order the vessel to discharge and/or backload a part or full cargo at any nominated port within the 611
loading / discharging ranges specified within Part I clauses (D/E) and within the rotation of the ports previously nominated, 612
provided that any cargo loaded is of the description specified in Part I clause (F) and that the master in his reasonable discretion 613
determines that the cargo can be loaded, segregated and discharged without risk of contamination by, or of any other cargo. 614

Charterers shall pay in respect of loading, carrying and discharging such cargo as follows: 615

(a)   a lumpsum freight calculated at the demurrage rate specified in Part I clause (J) on any additional port time used 616
by the vessel; and 617

(b)   any additional expenses, including bunkers consumed (at replacement cost) over above those required to load and 618
discharge one full cargo and port costs which included additional agency costs: and

(c)   if the vessel is fixed on a Worldscale rate in Part I clause (G) then freight shall always be paid for the whole 619
voyage at the rate(s) specified in Part I clause (G) on the largest cargo quantity carried on any ocean leg. 620

Bunkers 39. Owners shall give Charterers or any other company in the Royal Dutch/Shell Group of Companies first option to quote 621
for the supply of bunker requirements for the performance of this Charter. 622

Oil pollution 40.(1) Owners shall ensure that the master shall: 623
prevention/ (a)   comply with MARPOL 73/78 including any amendments thereof; 624
Ballast (b)   collect the drainings and any tank washings into a suitable tank or tanks and, after maximum separation of free 625
management water, discharge the bulk of such water overboard, consistent with the above regulations; and 626

(c)   thereafter notify Charterers promptly of the amounts of oil and free water so retained on board and details of any 627
other washings retained on board from earlier voyages (together called the "collected washings"). 628

(d)   not to load on top of such 'collected washings' without specific instructions from Charterers. 629

(e)   provide Charterers with a slops certificate to be made up and signed by the master and an independent 630
surveyor/terminal representative. The certificate shall indicate: 631
Origin and composition of slops, Volume, Free water and API measured in barrels at 60 deg F. 632

(2) On being so notified, Charterers, in accordance with their rights under this clause (which shall include without 633
limitation the right to determine the disposal of the collected washings), shall before the vessel's arrival at the loading berth 634
(or if already arrived as soon as possible thereafter) give instructions as to how the collected washings shall be dealt with. 635
Owners shall ensure that the master on the vessel's arrival at the loading berth (or if already arrived as soon as possible thereafter) 636
shall arrange in conjunction with the cargo suppliers for the measurement of the quantity of the collected washings and shall 637
record the same in the vessel's ullage record. 638

(3) Charterers may require the collected washings to be discharged ashore at the loading port, in which case no freight 639
shall be payable on them. 640

(4) Alternatively Charterers may require either that the cargo be loaded on top of the collected washings and the 641
collected washings be discharged with the cargo, or that they be kept separate from the cargo in which case Charterers shall pay 642
for any deadfreight incurred thereby in accordance with Part II clause 8 and shall, if practicable, accept discharge of the collected 643
washings at the discharging port or ports. 644
In either case, provided that the master has reduced the free water in the collected washings to a minimum consistent with the 645
retention on board of the oil residues in them and consistent with sub-clause (1)(a) above, freight in accordance with Part II 646
clause 5shall be payable on the quantity of the collected washings as if such quantity were included in a bill of lading and the 647
figure therefore furnished by the shipper provided, however, that 648

(i)   if there is a provision in this Charter for a lower freight rate to apply to cargo in excess of an agreed quantity, 649
freight on the collected washings shall be paid at such lower rate (provided such agreed quantity of cargo has been 650
loaded) and 651

(ii)   if there is provision in this Charter for a minimum cargo quantity which is less than a full cargo, then whether or 652
not such minimum cargo quantity is furnished, freight on the collected washings shall be paid as if such minimum 653
cargo quantity had been furnished, provided that no freight shall be payable in respect of any collected washings 654
which are kept separate from the cargo and not discharged at the discharge port. 655

(5) Whenever Charterers require the collected washings to be discharged ashore pursuant to this clause, Charterers shall 656

PART II

	provide and pay for the reception facilities, and the cost of any shifting there for shall be for Charterers' account. Any time lost	657

provide and pay for the reception facilities, and the cost of any shifting there for shall be for Charterers' account. Any time lost discharging the collected washings and/or shifting therefore shall count against laytime or, if the vessel is on demurrage, for demurrage.

(6) Owners warrant that the vessel will arrive at the load port with segregated/ clean ballast as defined by Annex I of MARPOL 73/78 including any amendments thereof.

Oil response pollution and insurance

41. (1) Owners warrant that throughout the duration of this Charter the vessel will be:

(i)   owned or demise chartered by a member of the 'International Tanker Owners Pollution Federation Limited, and

(ii)   entered in the Protection and Indemnity (P&I) Club stated in Part I clause (A) I (xii) .

(2) It is a condition of this Charter that Owners have in place insurance cover for oil pollution for the maximum on offer through the International Group of P&I Clubs but always a minimum of United States Dollars1,000,000,000 (one thousand million). If requested by Charterers, Owners shall immediately furnish to Charterers full and proper evidence of the coverage.

(3) Owners warrant that the vessel carries on board a certificate of insurance as required by the Civil Liability Convention for Oil Pollution damage. Owners further warrant that said certificate will be maintained effective throughout the duration of performance under this Charter. All time, costs and expense as a result of Owners' failure to comply with the foregoing shall be for Owners' account.

(4) Owners warrant that where the vessel is a "Relevant Ship", they are a "Participating Owner", both as defined in the Small Tanker Oil Pollution Indemnification Agreement ("STOPIA") and that the vessel is entered in STOPIA, and shall so remain during the currency of this Charter, provided always that STOPIA is not terminated in accordance with Clause VIII of its provisions.

Lien

42.   Owners shall have an absolute lien upon the cargo and all subfreights for all amounts due under this charter and the cost of recovery thereof including any expenses whatsoever arising from the exercise of such lien.

Drugs and alcohol

43. Owners are aware of the problem of drug and alcohol abuse and warrant that they have a written policy in force, covering the vessel, which meets or exceeds the standards set out in the "Guidelines for the Control of Drugs and Alcohol on board Ship" as published by OCIMF dated June 1995.
Owners further warrant that this policy shall remain in force during the period of this Charter and such policy shall be adhered to throughout this Charter.

ITWF

44. Owners warrant that the terms of employment of the vessel's staff and crew will always remain acceptable to the International Transport Workers Federation on a worldwide basis. All time, costs and expenses incurred as a result of Owners' failure to comply with foregoing shall be for Owners' account.

Letters of protest/ Deficiencies

45.   It is a condition of this Charter that from the time the vessel sails to the first load port there will be no Letter(s) of Protest ("LOP"'s) or deficiencies outstanding against the vessel. This refers to LOP's or deficiencies issued by Terminal Inspectorate or similar Port or Terminal or Governmental Authorities.

Document- ation

46. Owners shall ensure that the master and agents produce documentation and provide Charterers with copies of all such documentation relevant to each port and berth call and all transhipments at sea, including but not limited to:
Notice of Readiness / Statement of Facts / Shell Form 19x (if Charterers nominate agents under Part II clause 24) / Time sheet(s) / LOPs/ Hourly pumping logs /COW performance logs by facsimile (to the number advised in the voyage instructions). These documents to be faxed within 48 hours from sailing from each load or discharge port or transhipment area. If the vessel does not have a facsimile machine on board the master shall advise Charterers, within 48 hours from sailing from each port under this Charter, of the documents he has available and ensure copies of such documents are faxed by agents to Charterers from the relevant port of call or at latest from the next port of call. Complying with this clause does not affect the terms of Part II clause 15(3) with regard to notification and submission of a fully documented claim for demurrage or a claim described in Part II clause 6(3) of this Charter. Any documents to be faxed under this clause may be, alternatively, scanned and e-mailed to Charterers.
If any actions or facilities of Suppliers / Receivers / Terminal/ Transhipment vessels or Charterers, as applicable, impinge on the vessel's ability to perform the warranties and / or guarantees of performance under this Charter the master must issue a LOP to such effect. If the master fails to issue such LOP then Owners shall be deemed to have waived any rights to claim. Master and agents shall ensure that all documents concerning port/berth and cargo activities at all ports/berths and transhipment at sea places are signed by both an officer of the vessel and a representative of either Suppliers / Receivers / Terminal / Transhipment vessels or Charterers, as applicable.
If such a signature from Suppliers / Receivers / Terminal/ Transhipment vessels or Charterers, as applicable, is not obtainable the master or his agents should issue a LOP to such effect.
All LOP's issued by master or his agents or received by master or his agents must be forwarded to Charterers as per the terms of this clause.

Administra- tion

47. The agreed terms and conditions of this Charter shall be recorded and evidenced by the production of a fixture note sent to both Charterers and Owners within 24 hours of the fixture being concluded. This fixture note shall state the name and date of the standard pre-printed Charter Party Form, on which the Charter is based, along with all amendments / additions/ deletions to such charter party form. All further additional clauses agreed shall be reproduced in the fixture note with full wording. This fixture note shall be approved and acknowledged as correct by both Owners and Charterers to either the Ship Broker through whom they negotiated or, if no Ship Broker was involved, to each other within two working days after fixture concluded. No formal written and signed Charter Party will be produced unless specifically requested by Charterers or Owners or is required

PART II

	by additional clauses of this Charter.	714

Cargo retention

48. If on completion of discharge any liquid cargo of a pumpable nature remains on board (the presence and quantity of 715
such cargo having been established, by application of the wedge formula in respect of any tank the contents of which do not 716
reach the forward bulkhead, by an independent surveyor, appointed by Charterers and paid jointly by Owners and Charterers), 717
Charterers shall have the right to deduct from freight an amount equal to the FOB loading port value of such cargo, cargo 718
insurance plus freight thereon; provided, however, that any action or lack of action hereunder shall be without prejudice to any 719
other rights or obligations of Charterers, under this Charter or otherwise, and provided further that if Owners are liable to any 720
third party in respect of failure to discharge such pumpable cargo, or any part thereof, Charterers shall indemnify Owners against 721
such liability up to the total amount deducted under this clause. 722

Hydrogen sulphide

49. Owners shall comply with the requirements in ISGOTT (as amended from time to time) concerning Hydrogen Sulphide 723
and shall ensure that prior to arrival at the load port the Hydrogen Sulphide (ppm by volume in vapour) level in all bunker, 724
ballast and empty cargo spaces is below the Threshold Limit Value ("TLV") - Time Weighted Average ("TWA"). 725
If on arrival at the loading terminal, the loading authorities, inspectors or other authorised and qualified personnel declare that 726
the Hydrogen Sulphide levels in the vessels' tanks exceed the TLV- TWA and request the vessel to reduce the said level to 727
within the TLV-TWA then the original notice of readiness shall not be valid. A valid notice of readiness can only be tendered 728
and laytime, or demurrage time, if on demurrage, to the relevant authorities can only start to run in accordance with Part II clause 729
13 when the TLV-TWA is acceptable. 730
If the vessel is unable to reduce the levels of Hydrogen Sulphide within a reasonable time Charterers shall have the option of 731
cancelling this Charter without penalty and without prejudice to any claims which Charterers may have against Owners under 732
this Charter. 733

Port regulations

50. Owners warrant that the vessel will fully comply with all port and terminal regulations at any named port in this Charter, 734
and any ports to which Charterers may order the vessel to under this Charter in accordance with Part I clauses (D/E) provided 735
that Owners have a reasonable opportunity to acquaint themselves with the regulations at such ports. 736

Single Point/ Buoy and jetty mooring

51. (1) Owners warrant that: 737
    (a)   the vessel complies with the OCIMF recommendations, current at the date of this Charter, 738
          for equipment employed in the mooring of ships at single point moorings in particular 739
          for tongue type or hinged bar type chain stoppers and that the messenger from the Chain Stopper(s) 740
          is secured on a winch drum (not a drum end) and that the operation is totally hands free. 741
    (b)   the vessel complies and operates in accordance with the recommendations, current at the date 742
    of this Charter, contained in the latest edition of OCIMF's "Mooring Equipment Procedures" 743
    (2) If requested by Charterers, or in the event of an emergency situation arising whilst the vessel is at a 744
Single Buoy Mooring ("SBM"), the vessel shall pump sea water, either directly from the sea or from vessel's 745
clean ballast tanks, to flush SBMs floating hoses prior to, during or /after loading and/or discharge of the 746
cargo; this operation to be carried out at Charterers' expense and with time counting against laytime, or 747
demurrage, if on demurrage. Subject to Owners exercising due diligence in carrying out such an operation 748
Charterers hereby indemnify Owners for any cargo loss or contamination directly resulting from this request. 749
If master or Owners are approached by Suppliers/Receivers or Terminal Operators to undertake such an 750
operation Owners shall obtain Charterers' agreement before proceeding. 751

ISPS/MTSA

52. (1) (a) From the date of coming into force of the International Code for the Security of Ships and of Port 752
Facilities and the relevant amendments to Chapter XI of SOLAS ("ISPS Code") and the US Maritime 753
Transportation Security Act 2002 ("MTSA") in relation to the vessel, and thereafter during the currency of 754
this Charter, Owners shall procure that both the vessel and "the Company" (as defined by the ISPS Code) 755
and the "owner" (as defined by the MTSA) shall comply with the requirements of the ISPS Code relating to 756
the vessel and "the Company" and the requirements of MTSA relating to the vessel and the "owner". 757
Upon request Owners shall provide a copy of the relevant International Ship Security Certificate to 758
Charterers. Owners shall provide documentary evidence of compliance with this clause 52 (1) (a). 759
(b) Except as otherwise provided in this Charter, loss, damage, expense or delay caused by failure on the part 760
of Owners or "the Company"/"owner" to comply with the requirements of the ISPS Code/MTSA or this 761
clause shall be for Owners' account. 762
    (2) (a) Charterers shall provide the Owners with their full style contact details and other relevant information 763
reasonably required by Owners to comply with the requirements of the ISPS Code/MTSA. Additionally, 764
Charterers shall ensure that the contact details of any sub-Charterers are likewise provided to Owners. 765
Furthermore, Charterers shall ensure that all sub-charter parties they enter into shall contain the following 766
provision: 767
"The Charterers shall provide the Owners with their full style contact details and, where sub-letting is 768
permitted under the terms of the charter party, shall ensure that contact details of all sub-Charterers are likewise 769
provided to the Owners".
(b) Except as otherwise provided in this Charter, loss, damage, expense or delay caused by failure on the part 770
of Charterers to comply with this sub clause (2) shall be for Charterers' account. 771

PART II

(3) (a) Without prejudice to the foregoing, Owners right to tender notice of readiness and Charterers' liability 772
for demurrage in respect of any time delays caused by breaches of this clause 52 shall be dealt with in 773
accordance with Part II clauses 13, (Notice of readiness/Running time), 14, (Suspension of Time), and 774
15,(Demurrage), of the charter. 775
(b) Except where the delay is caused by Owners and/or Charterers failure to comply, respectively, with 776
clauses (1) and (2) of this clause 52, then any delay arising or resulting from measures imposed by a port 777
facility or by any relevant authority, under the ISPS Code/MTSA, shall count as half rate laytime, or, if the 778
vessel is on demurrage, half rate demurrage. 779
(4) Except where the same are imposed as a cause of Owners and/or Charterers failure to comply, respectively, 780
with clauses (1) and (2) of this clause 52 , then any costs or expenses related to security regulations or 781
measures required by the port facility or any relevant authority in accordance with the ISPS Code/MTSA 782
including, but not limited to, security guards, launch services, tug escorts, port security fees or taxes and 783
inspections, shall be shared equally between Owners and Charterers. All measures required by the Owners to 784
comply with the Ship Security Plan shall be for Owners' account. 785
(5) If either party makes any payment which is for the other party's account according to this clause, the other 786
party shall indemnify the paying party. 787

Business principles	53. Owners will co-operate with Charterers to ensure that the "Business Principles", as amended from time to time, of the Royal Dutch/Shell Group of Companies, which are posted on the Shell Worldwide Web (www.Shell.com), are complied with.	788 789 790
Law and litigation	54. (a) This Charter shall be construed and the relations between the parties determined in accordance with the laws of England.	791 792
Arbitration	(b) All disputes arising out of this Charter shall be referred to Arbitration in London in accordance with the Arbitration Act 1996 (or any re-enactment or modification thereof for the time being in force) subject to the following appointment procedure:	793 794 795
	(i) The parties shall jointly appoint a sole arbitrator not later than 28 days after service of a request in writing by either party to do so.	796 797
	(ii) If the parties are unable or unwilling to agree the appointment of a sole arbitrator in accordance with (i) then each party shall appoint one arbitrator, in any event not later than 14 days after receipt of a further request in writing by either party to do so. The two arbitrators so appointed shall appoint a third arbitrator before any substantive hearing or forthwith if they cannot agree on a matter relating to the arbitration.	798 799 800 801
	(iii) If a party fails to appoint an arbitrator within the time specified in (ii) (the "Party in Default"), the party who has duly appointed his arbitrator shall give notice in writing to the Party in Default that he proposes to appoint his arbitrator to act as sole arbitrator.	802 803 804
	(iv) If the Party in Default does not within 7 days of the notice given pursuant to (iii) make the required appointment and notify the other party that he has done so the other party may appoint his arbitrator as sole arbitrator whose award shall be binding on both parties as if he had been so appointed by agreement.	805 806 807
	(v) Any award of the arbitrator(s) shall be final and binding and not subject to appeal.	808
	(vi) For the purposes of this clause 54 any requests or notices in writing shall be sent by fax, e-mail or telex and shall be deemed received on the day of transmission.	809 810
	(c) It shall be a condition precedent to the right of any party to a stay of any legal proceedings in which maritime property has been, or may be, arrested in connection with a dispute under this Charter, that that party furnishes to the other party security to which that other party would have been entitled in such legal proceedings in the absence of a stay.	811 812 813 814
Small claims	(d) In cases where neither the claim nor any counterclaim exceeds the sum of United States Dollars 50,000 (or such other sum as Owners/Charterers may agree) the arbitration shall be conducted in accordance with the London Maritime Arbitrators' Association Small Claims Procedure current at the time when the arbitration proceedings are commenced.	815 816 817 818
Address commission	55. Charterers shall deduct address commission of 1.25% from all payments under this Charter.	819 820
Construction	56. The side headings have been included in this Charter for convenience of reference and shall in no way affect the construction hereof.	821 822

Issued March 2005   **"SHELLVOY 6"**

PART III

Australia	(1)(a)	The vessel shall not transit the Great Barrier Reef Inner Passage, whether in ballast en route to a	1
		loadport or laden, between the Torres Strait and Cairns, Australia. If the vessel transits the Torres Strait, the	2
		vessel shall use the outer reef passage as approved by the Australian Hydrographer. Owners shall always	3
		employ a pilot, when transiting the Torres Strait and for entry and departure through the Reef for ports	4
		North of Brisbane.	5
	(b)	The vessel shall discharge all ballast water on board the vessel and take on fresh ballast water,	6
		always in accordance with safe operational procedures, prior to entering Australian waters.	7
	(c)	On entering, whilst within and whilst departing from the port of Sydney Owners and master shall	8
		ensure that the water line to highest fixed point distance does not exceed 51.8 (fifty one point eight) metres.	9
	(d)	If Charterers or Terminal Operators instruct the vessel to slow the cargo operations down or stop	10
		entirely the cargo operations in Sydney during the hours of darkness due to excessive noise caused by the	11
		vessel then all additional time shall be for Owners' account.	12
Goods Services	(e)(i)	Goods Services Tax ("GST") imposed in Australia has application to any supply made under this	13
Tax		Charter, the parties agree that the Charterer shall account for GST in accordance with Division 83 of the	14
		GST Act even if the Owner becomes registered. The Owner acknowledges that it will not recover from the	15
		Charterer an additional amount on account of GST.	16
	(ii)	The Owner acknowledges that it is a non-resident and that it does not make supplies through an	17
		enterprise carried on in Australia as defined in section 995-1 of the Income Tax Assessment Act 1997.	18
	(iii)	The Charterer acknowledges that it is registered. Where appropriate, terms in this clause have the	19
		meaning set out in section 195-1 of the GST Act.	20
Brazil	(2) (a)	Owners acknowledge the vessel will have, if Charterers so require, to enter a port or place of	21
		clearance within mainland Brazil, to obtain necessary clearance from the Brazilian authorities and/or to	22
		pick-up personnel required to be on board during the loading of the cargo at Fluminense FPSO.	23
		The vessel then proceeds to the Fluminense FPSO where she can tender her notice of readiness.	24
		Time at the port of clearance, taken from arrival at pilot station to dropping outward pilot to be for	25
		Charterers' account and payable at the agreed demurrage rate together with freight.	26
		However this time not to count as laytime or demurrage if on demurrage.	27
	(b)	Freight payment under Part II clause 5 of this Charter shall be made within 5 banking days of	28
		receipt by Charterers of notice of completion of final discharge	29
Canada		(3) Owners warrant that the vessel complies with all the Canadian Oil Spill response regulations currently	30
		in force and that the Owner is a member of a certified oil spill response organisation and that the	31
		Owners/vessel shall continue to be members of such organisation and comply with the regulations and	32
		requirements of such organisation throughout the period of this Charter.	33
Egypt	(4)(a)	Any costs incurred by Charterers for vessel garbage or in vessel deballasting at Sidi Kerir shall be	34
		for Owners' account and Charterers shall deduct such costs from freight	35
	(b)	Charterers shall have the option for the discharge range Euromed and/or United Kingdom/ Continent	36
		(Gibraltar Hamburg range) to instruct the vessel to transit via Suez Canal. In the event that Charterers	37
		exercise this option the following shall apply:	38
		Charterers option to part discharge Ain Sukhna and reload Sidi Kerir.	39
		Charterers will pay the following with freight against Owners' fully documented claim:	40
	(c)	time incurred at the demurrage rate on the passage from the point at which the vessel deviates from the	41
		direct sailing route between last loadport and Port Suez, till the tendering of notice of readiness at Ain	42
		Sukhna, less any time lost by reason of delay beyond Charterers' reasonable control;	43
	(d)	time incurred at the demurrage rate on the passage from disconnection of hoses at Sidi Kerir to the	44
		point at which the vessel rejoins the direct sailing route between Port Said and the first discharge port UK	45
		Continent or Mediterranean, less any time lost by reason of delay beyond Charterers' reasonable control;	46
	(e)	time incurred at the demurrage rate between tendering of notice of readiness at Ain Sukhna and	47
		disconnection of hoses there;	48
	(f)	time incurred at the demurrage rate between tendering of notice of readiness at Sidi Kerir and	49
		disconnection of hoses there:	50
	(g)	all bunkers consumed during the periods (c) to (f) above at replacement cost;	51
	(h)	all port charges incurred at Ain Sukhna and Sidi Kerir.	52
		Freight rate via Suez shall be based on the Suez/Suez flat rate without the fixed Suez rate differential, other	53
		than as described below (the Worldscale rates in Part I clause (G) of this Charter to apply). All canal dues	54
		related to Suez laden transit, including Suez Canal port costs, agency fees and expenses, including but not	55
		limited to escort tugs and other expenses for canal laden transit, to be for Charterers' account and to be	56
		settled directly by them. Charterers' to pay Owners the 'ballast transit only' fixed rate differential as per	57
		Worldscale together with freight.	58
India	(5)	(a) In assessing the pumping efficiency under this Charter at ports in India, Owners agree to accept the	59
		record of pressure maintained as stated in receiver's statement of facts signed by the ship's representative.	60

(b) Owners shall be aware of and comply with the mooring requirements of Indian ports. All time,	61
costs and expenses as a result of Owners' failure to comply with the foregoing shall be for Owners'	62
account.	63
(c) Charterers shall not be liable for demurrage unless the following conditions are satisfied:	64
(i) the requirements of Part II clause 15 (3) are met in full; and	65
(ii) a copy of this Charter signed by Owners is received by Charterers at least 2 (two) working days	66
prior to the vessel's arrival in an Indian port.	67
Charterers undertake to pay agreed demurrage liabilities promptly if the above conditions have been	68
satisfied.	69

Japan (6) (a) Owners shall supply Charterers with copies of:- — 70
(i) General Arrangement/Capacity plan; and — 71
(ii) Piping/Fire Fighting Diagrams — 72
as soon as possible, but always within 4 working days after subjects lifted on this Charter. — 73
(b) If requested by Charterers, Owners shall ensure a Superintendent, fully authorised by Owners to — 74
act on Owners' and/or master's behalf, is available at all ports within Japan to attend safety meetings prior — 75
to vessel's arrival at the port(s) and be in attendance throughout the time in each port and during each cargo — 76
operation. — 77
(c) Vessel to record and print out the position with date/time by Global Positioning System when — 78
vessel enters Japanese Territorial Waters ("JTW") in order to perform vessel's declaration of entering JTW — 79
for crude oil stock piling purpose. — 80
(d) If under Part I clause (E) of this Charter Japan, or in particular ports or berths in Tokyo Bay and/or — 81
the SBM at UBE Refinery, are discharge options and if the vessel is over 220,000 metric tons deadweight — 82
and has not previously discharged in Tokyo Bay or the SBM at UBE Refinery then: — 83
(i) Owners shall submit an application of Safety Pledge Letter confirming that all safety measures — 84
will be complied with; and — 85
(ii) Present relevant ship data to the Japanese Maritime Safety Agency. — 86
Owners shall comply with the above requirements as soon as possible but always within 4 working days — 87
after subjects lifted on this Charter. — 88
(e) If Charterers instruct the vessel to make adjustment to vessel's arrival date/time at discharge port(s) in — 89
Japan, any adjustments shall be compensated in accordance with Part I clause (L) of this Charter. — 90
If vessel is ordered to drift off Japan, at a location in Owners'/master's option, then the following shall — 91
apply:- — 92
(i) Time from vessel's arrival at drifting location to the time vessel departs, on receipt of Charterers' — 93
instructions, from such location shall be for Charterers' account at the demurrage rate stipulated in Part I — 94
clause (J) of this Charter. — 95
(ii) Bunkers consumed whilst drifting as defined in sub clause (e)(i) above shall be for Charterers' — 96
account at replacement cost. — 97
Owners shall provide full documentation to support any claim under this clause. — 98

New Zealand (7) (a) Owners of vessels carrying Persistent Oil - as defined by the International Group of P&I Clubs - — 99
which shall always incorporate Crude and Fuel Oil, Non Persistent Oil as defined by the International — 100
Group of P&I Clubs - which shall always incorporate Petroleum Products; and Chemicals, warrant that the — 101
vessel shall comply at all times with the Maritime Safety Authority of New Zealand's Voluntary Routeing — 102
Code for Shipping whilst transiting the New Zealand coast and / or en route to or from ports in — 103
New Zealand and whether laden or in ballast. — 104
(b) the following voyage routing will apply: — 105
(i) vessel is to keep a minimum of 5 miles off the New Zealand coast (and outlying islands) until — 106
approaching the port's pilot station, with the following exceptions: — 107
a) to pass a minimum of 4 miles off the coast when transiting Cook Strait; — 108
b) to pass a minimum of 5 miles to the east of Poor Knights Islands and High Peaks Rocks; — 109
c) to pass a minimum of 3 miles from land when transiting the Colville or Jellicoe Channels. — 110
If due to safe navigation and or other weather related reasons the vessel proceeds on a different route to — 111
those set out above, the Owners and master shall immediately advise Charterers and Owner's agents in — 112
New Zealand of the route being followed and the reasons for such deviation from the above warranted route. — 113

Thailand (8) If Part I clause (E) of this Charter includes option to discharge at a port/berth in Thailand then the — 114
following, which is consistent with industry practice for ships discharging in Thailand, shall apply over and — 115
above any other terms contained within this Charter:- — 116
(a) Laytime shall be 96 running hours — 117
(b) Freight payment under Part II clause 5 of this Charter shall be made within 15 days of receipt — 118
by Charterers of notice of completion of final discharge of cargo. — 119
(c) Cargo quantity and quality measurements shall be carried out at load and discharge ports by — 120
mutually appointed independent surveyors, with costs to be shared equally between Owners and Charterers. — 121

PART III

	This is additional to any independent surveyors used for the Cargo Retention clause 48 in Part II of this Charter.	122 123
United Kingdom	(9) (a) It is a condition of this Charter that Owners ensure that the vessel fully complies with the latest Sullom Voe regulations, including but not limited to:-	124 125

<table>
<tr><td>United
Kingdom</td><td>(9) (a) It is a condition of this Charter that Owners ensure that the vessel fully complies with the latest Sullom Voe regulations, including but not limited to:-
        i) current minimum bulk loading rates; and
        ii) pilot boarding ladder arrangements.
Owners shall also comply with Charterers' instructions regarding the disposal of ballast from the vessel. Charterers shall accept any deadfreight claim that may arise by complying with such instructions.
    (b) It is also a condition of this Charter that Owners ensure that the vessel fully complies with the latest Tranmere and Shellhaven regulations, including but not limited to:-
        i) being able to ballast concurrently with discharge ; or
        ii) maintaining double valve segregation at all times between cargo and ballast if the vessel has
        to part discharge, stop to ballast, then resume discharge.
    (c) In the event of loading or discharge at Tranmere, Shell U.K. Ltd. shall appoint tugs, pilots and boatmen on behalf of Owners. The coordinator of these services shall be OBC., who will submit all bills to Owners direct, irrespective of whether OBC are appointed agents or not. Owners warrant they will put OBC in funds accordingly.</td><td>124
125
126
127
128
129
130
131
132
133
134
135
136
137
138</td></tr>
<tr><td>United
States of
America</td><td>(10) (a) It is a condition of this Charter that in accordance with U.S. Customs Regulations, 19 CFR 4.7a and 178.2 as amended, Owners have obtained a Standard Carrier Alpha Code (SCAC) and shall include same in the Unique Identifier which they shall enter, in the form set out in the above Customs Regulations, on all the bills of lading, Cargo manifest, Cargo declarations and other cargo documents issued under this Charter allowing carriage of goods to ports in the U.S.
Owners shall be liable for all time, costs and expenses and shall indemnify Charterers against all consequences whatsoever arising directly or indirectly from Owners' failure to comply with the above provisions of this clause.
Owners warrant that they are aware of the requirements of the U.S Bureau of Customs and Border Protection ruling issued on December 5th 2003 under Federal Register Part II Department of Homeland Security 19 CFR Parts 4, 103, et al. and will comply fully with these requirements for entering U.S ports.</td><td>139
140
141
142
143
144
145
146
147
148
149
150</td></tr>
<tr><td>Coastguard
compliance</td><td>   (b) Owners warrant that during the term of this Charter the vessel will comply with all applicable U.S. Coast Guard (USCG) Regulations in effect as of the date the vessel is tendered for first loading hereunder. If waivers are held to any USCG regulation Owners to advise Charterers of such waivers, including period of validation and reason(s) for waiver. All time costs and expense as a result of Owners' failure to comply with the foregoing shall be for Owners' account.
    (c) Owners warrant that they will
      (i) comply with the U.S. Federal Water Pollution Control Act as amended, and any
      amendments or successors to said Act</td><td>151
152
153
154
155
156
157
158</td></tr>
<tr><td>Laws and
regulation</td><td>   (ii) comply with all U.S. State Laws and regulations applicable during this Charter, as they
      apply to the U.S. States that Charterers may order vessel to under Part I clauses (D/E) of this Charter.
      (iii) have secured, carry aboard the vessel, and keep current any certificates or other evidence of
      financial responsibility required under applicable U.S. Federal or State Laws and regulations and
      documentation recording compliance with the requirements of OPA 90, any amendments or succeeding
      legislation, and any regulations promulgated thereunder. Owners shall confirm that these documents
      will be valid throughout this Charter.</td><td>159
160
161
162
163
164
165</td></tr>
<tr><td>W-8BEN</td><td>   (d) If the recipient of the freight due under this Charter does not file taxes within the US, then such recipient shall complete an IRS Form W-8BEN and forward the original by mail to Charterers, attention "Freight Payments". Should this not be received in a timely manner, then Charterers shall not be liable for interest on late payment of freight, or be in default of this Charter for such late payment.</td><td>166
167
168
169</td></tr>
<tr><td>Vapour Recovery
System</td><td>Owners warrant that the vessel's vapour recovery system complies with the requirements of the United States Coastguard.</td><td>170
171</td></tr>
<tr><td>Vietnam</td><td>(11) If required by Charterers, when loading Bach Ho crude oil, Owners will instruct the master to start the cargo heating system(s) prior to loading commencing.</td><td>172
173</td></tr>
</table>

**Code word for this Charter Party
"SHELLTIME 4"**

Issued December 1984

Time Charter Party

LONDON.   19

IT IS THIS DAY AGREED between   1

of   (hereinafter referred to as "Owners"), being owners of the   2

good   vessel called   3

(hereinafter referred to as "the vessel") described as per Clause 1 hereof and   4

of   (hereinafter referred to as "Charterers"):   5

Description and Condition of Vessel	1. At the date of delivery of the vessel under this charter 6
	    (a) she shall be classed: 7
	    (b) she shall be in every way fit to carry crude petroleum and/or its products; 8

    (c) she shall be tight, staunch, strong, in good order and condition, and in every way fit for the   9
service, with her machinery, boilers, hull and other equipment (including but not limited to hull stress calculator   10
and radar) in a good and efficient state: 11
    (d) her tanks, valves and pipelines shall be oil-tight;   12
    (e) she shall be in every way fitted for burning   13

at sea - fueloil with a maximum viscosity of   Centistokes at 50 degrees Centigrade/any   14
    commercial grade of fueloil ("ACGFO") for main propulsion, marine diesel oil/ACGFO   15
    for auxiliaries   16
in port - marine diesel oil/ACGFO for auxiliaries;   17

    (f) she shall comply with the regulations in force so as to enable her to pass through the Suez and   18
Panama Canals by day and night without delay;   19
    (g) she shall have on board all certificates, documents and equipment required from time to time by   20
any applicable law to enable her to perform the charter service without delay;   21
    (h) she shall comply with the description in Form B appended hereto, provided however that if there   22
is any conflict between the provisions of Form B and any other provision, including this Clause 1, of this charter   23
such other provision shall govern.   24

Shipboard Personnel and their Duties	2. (a) At the date of delivery of the vessel under this charter 25 (i) she shall have a full and efficient complement of master, officers and crew for a vessel of her 26

tonnage, who shall in any event be not less than the number required by the laws of the flag state and who shall be   27
trained to operate the vessel and her equipment competently and safely;   28
    (ii) all shipboard personnel shall hold valid certificates of competence in accordance with the   29
requirements of the law of the flag state;   30
    (iii) all shipboard personnel shall be trained in accordance with the relevant provisions of the   31
International Convention on Standards of Training, Certification and Watchkeeping for Seafarers, 1978;   32
    (iv) there shall be on board sufficient personnel with a good working knowledge of the English   33
language to enable cargo operations at loading and discharging places to be carried out efficiently and safely and   34
to enable communications between the vessel and those loading the vessel or accepting discharge therefrom to be   35
carried out quickly and efficiently.   36
    (b) Owners guarantee that throughout the charter service the master shall with the vessel's officers   37
and crew, unless otherwise ordered by Charterers,   38
    (i) prosecute all voyages with the utmost despatch;   39
    (ii) render all customary assistance; and   40
    (iii) load and discharge cargo as rapidly as possible when required by Charterers or their agents   41
to do so, by night or by day, but always in accordance with the laws of the place of loading or discharging (as the   42
case may be) and in each case in accordance with any applicable laws of the flag state.   43

Duty to Maintain	3. (i) Throughout the charter service Owners shall, whenever the passage of time, wear and tear or any 44

event (whether or not coming within Clause 27 hereof) requires steps to be taken to maintain or restore the   45
conditions stipulated in Clauses 1 and 2(a), exercise due diligence so to maintain or restore the vessel.   46
    (ii) If at any time whilst the vessel is on hire under this charter the vessel fails to comply with the   47
requirements of Clauses 1.2(a) or 10 then hire shall be reduced to the extent necessary to indemnify Charterers   48
for such failure. If and to the extent that such failure affects the time taken by the vessel to perform any services   49
under this charter, hire shall be reduced by an amount equal to the value, calculated at the rate of hire, of the time   50
so lost.   51
    Any reduction of hire under this sub-Clause (ii) shall be without prejudice to any other remedy   52
available to Charterers, but where such reduction of hire is in respect of time lost, such time shall be excluded   53
from any calculation under Clause 24.   54
    (iii) If Owners are in breach of their obligation under Clause 3(i) Charterers may so notify Owners in   55
writing: and if, after the expiry of 30 days following the receipt by Owners of any such notice, Owners have failed   56

	to demonstrate to Charterers' reasonable satisfaction the exercise of due diligence as required in Clause 3(i), the	57
	vessel shall be off-hire, and no further hire payments shall be due, until Owners have so demonstrated that they	58
	are exercising such due diligence.	59
	Furthermore, at any time while the vessel is off-hire under this Clause 3 Charterers have the	60
	option to terminate this charter by giving notice in writing with effect from the date on which such notice of	61
	termination is received by Owners or from any later date stated in such notice. This sub-Clause (iii) is without	62
	prejudice to any rights of Charterers or obligations of Owners under this charter or otherwise (including without	63
	limitation Charterers rights under Clause 21 hereof).	64

Period Trading Limits	4. Owners agree to let and Charterers agree to hire the vessel for a period of	65
	commencing from the time and date of delivery of the vessel, for the purpose of carrying all lawful merchandise	66
	(subject always to Clause 28) including in particular	67
	in any part of the world, as Charterers shall direct, subject to the limits of the current British Institute Warranties	68
	and any subsequent amendments thereof. Notwithstanding the foregoing, but subject to Clause 35. Charterers	69
	may order the vessel to ice-bound waters or to any part of the world outside such limits provided that Owners	70
	consent thereto (such consent not to be unreasonably withheld) and that Charterers pay for any insurance	71
	premium required by the vessel's underwriters as a consequence of such order.	72
	Charterers shall use due diligence to ensure that the vessel is only employed between and at safe places	73
	(which expression when used in this charter shall include ports, berths, wharves, docks, anchorages, submarine	74
	lines, alongside vessels or lighters, and other locations including locations at sea) where she can safely lie always	75
	afloat. Notwithstanding anything contained in this or any other clause of this charter. Charterers do not warrant	76
	the safety of any place to which they order the vessel and shall be under no liability in respect thereof except for	77
	loss or damage caused by their failure to exercise due diligence as aforesaid. Subject as above, the vessel shall be	78
	loaded and discharged at any places as Charterers may direct, provided that Charterers shall exercise due	79
	diligence to ensure that any ship-to-ship transfer operations shall conform to standards not less than those set out	80
	in the latest published edition of the ICS/OCIMF Ship-to-Ship Transfer Guide.	81
	The vessel shall be delivered by Owners at a port in	82
	at Owners' option and redelivered to Owners at a port in	83
	at Charterers' option.	84

Laydays/ Cancelling	5. The vessel shall not be delivered to Charterers before and Charterers shall	85
	have the option of cancelling this charter if the vessel is not ready and at their disposal on or before	86

Owners to Provide	6. Owners undertake to provide and to pay for all provisions, wages, and shipping and discharging fees	87
	and all other expenses of the master, officers and crew; also, except as provided in Clauses 4 and 34 hereof, for all	88
	insurance on the vessel, for all deck, cabin and engine-room stores, and for water; for all drydocking, overhaul,	89
	maintenance and repairs to the vessel; and for all fumigation expenses and de-rat certificates. Owners'	90
	obligations under this Clause 6 extend to all liabilities for customs or import duties arising at any time during the	91
	performance of this charter in relation to the personal effects of the master, officers and crew, and in relation to	92
	the stores, provisions and other matters aforesaid which Owners are to provide and pay for and Owners shall	93
	refund to Charterers any sums Charterers or their agents may have paid or been compelled to pay in respect of	94
	any such liability. Any amounts allowable in general average for wages and provisions and stores shall be credited	95
	to Charterers insofar as such amounts are in respect of a period when the vessel is on-hire.	96

Charterers to Provide	7. Charterers shall provide and pay for all fuel (except fuel used for domestic services), towage and	97
	pilotage and shall pay agency fees, port charges, commissions, expenses of loading and unloading cargoes. canal	98
	dues and all charges other than those payable by Owners in accordance with Clause 6 hereof, provided that all	99
	charges for the said items shall be for Owners' account when such items are consumed, employed or incurred for	100
	Owners' purposes or while the vessel is off-hire (unless such items reasonably relate to any service given or	101
	distance made good and taken into account under Clause 21 or 22); and provided further that any fuel used in	102
	connection with a general average sacrifice or expenditure shall be paid for by Owners.	103

Rate of Hire	8. Subject as herein provided, Charterers shall pay for the use and hire of the vessel at the rate of	104
	per day, and pro rata for any part of a day, from the time and date of her delivery (local	105
	time) until the time and date of her redelivery (local time) to Owners.	106

Payment of Hire	9. Subject to Clause 3(iii), payment of hire shall be made in immediately available funds to:	107
	Account	108
	in per calendar month in advance, less:	109
	(i) any hire paid which Charterers reasonably estimate to relate to off-hire periods, and	110
	(ii) any amounts disbursed on Owners' behalf, any advances and commission thereon, and	111
	charges which are for Owners' account pursuant to any provision hereof, and	112
	(iii) any amounts due or reasonably estimated to become due to Charterers under Clause 3(ii) or	113
	24 hereof,	114
	any such adjustments to be made at the due date for the next monthly payment after the facts have been	115
	ascertained. Charterers shall not be responsible for any delay or error by Owners' bank in crediting Owners'	116
	account provided that Charterers have made proper and timely payment.	117
	In default of such proper and timely payment,	118
	(a) Owners shall notify Charterers of such default and Charterers shall within seven days of receipt of	119
	such notice pay to Owners the amount due including interest, failing which Owners may withdraw the vessel from	120
	the service of Charterers without prejudice to any other rights Owners may have under this charter or otherwise;	121
	and	122
	(b) Interest on any amount due but not paid on the due date shall accrue from the day after that date	123
	up to and including the day when payment is made, at a rate per annum which shall be 1% above the U.S. Prime	124

Interest Rate as published by the Chase Manhattan Bank in New York at 12.00 New York time on the due date.   125
or, if no such interest rate is published on that day, the interest rate published on the next preceding day on which   126
such a rate was so published, computed on the basis of a 360 day year of twelve 30-day months, compounded   127
semi-annually.   128

Space Available to Charterers
10. The whole reach, burthen and decks of the vessel and any passenger accommodation (including   129
Owners' suite) shall be at Charterers' disposal, reserving only proper and sufficient space for the vessel's master,   130
officers, crew, tackle, apparel, furniture, provisions and stores, provided that the weight of stores on board shall   131
not, unless specially agreed, exceed   tonnes at any time during the charter period.   132

Overtime
11. Overtime pay of the master, officers and crew in accordance with ship's articles shall be for Charterers'   133
account when incurred, as a result of complying with the request of Charterers or their agents, for loading,   134
discharging, heating of cargo, bunkering or tank cleaning.   135

Instructions and Logs
12. Charterers shall from time to time give the master all requisite instructions and sailing directions, and   136
he shall keep a full and correct log of the voyage or voyages, which Charterers or their agents may inspect as   137
required. The master shall when required furnish Charterers or their agents with a true copy of such log and with   138
properly completed loading and discharging port sheets and voyage reports for each voyage and other returns as   139
Charterers may require. Charterers shall be entitled to take copies at Owners' expense of any such documents   140
which are not provided by the master.   141

Bills of Lading
13. (a) The master (although appointed by Owners) shall be under the orders and direction of   142
Charterers as regards employment of the vessel, agency and other arrangements, and shall sign bills of lading as   143
Charterers or their agents may direct (subject always to Clauses 35(a) and 40) without prejudice to this charter.   144
Charterers hereby indemnify Owners against all consequences or liabilities that may arise   145
    (i) from signing bills of lading in accordance with the directions of Charterers, or their agents, to   146
the extent that the terms of such bills of lading fail to conform to the requirements of this charter, or (except as   147
provided in Clause 13(b)) from the master otherwise complying with Charterers or their agents orders: 148
    (ii) from any irregularities in papers supplied by Charterers or their agents.   149
    (b) Notwithstanding the foregoing, Owners shall not be obliged to comply with any orders from   150
Charterers to discharge all or part of the cargo   151
    (i) at any place other than that shown on the bill of lading and/or   152
    (ii) without presentation of an original bill of lading   153
    unless they have received from Charterers both written confirmation of such orders and an   154
indemnity in a form acceptable to Owners.   155

Conduct of Vessel's Personnel
14. If Charterers complain of the conduct of the master or any of the officers or crew, Owners shall   156
immediately investigate the complaint. If the complaint proves to be well founded, Owners shall, without delay,   157
make a change in the appointments and Owners shall in any event communicate the result of their investigations   158
to Charterers as soon as possible.   159

Bunkers at Delivery and Redelivery
15. Charterers shall accept and pay for all bunkers on board at the time of delivery, and Owners shall on   160
redelivery (whether it occurs at the end of the charter period or on the earlier termination of this charter) accept   161
and pay for all bunkers remaining on board, at the then-current market prices at the port of delivery or redelivery,   162
as the case may be, or if such prices are not available payment shall be at the then-current market prices at the   163
nearest port at which such prices are available; provided that if delivery or redelivery does not take place in a port   164
payment shall be at the price paid at the vessel's last port of bunkering before delivery or redelivery, as the case   165
may be. Owners shall give Charterers the use and benefit of any fuel contracts they may have in force from time to   166
time, if so required by Charterers, provided suppliers agree.   167

Stevedores, Pilots, Tugs
16. Stevedores when required shall be employed and paid by Charterers, but this shall not relieve Owners   168
from responsibility at all times for proper stowage, which must be controlled by the master who shall keep a strict   169
account of all cargo loaded and discharged. Owners hereby indemnify Charterers, their servants and agents   170
against all losses, claims, responsibilities and liabilities arising in any way whatsoever from the employment of   171
pilots, tugboats or stevedores, who although employed by Charterers shall be deemed to be the servants of and in   172
the service of Owners and under their instructions (even if such pilots, tugboat personnel or stevedores are in fact   173
the servants of Charterers their agents or any affiliated company); provided, however, that   174
    (i) the foregoing indemnity shall not exceed the amount to which Owners would have been   175
entitled to limit their liability if they had themselves employed such pilots, tugboats or stevedores, and   176
    (ii) Charterers shall be liable for any damage to the vessel caused by or arising out of the use of   177
stevedores, fair wear and tear excepted, to the extent that Owners are unable by the exercise of due diligence to   178
obtain redress therefor from stevedores.   179

Supernumeraries
17. Charterers may send representatives in the vessel's available accommodation upon any voyage made   180
under this charter, Owners finding provisions and all requisites as supplied to officers, except liquors. Charterers   181
paying at the rate of   per day for each representative while on board the vessel.   182

Sub-letting
18. Charterers may sub-let the vessel, but shall always remain responsible to Owners for due fulfilment of   183
this charter.   184

Final Voyage
19. If when a payment of hire is due hereunder Charterers reasonably expect to redeliver the vessel before   185
the next payment of hire would fall due, the hire to be paid shall be assessed on Charterers' reasonable estimate of   186
the time necessary to complete Charterers' programme up to redelivery, and from which estimate Charterers   187
may deduct amounts due or reasonably expected to become due for   188
    (i) disbursements on Owners' behalf or charges for Owners' account pursuant to any provision   189
hereof, and   190
    (ii) bunkers on board at redelivery pursuant to Clause 15.   191
    Promptly after redelivery any overpayment shall be refunded by Owners or any underpayment made   192
good by Charterers.   193
    If at the time this charter would otherwise terminate in accordance with Clause 4 the vessel is on a   194
ballast voyage to a port of redelivery or is upon a laden voyage, Charterers shall continue to have the use of the   195

vessel at the same rate and conditions as stand herein for as long as necessary to complete such ballast voyage, or   196
to complete such laden voyage and return to a port of redelivery as provided by this charter, as the case may be.   197

Loss of
Vessel

20.   Should the vessel be lost, this charter shall terminate and hire shall cease at noon on the day of her loss;   198
should the vessel be a constructive total loss, this charter shall terminate and hire shall cease at noon on the day on   199
which the vessel's underwriters agree that the vessel is a constructive total loss; should the vessel be missing, this   200
charter shall terminate and hire shall cease at noon on the day on which she was last heard of. Any hire paid in   201
advance and not earned shall be returned to Charterers and Owners shall reimburse Charterers for the value of   202
the estimated quantity of bunkers on board at the time of termination, at the price paid by Charterers at the last   203
bunkering port.   204

Off-hire

21.   (a)   On each and every occasion that there is loss of time (whether by way of interruption in the   205
vessel's service or, from reduction in the vessel's performance, or in any other manner)   206
(i)   due to deficiency of personnel or stores; repairs; gas-freeing for repairs; time in and waiting   207
to enter dry dock for repairs; breakdown (whether partial or total) of machinery, boilers or other parts of the   208
vessel or her equipment (including without limitation tank coatings); overhaul, maintenance or survey; collision,   209
stranding, accident or damage to the vessel; or any other similar cause preventing the efficient working of the   210
vessel; and such loss continues for more than three consecutive hours (if resulting from interruption in the vessel's   211
service) or cumulates to more than three hours (if resulting from partial loss of service); or   212
(ii)   due to industrial action, refusal to sail, breach of orders or neglect of duty on the part of the   213
master, officers or crew; or   214
(iii)   for the purpose of obtaining medical advice or treatment for or landing any sick or injured   215
person (other than a Charterers' representative carried under Clause 17 hereof) or for the purpose of landing the   216
body of any person (other than a Charterers' representative), and such loss continues for more than three   217
consecutive hours: or   218
(iv)   due to any delay in quarantine arising from the master, officers or crew having had   219
communication with the shore at any infected area without the written consent or instructions of Charterers or   220
their agents, or to any detention by customs or other authorities caused by smuggling or other infraction of local   221
law on the part of the master, officers, or crew; or   222
(v)   due to detention of the vessel by authorities at home or abroad attributable to legal action   223
against or breach of regulations by the vessel, the vessel's owners, or Owners (unless brought about by the act or   224
neglect of Charterers); then   225
without prejudice to Charterers' rights under Clause 3 or to any other rights of Charterers   226
hereunder or otherwise the vessel shall be off-hire from the commencement of such loss of time until she is again   227
ready and in an efficient state to resume her service from a position not less favourable to Charterers than that at   228
which such loss of time commenced; provided, however, that any service given or distance made good by the   229
vessel whilst off-hire shall be taken into account in assessing the amount to be deducted from hire.   230
(b)   If the vessel fails to proceed at any guaranteed speed pursuant to Clause 24, and such failure   231
arises wholly or partly from any of the causes set out in Clause 21(a) above, then the period for which the vessel   232
shall be off-hire under this Clause 21 shall be the difference between   233
(i)   the time the vessel would have required to perform the relevant service at such guaranteed   234
speed, and   235
(ii)   the time actually taken to perform such service (including any loss of time arising from   236
interruption in the performance of such service).   237
For the avoidance of doubt, all time included under (ii) above shall be excluded from any   238
computation under Clause 24.   239
(c)   Further and without prejudice to the foregoing, in the event of the vessel deviating (which   240
expression includes without limitation putting back, or putting into any port other than that to which she is bound   241
under the instructions of Charterers) for any cause or purpose mentioned in Clause 21(a), the vessel shall be   242
off-hire from the commencement of such deviation until the time when she is again ready and in an efficient state   243
to resume her service from a position not less favourable to Charterers than that at which the deviation   244
commenced, provided, however, that any service given or distance made good by the vessel whilst so off-hire   245
shall be taken into account in assessing the amount to be deducted from hire. If the vessel, for any cause or   246
purpose mentioned in Clause 21 (a), puts into any port other than the port to which she is bound on the   247
instructions of Charterers, the port charges, pilotage and other expenses at such port shall be borne by Owners.   248
Should the vessel be driven into any port or anchorage by stress of weather hire shall continue to be due and   249
payable during any time lost thereby.   250
(d)   If the vessel's flag state becomes engaged in hostilities, and Charterers in consequence of such   251
hostilities find it commercially impracticable to employ the vessel and have given Owners written notice thereof   252
then from the date of receipt by Owners of such notice until the termination of such commercial impracticability   253
the vessel shall be off-hire and Owners shall have the right to employ the vessel on their own account.   254
(e)   Time during which the vessel is off-hire under this charter shall count as part of the charter   255
period.   256

Periodical
Drydocking

22.   (a)   Owners have the right and obligation to drydock the vessel at regular intervals of   257
On each occasion Owners shall propose to Charterers a date on which they wish to   258
drydock the vessel, not less than   before such date, and Charterers shall offer a port for   259
such periodical drydocking and shall take all reasonable steps to make the vessel available as near to such date as   260
practicable.   261
Owners shall put the vessel in drydock at their expense as soon as practicable after Charterers   262
place the vessel at Owners' disposal clear of cargo other than tank washings and residues. Owners shall be   263
responsible for and pay for the disposal into reception facilities of such tank washings and residues and shall have   264
the right to retain any monies received therefor, without prejudice to any claim for loss of cargo under any bill of   265
lading or this charter.   266
(b)   If a periodical drydocking is carried out in the port offered by Charterers (which must have   267
suitable accommodation for the purpose and reception facilities for tank washings and residues), the vessel shall   268
be off-hire from the time she arrives at such port until drydocking is completed and she is in every way ready to   269
resume Charterers' service and is at the position at which she went off-hire or a position no less favourable to   270
Charterers, whichever she first attains. However,   271
(i)   provided that Owners exercise due diligence in gas-freeing, any time lost in gas-freeing to   272
the standard required for entry into drydock for cleaning and painting the hull shall not count as off-hire, whether   273

lost on passage to the drydocking port or after arrival there (notwithstanding Clause 21), and 274

(ii) any additional time lost in further gas-freeing to meet the standard required for hot work or 275 entry to cargo tanks shall count as off-hire, whether lost on passage to the drydocking port or after arrival there. 276

Any time which, but for sub-Clause (i) above, would be off-hire, shall not be included in any 277 calculation under Clause 24. 278

The expenses of gas-freeing, including without limitation the cost of bunkers, shall be for 279 Owners account. 280

(c) If Owners require the vessel, instead of proceeding to the offered port, to carry out periodical 281 drydocking at a special port selected by them, the vessel shall be off-hire from the time when she is released to 282 proceed to the special port until she next presents for loading in accordance with Charterers' instructions, 283 provided, however, that Charterers shall credit Owners with the time which would have been taken on passage at 284 the service speed had the vessel not proceeded to drydock. All fuel consumed shall be paid for by Owners but 285 Charterers shall credit Owners with the value of the fuel which would have been used on such notional passage 286 calculated at the guaranteed daily consumption for the service speed, and shall further credit Owners with any 287 benefit they may gain in purchasing bunkers at the special port. 288

(d) Charterers shall, insofar as cleaning for periodical drydocking may have reduced the amount of 289 tank-cleaning necessary to meet Charterers' requirements, credit Owners with the value of any bunkers which 290 Charterers calculate to have been saved thereby, whether the vessel drydocks at an offered or a special port. 291

Ship Inspection

23. Charterers shall have the right at any time during the charter period to make such inspection of the 292 vessel as they may consider necessary. This right may be exercised as often and at such intervals as Charterers in 293 their absolute discretion may determine and whether the vessel is in port or on passage. Owners affording all 294 necessary co-operation and accommodation on board provided, however, 295

(i) that neither the exercise nor the non-exercise, nor anything done or not done in the exercise 296 or non-exercise, by Charterers of such right shall in any way reduce the master's or Owners' authority over, or 297 responsibility to Charterers or third parties for, the vessel and every aspect of her operation, nor increase 298 Charterers' responsibilities to Owners or third parties for the same; and 299

(ii) that Charterers shall not be liable for any act, neglect or default by themselves, their 300 servants or agents in the exercise or non-exercise of the aforesaid right. 301

Detailed Description and Performance

24. (a) Owners guarantee that the speed and consumption of the vessel shall be as follows:- 302

Average speed in knots	Maximum average bunker consumption		
	main propulsion	-	auxiliaries
	fuel oil/diesel oil		fuel oil/diesel oil
Laden	tonnes		tonnes
Ballast			

303
304
305
306

307

The foregoing bunker consumptions are for all purposes except cargo heating and tank cleaning 308 and shall be pro-rated between the speeds shown. 309

The service speed of the vessel is knots laden and knots in ballast and in the absence 310 of Charterers' orders to the contrary the vessel shall proceed at the service speed. However if more than one 311 laden and one ballast speed are shown in the table above Charterers shall have the right to order the vessel to 312 steam at any speed within the range set out in the table (the "ordered speed"). 313

If the vessel is ordered to proceed at any speed other than the highest speed shown in the table, 314 and the average speed actually attained by the vessel during the currency of such order exceeds such ordered 315 speed plus 0.5 knots (the "maximum recognised speed"), then for the purpose of calculating any increase or 316 decrease of hire under this Clause 24 the maximum recognised speed shall be used in place of the average speed 317 actually attained. 318

For the purposes of this charter the "guaranteed speed" at any time shall be the then-current 319 ordered speed or the service speed, as the case may be 320

The average speeds and bunker consumptions shall for the purposes of this Clause 24 be 321 calculated by reference to the observed distance from pilot station to pilot station on all sea passages during each 322 period stipulated in Clause 24 (c), but excluding any time during which the vessel is (or but for Clause 22(b) (i) 323 would be) off-hire and also excluding "Adverse Weather Periods", being (i) any periods during which reduction 324 of speed is necessary for safety in congested waters or in poor visibility (ii) any days, noon to noon, when winds 325 exceed force 8 on the Beaufort Scale for more than 12 hours. 326

(b) If during any year from the date on which the vessel enters service (anniversary to anniversary) 327 the vessel falls below or exceeds the performance guaranteed in Clause 24(a) then if such shortfall or excess 328 results 329

(i) from a reduction or an increase in the average speed of the vessel, compared to the speed 330 guaranteed in Clause 24(a). then an amount equal to the value at the hire rate of the time so lost or gained, as the 331 case may be, shall be deducted from or added to the hire paid: 332

(ii) from an increase or a decrease in the total bunkers consumed, compared to the total bunkers 333 which would have been consumed had the vessel performed as guaranteed in Clause 24(a), an amount equivalent 334 to the value of the additional bunkers consumed or the bunkers saved, as the case may be, based on the average 335 price paid by Charterers for the vessel's bunkers in such period, shall be deducted from or added to the hire paid. 336

The addition to or deduction from hire so calculated for laden and ballast mileage respectively 337 shall be adjusted to take into account the mileage steamed in each such condition during Adverse Weather 338 Periods, by dividing such addition or deduction by the number of miles over which the performance has been 339 calculated and multiplying by the same number of miles plus the miles steamed during the Adverse Weather 340 Periods, in order to establish the total addition to or deduction from hire to be made for such period. 341

Reduction of hire under the foregoing sub-Clause (b) shall be without prejudice to any other 342 remedy available to Charterers. 343

(c) Calculations under this Clause 24 shall be made for the yearly periods terminating on each 344 successive anniversary of the date on which the vessel enters service, and for the period between the last such 345

anniversary and the date of termination of this charter if less than a year. Claims in respect of reduction of hire 346
arising under this Clause during the final year or part year of the charter period shall in the first instance be settled 347
in accordance with Charterers' estimate made two months before the end of the charter period. Any necessary 348
adjustment after this charter terminates shall be made by payment by Owners to Charterers or by Charterers to 349
Owners as the case may require. 350
          Payments in respect of increase of hire arising under this Clause shall be made promptly after 351
receipt by Charterers of all the information necessary to calculate such increase. 352

Salvage

    25. Subject to the provisions of Clause 21 hereof, all loss of time and all expenses (excluding any damage to 353
or loss of the vessel or tortious liabilities to third parties) incurred in saving or attempting to save life or in 354
successful or unsuccessful attempts at salvage shall be borne equally by Owners and Charterers provided that 355
Charterers shall not be liable to contribute towards any salvage payable by Owners arising in any way out of 356
services rendered under this Clause 25. 357
          All salvage and all proceeds from derelicts shall be divided equally between Owners and Charterers 358
after deducting the master's, officers' and crew's share. 359

Lien

    26. Owners shall have a lien upon all cargoes and all freights, sub-freights and demurrage for any amounts 360
due under this charter: and Charterers shall have a lien on the vessel for all monies paid in advance and not 361
earned, and for all claims for damages arising from any breach by Owners of this charter. 362

Exceptions

    27. (a) The vessel, her master and Owners shall not, unless otherwise in this charter expressly provided, 363
be liable for any loss or damage or delay or failure arising or resulting from any act, neglect or default of the 364
master, pilots, mariners or other servants of Owners in the navigation or management of the vessel: fire, unless 365
caused by the actual fault or privity of Owners; collision or stranding; dangers and accidents of the sea; explosion, 366
bursting of boilers, breakage of shafts or any latent defect in hull, equipment or machinery: provided, however, 367
that Clauses 1, 2, 3 and 24 hereof shall be unaffected by the foregoing. Further, neither the vessel, her master or 368
Owners, nor Charterers shall, unless otherwise in this charter expressly provided, be liable for any loss or damage 369
or delay or failure in performance hereunder arising or resulting from act of God, act of war, seizure under legal 370
process, quarantine restrictions, strikes, lock-outs, riots, restraints of labour, civil commotions or arrest or 371
restraint of princes, rulers or people. 372
         (b) The vessel shall have liberty to sail with or without pilots, to tow or go to the assistance of vessels 373
in distress and to deviate for the purpose of saving life or property. 374
         (c) Clause 27(a) shall not apply to or affect any liability of Owners or the vessel or any other relevant 375
person in respect of 376
         (i) loss or damage caused to any berth, jetty, dock, dolphin, buoy, mooring line, pipe or crane 377
or other works or equipment whatsoever at or near any place to which the vessel may proceed under this charter, 378
whether or not such works or equipment belong to Charterers, or 379
         (ii) any claim (whether brought by Charterers or any other person) arising out of any loss of or 380
damage to or in connection with cargo. All such claims shall be subject to the Hague-Visby Rules or the Hague 381
Rules, as the case may be, which ought pursuant to Clause 38 hereof to have been incorporated in the relevant bill 382
of lading (whether or not such Rules were so incorporated) or, if no such bill of lading is issued, to the 383
Hague-Visby Rules. 384
         (d) In particular and without limitation, the foregoing subsections (a) and (b) of this Clause shall not 385
apply to or in any way affect any provision in this charter relating to off-hire or to reduction of hire. 386

Injurious Cargoes

    28. No acids, explosives or cargoes injurious to the vessel shall be shipped and without prejudice to the 387
foregoing any damage to the vessel caused by the shipment of any such cargo, and the time taken to repair such 388
damage, shall be for Charterers' account. No voyage shall be undertaken, nor any goods or cargoes loaded, that 389
would expose the vessel to capture or seizure by rulers or governments. 390

Grade of Bunkers

    29. Charterers shall supply marine diesel oil/fuel oil with a maximum viscosity of   Centistokes at 50 391
degrees Centigrade/ACGFO for main propulsion and diesel oil/ACGFO for the auxiliaries. If Owners require 392
the vessel to be supplied with more expensive bunkers they shall be liable for the extra cost thereof. 393
         Charterers warrant that all bunkers provided by them in accordance herewith shall be of a quality 394
complying with the International Marine Bunker Supply Terms and Conditions of Shell International Trading 395
Company and with its specification for marine fuels as amended from time to time. 396

Disbursements

    30. Should the master require advances for ordinary disbursements at any port, Charterers or their agents 397
shall make such advances to him, in consideration of which Owners shall pay a commission of two and a half per 398
cent, and all such advances and commission shall be deducted from hire. 399

Laying-up

    31. Charterers shall have the option, after consultation with Owners, of requiring Owners to lay up the 400
vessel at a safe place nominated by Charterers, in which case the hire provided for under this charter shall be 401
adjusted to reflect any net increases in expenditure reasonably incurred or any net saving which should 402
reasonably be made by Owners as a result of such lay-up, Charterers may exercise the said option any number of 403
times during the charter period. 404

Requisition

    32. Should the vessel be requisitioned by any government, de facto or de jure, during the period of this 405
charter, the vessel shall be off-hire during the period of such requisition. and any hire paid by such government in 406
respect of such requisition period shall be for Owners' account. Any such requisition period shall count as part of 407
the charter period. 408

Outbreak of War

    33. If war or hostilities break out between any two or more of the following countries: U.S.A., U.S.S.R., 409
P.R.C., U.K., Netherlands-both Owners and Charterers shall have the right to cancel this charter. 410

Additional War Expenses

    34. If the vessel is ordered to trade in areas where there is war (de facto or de jure) or threat of war, 411
Charterers shall reimburse Owners for any additional insurance premia, crew bonuses and other expenses which 412
are reasonably incurred by Owners as a consequence of such orders, provided that Charterers are given notice of 413
such expenses as soon as practicable and in any event before such expenses are incurred, and provided further 414
that Owners obtain from their insurers a waiver of any subrogated rights against Charterers in respect of any 415
claims by Owners under their war risk insurance arising out of compliance with such orders. 416

War Risks	35. (a) The master shall not be required or bound to sign bills of lading for any place which in his or Owners' reasonable opinion is dangerous or impossible for the vessel to enter or reach owing to any blockade, war, hostilities, warlike operations, civil war, civil commotions or revolutions.

35. (a) The master shall not be required or bound to sign bills of lading for any place which in his or Owners' reasonable opinion is dangerous or impossible for the vessel to enter or reach owing to any blockade, war, hostilities, warlike operations, civil war, civil commotions or revolutions.

(b) If in the reasonable opinion of the master or Owners it becomes, for any of the reasons set out in Clause 35(a) or by the operation of international law, dangerous, impossible or prohibited for the vessel to reach or enter, or to load or discharge cargo at, any place to which the vessel has been ordered pursuant to this charter (a "place of peril"), then Charterers or their agents shall be immediately notified by telex or radio messages, and Charterers shall thereupon have the right to order the cargo, or such part of it as may be affected, to be loaded or discharged, as the case may be, at any other place within the trading limits of this charter (provided such other place is not itself a place of peril). If any place of discharge is or becomes a place of peril, and no orders have been received from Charterers or their agents within 48 hours after dispatch of such messages, then Owners shall be at liberty to discharge the cargo or such part of it as may be affected at any place which they or the master may in their or his discretion select within the trading limits of this charter and such discharge shall be deemed to be due fulfilment of Owners' obligations under this charter so far as cargo so discharged is concerned.

(c) The vessel shall have liberty to comply with any directions or recommendations as to departure, arrival, routes, ports of call, stoppages, destinations, zones, waters, delivery or in any other wise whatsoever given by the government of the state under whose flag the vessel sails or any other government or local authority or by any person or body acting or purporting to act as or with the authority of any such government or local authority including any de facto government or local authority or by any person or body acting or purporting to act as or with the authority of any such government or local authority or by any committee or person having under the terms of the war risks insurance on the vessel the right to give any such directions or recommendations. If by reason of or in compliance with any such directions or recommendations anything is done or is not done, such shall not be deemed a deviation.

If by reason of or in compliance with any such direction or recommendation the vessel does not proceed to any place of discharge to which she has been ordered pursuant to this charter, the vessel may proceed to any place which the master or Owners in his or their discretion select and there discharge the cargo or such part of it as may be affected. Such discharge shall be deemed to be due fulfilment of Owners obligations under this charter so far as cargo so discharged is concerned.

Charterers shall procure that all bills of lading issued under this charter shall contain the Chamber of Shipping War Risks Clause 1952.

Both to Blame Collision Clause

36. If the liability for any collision in which the vessel is involved while performing this charter falls to be determined in accordance with the laws of the United States of America, the following provision shall apply:

"If the ship comes into collision with another ship as a result of the negligence of the other ship and any act, neglect or default of the master, mariner, pilot or the servants of the carrier in the navigation or in the management of the ship, the owners of the cargo carried hereunder will indemnify the carrier against all loss, or liability to the other or non-carrying ship or her owners in so far as such loss or liability represents loss of, or damage to, or any claim whatsoever of the owners of the said cargo, paid or payable by the other or non-carrying ship or her owners to the owners of the said cargo and set off, recouped or recovered by the other or non-carrying ship or her owners as part of their claim against the carrying ship or carrier."

"The foregoing provisions shall also apply where the owners, operators or those in charge of any ship or ships or objects other than, or in addition to, the colliding ships or objects are at fault in respect of a collision or contact."

Charterers shall procure that all bills of lading issued under this charter shall contain a provision in the foregoing terms to be applicable where the liability for any collision in which the vessel is involved falls to be determined in accordance with the laws of the United States of America.

New Jason Clause

37. General average contributions shall be payable according to the York/Antwerp Rules, 1974, and shall be adjusted in London in accordance with English law and practice but should adjustment be made in accordance with the law and practice of the United States of America, the following provision shall apply:

"In the event of accident, danger, damage or disaster before or after the commencement of the voyage, resulting from any cause whatsoever, whether due to negligence or not, for which, or for the consequence of which, the carrier is not responsible by statute, contract or otherwise, the cargo, shippers, consignees or owners of the cargo shall contribute with the carrier in general average to the payment of any sacrifices, losses or expenses of a general average nature that may be made or incurred and shall pay salvage and special charges incurred in respect of the cargo."

"If a salving ship is owned or operated by the carrier, salvage shall be paid for as fully as if the said salving ship or ships belonged to strangers. Such deposit as the carrier or his agents may deem sufficient to cover the estimated contribution of the cargo and any salvage and special charges thereon shall, if required, be made by the cargo, shippers, consignees or owners of the cargo to the carrier before delivery."

Charterers shall procure that all bills of lading issued under this charter shall contain a provision in the foregoing terms, to be applicable where adjustment of general average is made in accordance with the laws and practice of the United States of America.

Clause Paramount

38. Charterers shall procure that all bills of lading issued pursuant to this charter shall contain the following clause:

"(1) Subject to sub-clause (2) hereof, this bill of lading shall be governed by, and have effect subject to, the rules contained in the International Convention for the Unification of Certain Rules relating to Bills of Lading signed at Brussels on 25th August 1924 (hereafter the "Hague Rules") as amended by the Protocol signed at Brussels on 23rd February 1968 (hereafter the "Hague-Visby Rules"). Nothing contained herein shall be deemed to be either a surrender by the carrier of any of his rights or immunities or any increase of any of his responsibilities or liabilities under the "Hague-Visby Rules."

"(2) If there is governing legislation which applies the Hague Rules compulsorily to this bill of lading, to the exclusion of the Hague-Visby Rules, then this bill of lading shall have effect subject to the Hague Rules. Nothing herein contained shall be deemed to be either a surrender by the carrier of any of his rights or immunities or an increase of any of his responsibilities or liabilities under the Hague Rules."

"(3) If any term of this bill of lading is repugnant to the Hague-Visby Rules, or Hague Rules if applicable, such term shall be void to that extent but no further."

"(4) Nothing in this bill of lading shall be construed as in any way restricting, excluding or waiving the right of any relevant party or person to limit his liability under any available legislation and/or law."

417
418
419
420
421
422
423
424
425
426
427
428
429
430
431
432
433
434
435
436
437
438
439
440
441
442
443
444
445
446
447
448
449
450
451
452
453
454
455
456
457
458
459
460
461
462
463
464
465
466
467
468
469
470
471
472
473
474
475
476
477
478
479
480
481
482
483
484
485
486
487
488
489
490
491
492
493

TOVALOP	39. Owners warrant that the vessel is:	494
	(i) a tanker in TOVALOP and	495
	(ii) properly entered in P & I Club	496

and will so remain during the currency of this charter. 497
            When an escape or discharge of Oil occurs from the vessel and causes or threatens to cause Pollution 498
Damage, or when there is the threat of an escape or discharge of Oil (i.e. a grave and imminent danger of the 499
escape or discharge of Oil which, if it occurred, would create a serious danger of Pollution Damage, whether or 500
not an escape or discharge in fact subsequently occurs), then Charterers may, at their option, upon notice to 501
Owners or master, undertake such measures as are reasonably necessary to prevent or minimise such Pollution 502
Damage or to remove the Threat, unless Owners promptly undertake the same. Charterers shall keep Owners 503
advised of the nature and result of any such measures taken by them and, if time permits, the nature of the 504
measures intended to be taken by them. Any of the aforementioned measures taken by Charterers shall be 505
deemed taken on Owners' authority as Owners' agent, and shall be at Owners' expense except to the extent that: 506
            (1)   any such escape or discharge or Threat was caused or contributed to by Charterers, or 507
            (2)   by reason of the exceptions set out in Article III, paragraph 2, of the 1969 International 508
Convention on Civil Liability for Oil Pollution Damage, Owners are or, had the said Convention applied to such 509
escape or discharge or to the Threat, would have been exempt from liability for the same, or 510
            (3)   the cost of such measures together with all other liabilities, costs and expenses of Owners arising 511
out of or in connection with such escape or discharge or Threat exceeds one hundred and sixty United States 512
Dollars (US \$160) per ton of the vessel's Tonnage or sixteen million eight hundred thousand United States 513
Dollars (US \$16,800,000), whichever is the lesser, save and insofar as Owners shall be entitled to recover such 514
excess under either the 1971 International Convention on the Establishment of an International Fund for 515
Compensation for Oil Pollution Damage or under CRISTAL; 516
            PROVIDED ALWAYS that if Owners in their absolute discretion consider said measures 517
should be discontinued. Owners shall so notify Charterers and thereafter Charterers shall have no right to 518
continue said measures under the provisions of this Clause 39 and all further liability to Charterers under this 519
Clause 39 shall thereupon cease. 520
            The above provisions are not in derogation of such other rights as Charterers or Owners may have 521
under this charter or may otherwise have or acquire by law or any International Convention or TOVALOP. 522
            The term "TOVALOP" means the Tanker Owners' Voluntary Agreement Concerning Liability 523
for Oil Pollution dated 7th January 1969, as amended from time to time, and the term "CRISTAL" means the 524
Contract Regarding an Interim Supplement to Tanker Liability for Oil Pollution dated 14th January 1971, as 525
amended from time to time. The terms "Oil", "Pollution Damage", and "Tonnage" shall for the purposes of this 526
Clause 39 have the meanings ascribed to them in TOVALOP. 527

Export Restrictions	40. The master shall not be required or bound to sign bills of lading for the carriage of cargo to any place to	528

which export of such cargo is prohibited under the laws, rules or regulations of the country in which the cargo was 529
produced and/or shipped. 530
            Charterers shall procure that all bills of lading issued under this charter shall contain the following 531
clause: 532
            "If any laws rules or regulations applied by the government of the country in which the cargo was 533
            produced and/or shipped, or any relevant agency thereof, impose a prohibition on export of the cargo 534
            to the place of discharge designated in or ordered under this bill of lading, carriers shall be entitled to 535
            require cargo owners forthwith to nominate an alternative discharge place for the discharge of the 536
            cargo, or such part of it as may be affected, which alternative place shall not be subject to the 537
            prohibition, and carriers shall be entitled to accept orders from cargo owners to proceed to and 538
            discharge at such alternative place. If cargo owners fail to nominate an alternative place within 72 539
            hours after they or their agents have received from carriers notice of such prohibition, carriers shall be 540
            at liberty to discharge the cargo or such part of it as may be affected by the prohibition at any safe place 541
            on which they or the master may in their or his absolute discretion decide and which is not subject to the 542
            prohibition, and such discharge shall constitute due performance of the contract contained in this bill 543
            of lading so far as the cargo so discharged is concerned". 544
            The foregoing provision shall apply mutatis mutandis to this charter, the references to a bill of lading 545
being deemed to be references to this charter. 546

Law and Litigation	41. (a) This charter shall be construed and the relations between the parties determined in accordance	547

with the laws of England. 548
            (b)   Any dispute arising under this charter shall be decided by the English Courts to whose 549
jurisdiction the parties hereby agree. 550
            (c)   Notwithstanding the foregoing, but without prejudice to any party's right to arrest or maintain 551
the arrest of any maritime property, either party may, by giving written notice of election to the other party, elect 552
to have any such dispute referred to the arbitration of a single arbitrator in London in accordance with the 553
provisions of the Arbitration Act 1950, or any statutory modification or re-enactment thereof for the time being 554
in force. 555
            (i)   A party shall lose its right to make such an election only if: 556
                  (a)   it receives from the other party a written notice of dispute which - 557
                        (1)   states expressly that a dispute has arisen out of this charter: 558
                        (2)   specifies the nature of the dispute: and 559
                        (3)   refers expressly to this clause 41(c) 560
                  and 561
                  (b)   it fails to give notice of election to have the dispute referred to arbitration not later than 562
                        30 days from the date of receipt of such notice of dispute. 563
            (ii) The parties hereby agree that either party may - 564
                  (a)   appeal to the High Court on any question of law arising out of an award: 565
                  (b)   apply to the High Court for an order that the arbitrator state the reasons for his award: 566
                  (c)   give notice to the arbitrator that a reasoned award is required: and 567
                  (d)   apply to the High Court to determine any question of law arising in the course of the 568
                        reference. 569
            (d)   It shall be a condition precedent to the right of any party to a stay of any legal proceedings in 570
which maritime property has been, or may be, arrested in connection with a dispute under this charter, that that 571

---

party furnishes to the other party security to which that other party would have been entitled in such legal proceedings in the absence of a stay.

572
573

Construction   42.   The side headings have been included in this charter for convenience of reference and shall in no way affect the construction hereof.

574
575

This Charter Party is a computer generated copy of the SHELLTIME4 Charter Party form, printed using software which is the copyright of Strategic Software Limited.

This is a precise copy of the original document which can be modified, amended or added to only by the striking out of original characters, or the insertion of new characters, such characters being clearly highlighted by underlining or use of colour or use of a larger font and marked as having been made by the licensee or end user as appropriate and not by the author.

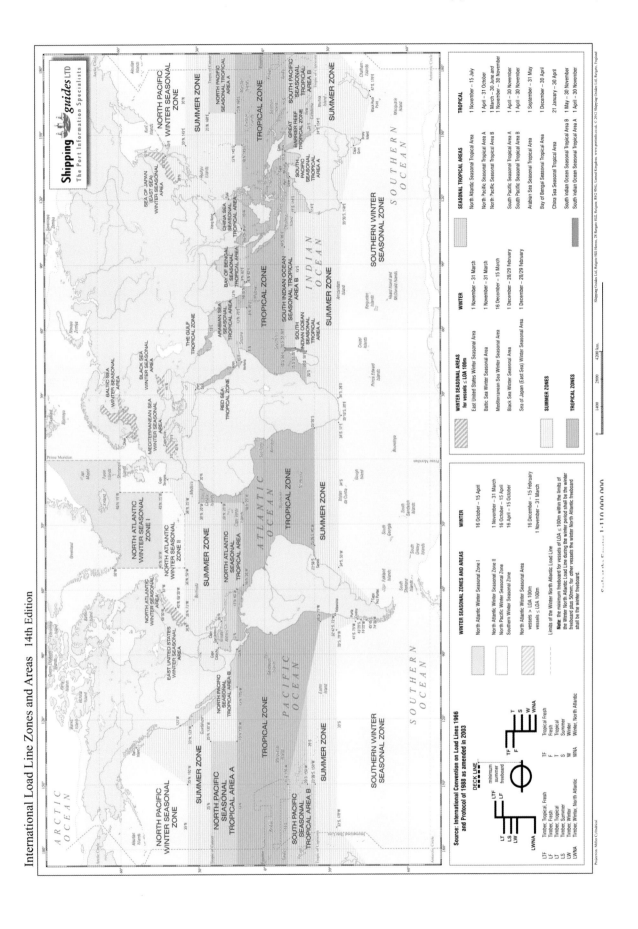

International Load Line Zones and Areas   14th Edition

S & P Particulars Sheet

Particulars of

Flag

Year Built and Builders

Tons gross/nett

Cubic Capacity (about)

DEADWEIGHT
including Bunkers of about   Draught   Loaded

Dimensions

Bunkers

Water Ballast

ENGINES

BOILERS

Donkey Boiler

Winches   Derricks   DECK PLAN   'Tween Decks

AVERAGE SPEED (about)   CONSUMPTION (about)

Passengers

No. of Bulkheads

    " of Holds

    " of Hatchways and dimensions

CLASS AND SURVEY

Remarks

(These particulars are given without any guarantee for their accuracy

Appendix 6 S & P 'Particulars Sheet'

Appendix 6 S & P 'Particulars Sheet'

MEMORANDUM OF AGREEMENT

Dated:

hereinafter called the Sellers, have agreed to sell, and   1

hereinafter called the Buyers, have agreed to buy   2

Name: 3

Classification Society/Class: 4

Built: By: 5

Flag: Place of Registration: 6

Call Sign: Grt/Nrt: 7

Register Number: 8

hereinafter called the Vessel, on the following terms and conditions: 9

Definitions   10

"Banking days" are days on which banks are open both in the country of the currency   11
stipulated for the Purchase Price in Clause 1 and in the place of closing stipulated in Clause 8.   12

"In writing" or "written" means a letter handed over from the Sellers to the Buyers or vice versa,   13
a registered letter, telex, telefax or other modern form of written communication.   14

"Classification Society" or "Class" means the Society referred to in line 4.   15

1.   Purchase Price   16

2.   Deposit   17

As security for the correct fulfilment of this Agreement the Buyers shall pay a deposit of 10 %   18
(ten per cent) of the Purchase Price within   banking days from the date of this   19
Agreement. This deposit shall be placed with   20

and held by them in a joint account for the Sellers and the Buyers, to be released in accordance   21
with joint written instructions of the Sellers and the Buyers. Interest, if any, to be credited to the   22
Buyers. Any fee charged for holding the said deposit shall be borne equally by the Sellers and the   23
Buyers.   24

3.   Payment   25

The said Purchase Price shall be paid in full free of bank charges to   26

on delivery of the Vessel, but not later than 3 banking days after the Vessel is in every respect   27
physically ready for delivery in accordance with the terms and conditions of this Agreement and   28
Notice of Readiness has been given in accordance with Clause 5.   29

4.   Inspections   30

a)*   The Buyers have inspected and accepted the Vessel's classification records. The Buyers   31
have also inspected the Vessel at/in   on   32
and have accepted the Vessel following this inspection and the sale is outright and definite,   33
subject only to the terms and conditions of this Agreement.   34

b)*   The Buyers shall have the right to inspect the Vessel's classification records and declare   35
whether same are accepted or not within   36

The Sellers shall provide for inspection of the Vessel at/in   37

The Buyers shall undertake the inspection without undue delay to the Vessel. Should the   38
Buyers cause undue delay they shall compensate the Sellers for the losses thereby incurred.   39

The Buyers shall inspect the Vessel without opening up and without cost to the Sellers. 40
During the inspection, the Vessel's deck and engine log books shall be made available for 41
examination by the Buyers. If the Vessel is accepted after such inspection, the sale shall 42
become outright and definite, subject only to the terms and conditions of this Agreement, 43
provided the Sellers receive written notice of acceptance from the Buyers within 72 hours 44
after completion of such inspection. 45
Should notice of acceptance of the Vessel's classification records and of the Vessel not be 46
received by the Sellers as aforesaid, the deposit together with interest earned shall be 47
released immediately to the Buyers, whereafter this Agreement shall be null and void. 48

*   *4a) and 4b) are alternatives; delete whichever is not applicable. In the absence of deletions,* 49
alternative 4a) to apply. 50

5.   **Notices, time and place of delivery** 51

a) The Sellers shall keep the Buyers well informed of the Vessel's itinerary and shall 52
provide the Buyers with   ,   , and   days notice of the estimated time of arrival at the 53
intended place of drydocking/underwater inspection/delivery. When the Vessel is at the place 54
of delivery and in every respect physically ready for delivery in accordance with this 55
Agreement, the Sellers shall give the Buyers a written Notice of Readiness for delivery. 56

b) The Vessel shall be delivered and taken over safely afloat at a safe and accessible berth or 57
anchorage at/in 58

in the Sellers' option. 59

Expected time of delivery: 60

Date of cancelling (see Clauses 5 c), 6 b) (iii) and 14): 61

c) If the Sellers anticipate that, notwithstanding the exercise of due diligence by them, the 62
Vessel will not be ready for delivery by the cancelling date they may notify the Buyers in 63
writing stating the date when they anticipate that the Vessel will be ready for delivery and 64
propose a new cancelling date. Upon receipt of such notification the Buyers shall have the 65
option of either cancelling this Agreement in accordance with Clause 14 within 7 running 66
days of receipt of the notice or of accepting the new date as the new cancelling date. If the 67
Buyers have not declared their option within 7 running days of receipt of the Sellers' 68
notification or if the Buyers accept the new date, the date proposed in the Sellers' notification 69
shall be deemed to be the new cancelling date and shall be substituted for the cancelling 70
date stipulated in line 61. 71

If this Agreement is maintained with the new cancelling date all other terms and conditions 72
hereof including those contained in Clauses 5 a) and 5 c) shall remain unaltered and in full 73
force and effect. Cancellation or failure to cancel shall be entirely without prejudice to any 74
claim for damages the Buyers may have under Clause 14 for the Vessel not being ready by 75
the original cancelling date. 76

d) Should the Vessel become an actual, constructive or compromised total loss before delivery 77
the deposit together with interest earned shall be released immediately to the Buyers 78
whereafter this Agreement shall be null and void. 79

6.   **Drydocking/Divers Inspection** 80

a)** The Sellers shall place the Vessel in drydock at the port of delivery for inspection by the 81
Classification Society of the Vessel's underwater parts below the deepest load line, the 82
extent of the inspection being in accordance with the Classification Society's rules. If the 83
rudder, propeller, bottom or other underwater parts below the deepest load line are found 84
broken, damaged or defective so as to affect the Vessel's class, such defects shall be made 85
good at the Sellers' expense to the satisfaction of the Classification Society without 86
condition/recommendation*. 87

b)** (i) The Vessel is to be delivered without drydocking. However, the Buyers shall 88
have the right at their expense to arrange for an underwater inspection by a diver approved 89
by the Classification Society prior to the delivery of the Vessel. The Sellers shall at their 90
cost make the Vessel available for such inspection. The extent of the inspection and the 91
conditions under which it is performed shall be to the satisfaction of the Classification 92

Society. If the conditions at the port of delivery are unsuitable for such inspection, the 93
Sellers shall make the Vessel available at a suitable alternative place near to the delivery 94
port. 95

(ii) If the rudder, propeller, bottom or other underwater parts below the deepest load line 96
are found broken, damaged or defective so as to affect the Vessel's class, then unless 97
repairs can be carried out afloat to the satisfaction of the Classification Society, the Sellers 98
shall arrange for the Vessel to be drydocked at their expense for inspection by the 99
Classification Society of the Vessel's underwater parts below the deepest load line, the 100
extent of the inspection being in accordance with the Classification Society's rules. If the 101
rudder, propeller, bottom or other underwater parts below the deepest load line are found 102
broken, damaged or defective so as to affect the Vessel's class, such defects shall be made 103
good by the Sellers at their expense to the satisfaction of the Classification Society 104
without condition/recommendation*. In such event the Sellers are to pay also for the cost of 105
the underwater inspection and the Classification Society's attendance. 106

(iii) If the Vessel is to be drydocked pursuant to Clause 6 b) (ii) and no suitable dry- 107
docking facilities are available at the port of delivery, the Sellers shall take the Vessel 108
to a port where suitable drydocking facilities are available, whether within or outside the 109
delivery range as per Clause 5 b). Once drydocking has taken place the Sellers shall deliver 110
the Vessel at a port within the delivery range as per Clause 5 b) which shall, for the 111
purpose of this Clause, become the new port of delivery. In such event the cancelling date 112
provided for in Clause 5 b) shall be extended by the additional time required for the 113
drydocking and extra steaming, but limited to a maximum of 14 running days. 114

c)   If the Vessel is drydocked pursuant to Clause 6 a) or 6 b) above 115

(i) the Classification Society may require survey of the tailshaft system, the extent of 116
the survey being to the satisfaction of the Classification surveyor. If such survey is not 117
required by the Classification Society, the Buyers shall have the right to require the tailshaft 118
to be drawn and surveyed by the Classification Society, the extent of the survey being in 119
accordance with the Classification Society's rules for tailshaft survey and consistent with 120
the current stage of the Vessel's survey cycle. The Buyers shall declare whether they 121
require the tailshaft to be drawn and surveyed not later than by the completion of the 122
inspection by the Classification Society. The drawing and refitting of the tailshaft shall be 123
arranged by the Sellers. Should any parts of the tailshaft system be condemned or found 124
defective so as to affect the Vessel's class, those parts shall be renewed or made good at 125
the Sellers' expense to the satisfaction of the Classification Society without 126
condition/recommendation*. 127

(ii) the expenses relating to the survey of the tailshaft system shall be borne 128
by the Buyers unless the Classification Society requires such survey to be carried out, in 129
which case the Sellers shall pay these expenses. The Sellers shall also pay the expenses 130
if the Buyers require the survey and parts of the system are condemned or found defective 131
or broken so as to affect the Vessel's class*. 132

(iii) the expenses in connection with putting the Vessel in and taking her out of 133
drydock, including the drydock dues and the Classification Society's fees shall be paid by 134
the Sellers if the Classification Society issues any condition/recommendation* as a result 135
of the survey or if it requires survey of the tailshaft system. In all other cases the Buyers 136
shall pay the aforesaid expenses, dues and fees. 137

(iv) the Buyers' representative shall have the right to be present in the drydock, but 138
without interfering with the work or decisions of the Classification surveyor. 139

(v) the Buyers shall have the right to have the underwater parts of the Vessel 140
cleaned and painted at their risk and expense without interfering with the Sellers' or the 141
Classification surveyor's work, if any, and without affecting the Vessel's timely delivery. If, 142
however, the Buyers' work in drydock is still in progress when the Sellers have 143
completed the work which the Sellers are required to do, the additional docking time 144
needed to complete the Buyers' work shall be for the Buyers' risk and expense. In the event 145
that the Buyers' work requires such additional time, the Sellers may upon completion of the 146
Sellers' work tender Notice of Readiness for delivery whilst the Vessel is still in drydock 147
and the Buyers shall be obliged to take delivery in accordance with Clause 3, whether 148
the Vessel is in drydock or not and irrespective of Clause 5 b). 149

*   Notes, if any, in the surveyor's report which are accepted by the Classification Society 150
without condition/recommendation are not to be taken into account. 151

**	*6 a) and 6 b) are alternatives; delete whichever is not applicable. In the absence of deletions, alternative 6 a) to apply.*	152 153

7.   Spares/bunkers, etc.   154

The Sellers shall deliver the Vessel to the Buyers with everything belonging to her on board and on   155
shore. All spare parts and spare equipment including spare tail-end shaft(s) and/or spare   156
propeller(s)/propeller blade(s), if any, belonging to the Vessel at the time of inspection used or   157
unused, whether on board or not shall become the Buyers' property, but spares on order are to be   158
excluded. Forwarding charges, if any, shall be for the Buyers' account. The Sellers are not required to   159
replace spare parts including spare tail-end shaft(s) and spare propeller(s)/propeller blade(s) which   160
are taken out of spare and used as replacement prior to delivery, but the replaced items shall be the   161
property of the Buyers. The radio installation and navigational equipment shall be included in the sale   162
without extra payment if they are the property of the Sellers. Unused stores and provisions shall be   163
included in the sale and be taken over by the Buyers without extra payment.   164

The Sellers have the right to take ashore crockery, plates, cutlery, linen and other articles bearing the   165
Sellers' flag or name, provided they replace same with similar unmarked items. Library, forms, etc.,   166
exclusively for use in the Sellers' vessel(s), shall be excluded without compensation. Captain's,   167
Officers' and Crew's personal belongings including the slop chest are to be excluded from the sale,   168
as well as the following additional items (including items on hire):   169

The Buyers shall take over the remaining bunkers and unused lubricating oils in storage tanks and   170
sealed drums and pay the current net market price (excluding barging expenses) at the port and date   171
of delivery of the Vessel.   172
Payment under this Clause shall be made at the same time and place and in the same currency as   173
the Purchase Price.   174

8.   Documentation   175

The place of closing: 176

In exchange for payment of the Purchase Price the Sellers shall furnish the Buyers with delivery   177
documents, namely: 178

a)   Legal Bill of Sale in a form recordable in   (the country in which the Buyers are   179
     to register the Vessel), warranting that the Vessel is free from all encumbrances, mortgages   180
     and maritime liens or any other debts or claims whatsoever, duly notarially attested and   181
     legalized by the consul of such country or other competent authority.   182

b)   Current Certificate of Ownership issued by the competent authorities of the flag state of   183
     the Vessel.   184

c)   Confirmation of Class issued within 72 hours prior to delivery.   185

d)   Current Certificate issued by the competent authorities stating that the Vessel is free from   186
     registered encumbrances.   187

e)   Certificate of Deletion of the Vessel from the Vessel's registry or other official evidence of   188
     deletion appropriate to the Vessel's registry at the time of delivery, or, in the event that the   189
     registry does not as a matter of practice issue such documentation immediately, a written   190
     undertaking by the Sellers to effect deletion from the Vessel's registry forthwith and furnish a   191
     Certificate or other official evidence of deletion to the Buyers promptly and latest within 4   192
     (four) weeks after the Purchase Price has been paid and the Vessel has been delivered.   193

f)   Any such additional documents as may reasonably be required by the competent authorities   194
     for the purpose of registering the Vessel, provided the Buyers notify the Sellers of any such   195
     documents as soon as possible after the date of this Agreement.   196

At the time of delivery the Buyers and Sellers shall sign and deliver to each other a Protocol of   197
Delivery and Acceptance confirming the date and time of delivery of the Vessel from the Sellers to the   198
Buyers.   199

At the time of delivery the Sellers shall hand to the Buyers the classification certificate(s) as well as all 200
plans etc., which are on board the Vessel. Other certificates which are on board the Vessel shall also 201
be handed over to the Buyers unless the Sellers are required to retain same, in which case the 202
Buyers to have the right to take copies. Other technical documentation which may 203
be in the Sellers' possession shall be promptly forwarded to the Buyers at their expense, if they so 204
request. The Sellers may keep the Vessel's log books but the Buyers to have the right to take 205
copies of same. 206

9.   Encumbrances
207

The Sellers warrant that the Vessel, at the time of delivery, is free from all charters, encumbrances, 208
mortgages and maritime liens or any other debts whatsoever. The Sellers hereby undertake 209
to indemnify the Buyers against all consequences of claims made against the Vessel which have 210
been incurred prior to the time of delivery. 211

10.   Taxes, etc.
212

Any taxes, fees and expenses in connection with the purchase and registration under the Buyers' flag 213
shall be for the Buyers' account, whereas similar charges in connection with the closing of the Sellers' 214
register shall be for the Sellers' account. 215

11.   Condition on delivery
216

The Vessel with everything belonging to her shall be at the Sellers' risk and expense until she is 217
delivered to the Buyers, but subject to the terms and conditions of this Agreement she shall be 218
delivered and taken over as she was at the time of inspection, fair wear and tear excepted. 219
However, the Vessel shall be delivered with her class maintained without condition/recommendation*, 220
free of average damage affecting the Vessel's class, and with her classification certificates and 221
national certificates, as well as all other certificates the Vessel had at the time of inspection, valid and 222
unextended without condition/recommendation* by Class or the relevant authorities at the time of 223
delivery. 224
"Inspection" in this Clause 11, shall mean the Buyers' inspection according to Clause 4 a) or 4 b), if 225
applicable, or the Buyers' inspection prior to the signing of this Agreement. If the Vessel is taken over 226
without inspection, the date of this Agreement shall be the relevant date. 227

*   Notes, if any, in the surveyor's report which are accepted by the Classification Society 228
     without condition/recommendation are not to be taken into account. 229

12.   Name/markings
230

Upon delivery the Buyers undertake to change the name of the Vessel and alter funnel markings. 231

13.   Buyers' default
232

Should the deposit not be paid in accordance with Clause 2, the Sellers have the right to cancel this 233
Agreement, and they shall be entitled to claim compensation for their losses and for all expenses 234
incurred together with interest. 235
Should the Purchase Price not be paid in accordance with Clause 3, the Sellers have the right to 236
cancel the Agreement, in which case the deposit together with interest earned shall be released to the 237
Sellers. If the deposit does not cover their loss, the Sellers shall be entitled to claim further 238
compensation for their losses and for all expenses incurred together with interest. 239

14.   Sellers' default
240

Should the Sellers fail to give Notice of Readiness in accordance with Clause 5 a) or fail to be ready 241
to validly complete a legal transfer by the date stipulated in line 61 the Buyers shall have 242
the option of cancelling this Agreement provided always that the Sellers shall be granted a 243
maximum of 3 banking days after Notice of Readiness has been given to make arrangements 244
for the documentation set out in Clause 8. If after Notice of Readiness has been given but before 245
the Buyers have taken delivery, the Vessel ceases to be physically ready for delivery and is not 246
made physically ready again in every respect by the date stipulated in line 61 and new Notice of 247

Readiness given, the Buyers shall retain their option to cancel. In the event that the Buyers elect 248
to cancel this Agreement the deposit together with interest earned shall be released to them 249
immediately. 250
Should the Sellers fail to give Notice of Readiness by the date stipulated in line 61 or fail to be ready 251
to validly complete a legal transfer as aforesaid they shall make due compensation to the Buyers for 252
their loss and for all expenses together with interest if their failure is due to proven 253
negligence and whether or not the Buyers cancel this Agreement. 254

15. Buyers' representatives 255

After this Agreement has been signed by both parties and the deposit has been lodged, the Buyers 256
have the right to place two representatives on board the Vessel at their sole risk and expense upon 257
arrival at   on or about 258
These representatives are on board for the purpose of familiarisation and in the capacity of 259
observers only, and they shall not interfere in any respect with the operation of the Vessel. The 260
Buyers' representatives shall sign the Sellers' letter of indemnity prior to their embarkation. 261

16. Arbitration 262

a)* This Agreement shall be governed by and construed in accordance with English law and 263
any dispute arising out of this Agreement shall be referred to arbitration in London in 264
accordance with the Arbitration Acts 1950 and 1979 or any statutory modification or 265
re-enactment thereof for the time being in force, one arbitrator being appointed by each 266
party. On the receipt by one party of the nomination in writing of the other party's arbitrator, 267
that party shall appoint their arbitrator within fourteen days, failing which the decision of the 268
single arbitrator appointed shall apply. If two arbitrators properly appointed shall not agree 269
they shall appoint an umpire whose decision shall be final. 270

b)* This Agreement shall be governed by and construed in accordance with Title 9 of the 271
United States Code and the Law of the State of New York and should any dispute arise out of 272
this Agreement, the matter in dispute shall be referred to three persons at New York, one to 273
be appointed by each of the parties hereto, and the third by the two so chosen; their 274
decision or that of any two of them shall be final, and for purpose of enforcing any award, this 275
Agreement may be made a rule of the Court. 276
The proceedings shall be conducted in accordance with the rules of the Society of Maritime 277
Arbitrators, Inc. New York. 278

c)* Any dispute arising out of this Agreement shall be referred to arbitration at 279
, subject to the procedures applicable there. 280

The laws of   shall govern this Agreement. 281

* *16 a), 16 b) and 16 c) are alternatives; delete whichever is not applicable. In the absence of* 282
deletions, alternative 16 a) to apply. 283

MEMORANDUM OF AGREEMENT

Norwegian Shipbrokers' Association's Memorandum of Agreement for sale and purchase of ships. Adopted by BIMCO in 1956. Code-name
SALEFORM 2012
Revised 1966, 1983 and 1986/87, 1993 and 2012

Dated:	1
(*Name of sellers*), hereinafter called the "Sellers", have agreed to sell, and	2
(*Name of buyers*), hereinafter called the "Buyers", have agreed to buy:	3
Name of vessel:	4
IMO Number:	5
Classification Society:	6
Class Notation:	7
Year of Build: Builder/Yard:	8
Flag: Place of Registration: GT/NT: /	9
hereinafter called the "Vessel", on the following terms and conditions:	10

Definitions — 11

"Banking Days" are days on which banks are open both in the country of the currency stipulated for — 12
the Purchase Price in Clause 1 (Purchase Price) and in the place of closing stipulated in Clause 8 — 13
(Documentation) and   (*add additional jurisdictions as appropriate*). — 14

"Buyers' Nominated Flag State" means   (*state flag state*). — 15

"Class" means the class notation referred to above. — 16

"Classification Society" means the Society referred to above. — 17

"Deposit" shall have the meaning given in Clause 2 (Deposit) — 18

"Deposit Holder" means   (*state name and location of Deposit Holder*) or, if left blank, the — 19
Sellers' Bank, which shall hold and release the Deposit in accordance with this Agreement. — 20

"In writing" or "written" means a letter handed over from the Sellers to the Buyers or vice versa, a — 21
registered letter, e-mail or telefax. — 22

"Parties" means the Sellers and the Buyers. — 23

"Purchase Price" means the price for the Vessel as stated in Clause 1 (Purchase Price). — 24

"Sellers' Account" means   (*state details of bank account*) at the Sellers' Bank. — 25

"Sellers' Bank" means   (*state name of bank, branch and details*) or, if left blank, the bank — 26
notified by the Sellers to the Buyers for receipt of the balance of the Purchase Price. — 27

1.   **Purchase Price** — 28
     The Purchase Price is   (*state currency and amount both in words and figures*). — 29

2.   **Deposit** — 30
     As security for the correct fulfilment of this Agreement the Buyers shall lodge a deposit of — 31
     % (per cent) or, if left blank, 10% (ten per cent), of the Purchase Price (the — 32
     "Deposit") in an interest bearing account for the Parties with the Deposit Holder within three (3) — 33
     Banking Days after the date that: — 34

     (i)   this Agreement has been signed by the Parties and exchanged in original or by — 35
           e-mail or telefax; and — 36

     (ii)   the Deposit Holder has confirmed in writing to the Parties that the account has been — 37
           opened. — 38

     The Deposit shall be released in accordance with joint written instructions of the Parties. — 39
     Interest, if any, shall be credited to the Buyers. Any fee charged for holding and releasing the — 40
     Deposit shall be borne equally by the Parties. The Parties shall provide to the Deposit Holder — 41

	all necessary documentation to open and maintain the account without delay.	42
3.	**Payment**	43
	On delivery of the Vessel, but not later than three (3) Banking Days after the date that Notice of	44
	Readiness has been given in accordance with <u>Clause 5</u> (Time and place of delivery and	45
	notices):	46

	(i)	the Deposit shall be released to the Sellers; and	47

	(ii)	the balance of the Purchase Price and all other sums payable on delivery by the Buyers	48
		to the Sellers under this Agreement shall be paid in full free of bank charges to the	49
		Sellers' Account.	50

4.	**Inspection**	51
	(a)* The Buyers have inspected and accepted the Vessel's classification records. The Buyers	52
	have also inspected the Vessel at/in *(state place)* on *(state date)* and have	53
	accepted the Vessel following this inspection and the sale is outright and definite, subject only	54
	to the terms and conditions of this Agreement.	55

(b)* The Buyers shall have the right to inspect the Vessel's classification records and declare	56
whether same are accepted or not within *(state date/period)*.	57

The Sellers shall make the Vessel available for inspection at/in *(state place/range)* within	58
(state date/period).	59

The Buyers shall undertake the inspection without undue delay to the Vessel. Should the	60
Buyers cause undue delay they shall compensate the Sellers for the losses thereby incurred.	61

The Buyers shall inspect the Vessel without opening up and without cost to the Sellers.	62

During the inspection, the Vessel's deck and engine log books shall be made available for	63
examination by the Buyers.	64

The sale shall become outright and definite, subject only to the terms and conditions of this	65
Agreement, provided that the Sellers receive written notice of acceptance of the Vessel from	66
the Buyers within seventy-two (72) hours after completion of such inspection or after the	67
date/last day of the period stated in <u>Line 59</u>, whichever is earlier.	68

Should the Buyers fail to undertake the inspection as scheduled and/or notice of acceptance of	69
the Vessel's classification records and/or of the Vessel not be received by the Sellers as	70
aforesaid, the Deposit together with interest earned, if any, shall be released immediately to the	71
Buyers, whereafter this Agreement shall be null and void.	72

*<u>4(a)</u> and <u>4(b)</u> are alternatives; delete whichever is not applicable. In the absence of deletions,	73
alternative <u>4(a)</u> shall apply.	74

5.	**Time and place of delivery and notices**	75
	(a) The Vessel shall be delivered and taken over safely afloat at a safe and accessible berth or	76
	anchorage at/in *(state place/range)* in the Sellers' option.	77

Notice of Readiness shall not be tendered before: *(date)*	78

Cancelling Date (see <u>Clauses 5(c)</u>, <u>6 (a)(i)</u>, <u>6 (a) (iii)</u> and <u>14</u>):	79

(b) The Sellers shall keep the Buyers well informed of the Vessel's itinerary and shall	80
provide the Buyers with twenty (20), ten (10), five (5) and three (3) days' notice of the date the	81
Sellers intend to tender Notice of Readiness and of the intended place of delivery.	82

When the Vessel is at the place of delivery and physically ready for delivery in accordance with	83
this Agreement, the Sellers shall give the Buyers a written Notice of Readiness for delivery.	84

(c) If the Sellers anticipate that, notwithstanding the exercise of due diligence by them, the	85
Vessel will not be ready for delivery by the Cancelling Date they may notify the Buyers in writing	86
stating the date when they anticipate that the Vessel will be ready for delivery and proposing a	87
new Cancelling Date. Upon receipt of such notification the Buyers shall have the option of	88
either cancelling this Agreement in accordance with <u>Clause 14</u> (Sellers' Default) within three (3)	89
Banking Days of receipt of the notice or of accepting the new date as the new Cancelling Date.	90
If the Buyers have not declared their option within three (3) Banking Days of receipt of the	91
Sellers' notification or if the Buyers accept the new date, the date proposed in the Sellers'	92
notification shall be deemed to be the new Cancelling Date and shall be substituted for the	93

2

Cancelling Date stipulated in <u>line 79</u>.	94

If this Agreement is maintained with the new Cancelling Date all other terms and conditions   95
hereof including those contained in <u>Clauses 5(b)</u> and <u>5(d)</u> shall remain unaltered and in full   96
force and effect.   97

(d) Cancellation, failure to cancel or acceptance of the new Cancelling Date shall be entirely   98
without prejudice to any claim for damages the Buyers may have under <u>Clause 14</u> (Sellers'   99
Default) for the Vessel not being ready by the original Cancelling Date.   100

(e) Should the Vessel become an actual, constructive or compromised total loss before delivery   101
the Deposit together with interest earned, if any, shall be released immediately to the Buyers   102
whereafter this Agreement shall be null and void.   103

6.   **Divers Inspection / Drydocking**   104
(a)*   105
(i)   The Buyers shall have the option at their cost and expense to arrange for an underwater   106
inspection by a diver approved by the Classification Society prior to the delivery of the   107
Vessel. Such option shall be declared latest nine (9) days prior to the Vessel's intended   108
date of readiness for delivery as notified by the Sellers pursuant to <u>Clause 5(b)</u> of this   109
Agreement. The Sellers shall at their cost and expense make the Vessel available for   110
such inspection. This inspection shall be carried out without undue delay and in the   111
presence of a Classification Society surveyor arranged for by the Sellers and paid for by   112
the Buyers. The Buyers' representative(s) shall have the right to be present at the diver's   113
inspection as observer(s) only without interfering with the work or decisions of the   114
Classification Society surveyor. The extent of the inspection and the conditions under   115
which it is performed shall be to the satisfaction of the Classification Society. If the   116
conditions at the place of delivery are unsuitable for such inspection, the Sellers shall at   117
their cost and expense make the Vessel available at a suitable alternative place near to   118
the delivery port, in which event the Cancelling Date shall be extended by the additional   119
time required for such positioning and the subsequent re-positioning. The Sellers may   120
not tender Notice of Readiness prior to completion of the underwater inspection.   121

(ii)   If the rudder, propeller, bottom or other underwater parts below the deepest load line are   122
found broken, damaged or defective so as to affect the Vessel's class, then (1) unless   123
repairs can be carried out afloat to the satisfaction of the Classification Society, the   124
Sellers shall arrange for the Vessel to be drydocked at their expense for inspection by   125
the Classification Society of the Vessel's underwater parts below the deepest load line,   126
the extent of the inspection being in accordance with the Classification Society's rules (2)   127
such defects shall be made good by the Sellers at their cost and expense to the   128
satisfaction of the Classification Society without condition/recommendation** and (3) the   129
Sellers shall pay for the underwater inspection and the Classification Society's   130
attendance.   131

Notwithstanding anything to the contrary in this Agreement, if the Classification Society   132
do not require the aforementioned defects to be rectified before the next class   133
drydocking survey, the Sellers shall be entitled to deliver the Vessel with these defects   134
against a deduction from the Purchase Price of the estimated direct cost (of labour and   135
materials) of carrying out the repairs to the satisfaction of the Classification Society,   136
whereafter the Buyers shall have no further rights whatsoever in respect of the defects   137
and/or repairs. The estimated direct cost of the repairs shall be the average of quotes   138
for the repair work obtained from two reputable independent shipyards at or in the   139
vicinity of the port of delivery, one to be obtained by each of the Parties within two (2)   140
Banking Days from the date of the imposition of the condition/recommendation, unless   141
the Parties agree otherwise. Should either of the Parties fail to obtain such a quote within   142
the stipulated time then the quote duly obtained by the other Party shall be the sole basis   143
for the estimate of the direct repair costs. The Sellers may not tender Notice of   144
Readiness prior to such estimate having been established.   145

(iii)   If the Vessel is to be drydocked pursuant to Clause <u>6(a)(ii)</u> and no suitable dry-docking   146
facilities are available at the port of delivery, the Sellers shall take the Vessel to a port   147
where suitable drydocking facilities are available, whether within or outside the delivery   148
range as per <u>Clause 5(a)</u>. Once drydocking has taken place the Sellers shall deliver the   149
Vessel at a port within the delivery range as per <u>Clause 5(a)</u> which shall, for the purpose   150
of this Clause, become the new port of delivery. In such event the Cancelling Date shall   151
be extended by the additional time required for the drydocking and extra steaming, but   152
limited to a maximum of fourteen (14) days.   153

3

(b)* The Sellers shall place the Vessel in drydock at the port of delivery for inspection by the | 154
Classification Society of the Vessel's underwater parts below the deepest load line, the extent | 155
of the inspection being in accordance with the Classification Society's rules. If the rudder, | 156
propeller, bottom or other underwater parts below the deepest load line are found broken, | 157
damaged or defective so as to affect the Vessel's class, such defects shall be made good at the | 158
Sellers' cost and expense to the satisfaction of the Classification Society without | 159
condition/recommendation**. In such event the Sellers are also to pay for the costs and | 160
expenses in connection with putting the Vessel in and taking her out of drydock, including the | 161
drydock dues and the Classification Society's fees. The Sellers shall also pay for these costs | 162
and expenses if parts of the tailshaft system are condemned or found defective or broken so as | 163
to affect the Vessel's class. In all other cases, the Buyers shall pay the aforesaid costs and | 164
expenses, dues and fees. | 165

(c) If the Vessel is drydocked pursuant to Clause 6 (a)(ii) or 6 (b) above: | 166

(i) The Classification Society may require survey of the tailshaft system, the extent of the | 167
survey being to the satisfaction of the Classification surveyor. If such survey is | 168
not required by the Classification Society, the Buyers shall have the option to require the | 169
tailshaft to be drawn and surveyed by the Classification Society, the extent of the survey | 170
being in accordance with the Classification Society's rules for tailshaft survey and | 171
consistent with the current stage of the Vessel's survey cycle. The Buyers shall declare | 172
whether they require the tailshaft to be drawn and surveyed not later than by the | 173
completion of the inspection by the Classification Society. The drawing and refitting of | 174
the tailshaft shall be arranged by the Sellers. Should any parts of the tailshaft system be | 175
condemned or found defective so as to affect the Vessel's class, those parts shall be | 176
renewed or made good at the Sellers' cost and expense to the satisfaction of | 177
Classification Society without condition/recommendation**. | 178

(ii) The costs and expenses relating to the survey of the tailshaft system shall be borne by | 179
the Buyers unless the Classification Society requires such survey to be carried out or if | 180
parts of the system are condemned or found defective or broken so as to affect the | 181
Vessel's class, in which case the Sellers shall pay these costs and expenses. | 182

(iii) The Buyers' representative(s) shall have the right to be present in the drydock, as | 183
observer(s) only without interfering with the work or decisions of the Classification | 184
Society surveyor. | 185

(iv) The Buyers shall have the right to have the underwater parts of the Vessel cleaned | 186
and painted at their risk, cost and expense without interfering with the Sellers' or the | 187
Classification Society surveyor's work, if any, and without affecting the Vessel's timely | 188
delivery. If, however, the Buyers' work in drydock is still in progress when the | 189
Sellers have completed the work which the Sellers are required to do, the additional | 190
docking time needed to complete the Buyers' work shall be for the Buyers' risk, cost and | 191
expense. In the event that the Buyers' work requires such additional time, the Sellers | 192
may upon completion of the Sellers' work tender Notice of Readiness for delivery whilst | 193
the Vessel is still in drydock and, notwithstanding Clause 5(a), the Buyers shall be | 194
obliged to take delivery in accordance with Clause 3 (Payment), whether the Vessel is in | 195
drydock or not. | 196

6 (a) and 6 (b) are alternatives; delete whichever is not applicable. In the absence of deletions, | 197
alternative 6 (a) shall apply. | 198

***Notes or memoranda, if any, in the surveyor's report which are accepted by the Classification* | 199
Society without condition/recommendation are not to be taken into account. | 200

Spares, bunkers and other items | 201
The Sellers shall deliver the Vessel to the Buyers with everything belonging to her on board | 202
and on shore. All spare parts and spare equipment including spare tail-end shaft(s) and/or | 203
spare propeller(s)/propeller blade(s), if any, belonging to the Vessel at the time of inspection | 204
used or unused, whether on board or not shall become the Buyers' property, but spares on | 205
order are excluded. Forwarding charges, if any, shall be for the Buyers' account. The Sellers | 206
are not required to replace spare parts including spare tail-end shaft(s) and spare | 207
propeller(s)/propeller blade(s) which are taken out of spare and used as replacement prior to | 208
delivery, but the replaced items shall be the property of the Buyers. Unused stores and | 209
provisions shall be included in the sale and be taken over by the Buyers without extra payment. | 210

Library and forms exclusively for use in the Sellers' vessel(s) and captain's, officers' and crew's | 211
personal belongings including the slop chest are excluded from the sale without compensation, | 212

4

as well as the following additional items: *(include list)*	213

Items on board which are on hire or owned by third parties, listed as follows, are excluded from the sale without compensation: *(include list)* — 214, 215

Items on board at the time of inspection which are on hire or owned by third parties, not listed above, shall be replaced or procured by the Sellers prior to delivery at their cost and expense. — 216, 217

The Buyers shall take over remaining bunkers and unused lubricating and hydraulic oils and greases in storage tanks and unopened drums and pay either: — 218, 219

(a) *the actual net price (excluding barging expenses) as evidenced by invoices or vouchers; or — 220

(b) *the current net market price (excluding barging expenses) at the port and date of delivery of the Vessel or, if unavailable, at the nearest bunkering port, — 221, 222

for the quantities taken over. — 223

Payment under this Clause shall be made at the same time and place and in the same currency as the Purchase Price. — 224, 225

"inspection" in this Clause 7, shall mean the Buyers' inspection according to Clause 4(a) or 4(b) (Inspection), if applicable. If the Vessel is taken over without inspection, the date of this Agreement shall be the relevant date. — 226, 227, 228

*(a) and (b) are alternatives, delete whichever is not applicable. In the absence of deletions alternative (a) shall apply. — 229, 230

Documentation — 231
The place of closing: — 232

(a) In exchange for payment of the Purchase Price the Sellers shall provide the Buyers with the following delivery documents: — 233, 234

(i)   Legal Bill(s) of Sale in a form recordable in the Buyers' Nominated Flag State, transferring title of the Vessel and stating that the Vessel is free from all mortgages, encumbrances and maritime liens or any other debts whatsoever, duly notarially attested and legalised or apostilled, as required by the Buyers' Nominated Flag State; — 235, 236, 237, 238

(ii)   Evidence that all necessary corporate, shareholder and other action has been taken by the Sellers to authorise the execution, delivery and performance of this Agreement; — 239, 240

(iii)   Power of Attorney of the Sellers appointing one or more representatives to act on behalf of the Sellers in the performance of this Agreement, duly notarially attested and legalised or apostilled (as appropriate); — 241, 242, 243

(iv)   Certificate or Transcript of Registry issued by the competent authorities of the flag state on the date of delivery evidencing the Sellers' ownership of the Vessel and that the Vessel is free from registered encumbrances and mortgages, to be faxed or e-mailed by such authority to the closing meeting with the original to be sent to the Buyers as soon as possible after delivery of the Vessel; — 244, 245, 246, 247, 248

(v)   Declaration of Class or (depending on the Classification Society) a Class Maintenance Certificate issued within three (3) Banking Days prior to delivery confirming that the Vessel is in Class free of condition/recommendation; — 249, 250, 251

(vi)   Certificate of Deletion of the Vessel from the Vessel's registry or other official evidence of deletion appropriate to the Vessel's registry at the time of delivery, or, in the event that the registry does not as a matter of practice issue such documentation immediately, a written undertaking by the Sellers to effect deletion from the Vessel's registry forthwith and provide a certificate or other official evidence of deletion to the Buyers promptly and latest within four (4) weeks after the Purchase Price has been paid and the Vessel has been delivered; — 252, 253, 254, 255, 256, 257, 258

(vii)   A copy of the Vessel's Continuous Synopsis Record certifying the date on which the Vessel ceased to be registered with the Vessel's registry, or, in the event that the registry does not as a matter of practice issue such certificate immediately, a written undertaking from the Sellers to provide the copy of this certificate promptly upon it being issued together with evidence of submission by the Sellers of a duly executed Form 2 stating the date on which the Vessel shall cease to be registered with the Vessel's registry; — 259, 260, 261, 262, 263, 264

5

(viii)	Commercial Invoice for the Vessel;	265
(ix)	Commercial Invoice(s) for bunkers, lubricating and hydraulic oils and greases;	266
(x)	A copy of the Sellers' letter to their satellite communication provider cancelling the Vessel's communications contract which is to be sent immediately after delivery of the Vessel;	267 268 269
(xi)	Any additional documents as may reasonably be required by the competent authorities of the Buyers' Nominated Flag State for the purpose of registering the Vessel, provided the Buyers notify the Sellers of any such documents as soon as possible after the date of this Agreement; and	270 271 272 273
(xii)	The Sellers' letter of confirmation that to the best of their knowledge, the Vessel is not black listed by any nation or international organisation.	274 275

(b) At the time of delivery the Buyers shall provide the Sellers with: 276

(i)	Evidence that all necessary corporate, shareholder and other action has been taken by the Buyers to authorise the execution, delivery and performance of this Agreement; and	277 278
(ii)	Power of Attorney of the Buyers appointing one or more representatives to act on behalf of the Buyers in the performance of this Agreement, duly notarially attested and legalised or apostilled (as appropriate).	279 280 281

(c) If any of the documents listed in Sub-clauses (a) and (b) above are not in the English language they shall be accompanied by an English translation by an authorised translator or certified by a lawyer qualified to practice in the country of the translated language. 282 283 284

(d) The Parties shall to the extent possible exchange copies, drafts or samples of the documents listed in Sub-clause (a) and Sub-clause (b) above for review and comment by the other party not later than   (*state number of days),* or if left blank, nine (9) days prior to the Vessel's intended date of readiness for delivery as notified by the Sellers pursuant to Clause 5(b) of this Agreement. 285 286 287 288 289

(e) Concurrent with the exchange of documents in Sub-clause (a) and Sub-clause (b) above, the Sellers shall also hand to the Buyers the classification certificate(s) as well as all plans, drawings and manuals, (excluding ISM/ISPS manuals), which are on board the Vessel. Other certificates which are on board the Vessel shall also be handed over to the Buyers unless the Sellers are required to retain same, in which case the Buyers have the right to take copies. 290 291 292 293 294

(f) Other technical documentation which may be in the Sellers' possession shall promptly after delivery be forwarded to the Buyers at their expense, if they so request. The Sellers may keep the Vessel's log books but the Buyers have the right to take copies of same. 295 296 297

(g) The Parties shall sign and deliver to each other a Protocol of Delivery and Acceptance confirming the date and time of delivery of the Vessel from the Sellers to the Buyers. 298 299

9. Encumbrances 300
The Sellers warrant that the Vessel, at the time of delivery, is free from all charters, encumbrances, mortgages and maritime liens or any other debts whatsoever, and is not subject to Port State or other administrative detentions. The Sellers hereby undertake to indemnify the Buyers against all consequences of claims made against the Vessel which have been incurred prior to the time of delivery. 301 302 303 304 305

10. Taxes, fees and expenses 306
Any taxes, fees and expenses in connection with the purchase and registration in the Buyers' Nominated Flag State shall be for the Buyers' account, whereas similar charges in connection with the closing of the Sellers' register shall be for the Sellers' account. 307 308 309

11. Condition on delivery 310
The Vessel with everything belonging to her shall be at the Sellers' risk and expense until she is delivered to the Buyers, but subject to the terms and conditions of this Agreement she shall be delivered and taken over as she was at the time of inspection, fair wear and tear excepted. 311 312 313

However, the Vessel shall be delivered free of cargo and free of stowaways with her Class maintained without condition/recommendation*, free of average damage affecting the Vessel's class, and with her classification certificates and national certificates, as well as all other certificates the Vessel had at the time of inspection, valid and unextended without condition/recommendation* by the Classification Society or the relevant authorities at the time 314 315 316 317 318

6

of delivery.	319

"inspection" in this <u>Clause 11</u>, shall mean the Buyers' inspection according to <u>Clause 4(a)</u> or 320
<u>4(b)</u> (Inspections), if applicable. If the Vessel is taken over without inspection, the date of this 321
Agreement shall be the relevant date. 322

Notes and memoranda, if any, in the surveyor's report which are accepted by the Classification 323
Society without condition/recommendation are not to be taken into account. 324

12. Name/markings
Upon delivery the Buyers undertake to change the name of the Vessel and alter funnel 326
markings. 327

13. Buyers' default
Should the Deposit not be lodged in accordance with <u>Clause 2</u> (Deposit), the Sellers have the 329
right to cancel this Agreement, and they shall be entitled to claim compensation for their losses 330
and for all expenses incurred together with interest. 331

Should the Purchase Price not be paid in accordance with <u>Clause 3</u> (Payment), the Sellers 332
have the right to cancel this Agreement, in which case the Deposit together with interest 333
earned, if any, shall be released to the Sellers. If the Deposit does not cover their loss, the 334
Sellers shall be entitled to claim further compensation for their losses and for all expenses 335
incurred together with interest. 336

14. Sellers' default
Should the Sellers fail to give Notice of Readiness in accordance with <u>Clause 5(b)</u> or fail to be 338
ready to validly complete a legal transfer by the Cancelling Date the Buyers shall have the 339
option of cancelling this Agreement. If after Notice of Readiness has been given but before 340
the Buyers have taken delivery, the Vessel ceases to be physically ready for delivery and is not 341
made physically ready again by the Cancelling Date and new Notice of Readiness given, the 342
Buyers shall retain their option to cancel. In the event that the Buyers elect to cancel this 343
Agreement, the Deposit together with interest earned, if any, shall be released to them 344
immediately. 345

Should the Sellers fail to give Notice of Readiness by the Cancelling Date or fail to be ready to 346
validly complete a legal transfer as aforesaid they shall make due compensation to the Buyers 347
for their loss and for all expenses together with interest if their failure is due to proven 348
negligence and whether or not the Buyers cancel this Agreement. 349

15. Buyers' representatives
After this Agreement has been signed by the Parties and the Deposit has been lodged, the 351
Buyers have the right to place two (2) representatives on board the Vessel at their sole risk and 352
expense. 353

These representatives are on board for the purpose of familiarisation and in the capacity of 354
observers only, and they shall not interfere in any respect with the operation of the Vessel. The 355
Buyers and the Buyers' representatives shall sign the Sellers' P&I Club's standard letter of 356
indemnity prior to their embarkation. 357

16. Law and Arbitration
(a) *This Agreement shall be governed by and construed in accordance with English law and 359
any dispute arising out of or in connection with this Agreement shall be referred to arbitration in 360
London in accordance with the Arbitration Act 1996 or any statutory modification or re- 361
enactment thereof save to the extent necessary to give effect to the provisions of this Clause. 362

The arbitration shall be conducted in accordance with the London Maritime Arbitrators 363
Association (LMAA) Terms current at the time when the arbitration proceedings are 364
commenced. 365

The reference shall be to three arbitrators. A party wishing to refer a dispute to arbitration shall 366
appoint its arbitrator and send notice of such appointment in writing to the other party requiring 367
the other party to appoint its own arbitrator within fourteen (14) calendar days of that notice and 368
stating that it will appoint its arbitrator as sole arbitrator unless the other party appoints its own 369
arbitrator and gives notice that it has done so within the fourteen (14) days specified. If the 370
other party does not appoint its own arbitrator and give notice that it has done so within the 371
fourteen (14) days specified, the party referring a dispute to arbitration may, without the 372
requirement of any further prior notice to the other party, appoint its arbitrator as sole arbitrator 373
and shall advise the other party accordingly. The award of a sole arbitrator shall be binding on 374
both Parties as if the sole arbitrator had been appointed by agreement. 375

7

In cases where neither the claim nor any counterclaim exceeds the sum of US$100,000 the arbitration shall be conducted in accordance with the LMAA Small Claims Procedure current at the time when the arbitration proceedings are commenced.	376 377 378

(b) *This Agreement shall be governed by and construed in accordance with Title 9 of the United States Code and the substantive law (not including the choice of law rules) of the State of New York and any dispute arising out of or in connection with this Agreement shall be referred to three (3) persons at New York, one to be appointed by each of the parties hereto, and the third by the two so chosen; their decision or that of any two of them shall be final, and for the purposes of enforcing any award, judgment may be entered on an award by any court of competent jurisdiction. The proceedings shall be conducted in accordance with the rules of the Society of Maritime Arbitrators, Inc.

379
380
381
382
383
384
385
386

In cases where neither the claim nor any counterclaim exceeds the sum of US$ 100,000 the arbitration shall be conducted in accordance with the Shortened Arbitration Procedure of the Society of Maritime Arbitrators, Inc.

387
388
389

(c) This Agreement shall be governed by and construed in accordance with the laws of *(state place)* and any dispute arising out of or in connection with this Agreement shall be referred to arbitration at   *(state place),* subject to the procedures applicable there.

390
391
392

16(a), 16(b) and 16(c) are alternatives; delete whichever is not applicable. In the absence of deletions, alternative 16(a) shall apply.

393
394

17. Notices
All notices to be provided under this Agreement shall be in writing.

395
396

Contact details for recipients of notices are as follows:

397

For the Buyers:

398

For the Sellers:

399

18. Entire Agreement
The written terms of this Agreement comprise the entire agreement between the Buyers and the Sellers in relation to the sale and purchase of the Vessel and supersede all previous agreements whether oral or written between the Parties in relation thereto.

400
401
402
403

Each of the Parties acknowledges that in entering into this Agreement it has not relied on and shall have no right or remedy in respect of any statement, representation, assurance or warranty (whether or not made negligently) other than as is expressly set out in this Agreement.

404
405
406

Any terms implied into this Agreement by any applicable statue or law are hereby excluded to the extent that such exclusion can legally be made. Nothing in this Clause shall limit or exclude any liability for fraud.

407
408
409

For and on behalf of the Sellers   For and on behalf of the Buyers

_____   _____

Name: Name:

Title: Title:

8

Explanatory Notes for SHIPMAN 2009 are available from BIMCO at www.bimco.org

Approved by the International Ship Managers' Association (InterManager)

InterManager

First published 1988. Revised 1998 and 2009.

Copyright, published by BIMCO, Copenhagen

BIMCO

SHIPMAN 2009
STANDARD SHIP MANAGEMENT AGREEMENT
PART I

1. Place and date of Agreement	2. Date of commencement of Agreement (Cls. 2, 12, 21 and 25)
3. Owners (name, place of registered office and law of registry) (Cl. 1) (i) Name: (ii) Place of registered office: (iii) Law of registry:	4. Managers (name, place of registered office and law of registry) (Cl. 1) (i) Name: (ii) Place of registered office: (iii) Law of registry:
5. The Company (with reference to the ISM/ISPS Codes) (state name and IMO Unique Company Identification number. If the Company is a third party then also state registered office and principal place of business) (Cls. 1 and 9(c)(i)) (i) Name: (ii) IMO Unique Company Identification number: (iii) Place of registered office: (iv) Principal place of business:	6. Technical Management (state "yes" or "no" as agreed) (Cl. 4) 7. Crew Management (state "yes" or "no" as agreed) (Cl. 5(a)) 8. Commercial Management (state "yes" or "no" as agreed) (Cl. 6)
9. Chartering Services period (only to be filled in if "yes" stated in Box 8) (Cl.6(a))	10. Crew Insurance arrangements (state "yes" or "no" as agreed) (i) Crew Insurances* (Cl. 5(b)): (ii) Insurance for persons proceeding to sea onboard (Cl. 5(b)(i)): *only to apply if Crew Management (Cl. 5(a)) agreed (see Box 7)
11. Insurance arrangements (state "yes" or "no" as agreed) (Cl. 7)	12. Optional insurances (state optional insurance(s) as agreed, such as piracy, kidnap and ransom, loss of hire and FD & D) (Cl. 10(a)(iv))
13. Interest (state rate of interest to apply after due date to outstanding sums) (Cl. 9(a))	14. Annual management fee (state annual amount) (Cl. 12(a))
15. Manager's nominated account (Cl.12(a))	16. Daily rate (state rate for days in excess of those agreed in budget) (Cl. 12(c)) 17. Lay-up period / number of months (Cl.12(d))
18. Minimum contract period (state number of months) (Cl. 21(a))	19. Management fee on termination (state number of months to apply) (Cl. 22(g))
20. Severance Costs (state maximum amount) (Cl. 22(h)(ii))	21. Dispute Resolution (state alternative Cl. 23(a), 23(b) or 23(c); if Cl. 23(c) place of arbitration must be stated) (Cl. 23)

SHIPMAN 2009
Standard ship management agreement

PART I

(continued)

22. Notices (state full style contact details for serving notice and communication to the Owners) (Cl. 24)	23. Notices (state full style contact details for serving notice and communication to the Managers) (Cl. 24)

It is mutually agreed between the party stated in Box 3 and the party stated in Box 4 that this Agreement consisting of PART I and PART II as well as Annexes "A" (Details of Vessel or Vessels), "B" (Details of Crew), "C" (Budget), "D" (Associated Vessels) and "E" (Fee Schedule) attached hereto, shall be performed subject to the conditions contained herein. In the event of a conflict of conditions, the provisions of PART I and Annexes "A", "B", "C", "D" and "E" shall prevail over those of PART II to the extent of such conflict but no further.

Signature(s) (Owners)	Signature(s) (Managers)

PART II
SHIPMAN 2009
Standard ship management agreement

SECTION 1 – Basis of the Agreement

1. Definitions

In this Agreement save where the context otherwise requires, the following words and expressions shall have the meanings hereby assigned to them:

"Company" (with reference to the ISM Code and the ISPS Code) means the organization identified in **Box 5** or any replacement organization appointed by the Owners from time to time (see Sub-clauses 9(b)(i) or 9(c) (ii), whichever is applicable).

"Crew" means the personnel of the numbers, rank and nationality specified in Annex "B" hereto.

"Crew Insurances" means insurance of liabilities in respect of crew risks which shall include but not be limited to death, permanent disability, sickness, injury, repatriation, shipwreck unemployment indemnity and loss of personal effects (see Sub-clause 5(b) (Crew Insurances) and Clause 7 (Insurance Arrangements) and Clause 10 (Insurance Policies) and **Boxes 10** and **11**).

"Crew Support Costs" means all expenses of a general nature which are not particularly referable to any individual vessel for the time being managed by the Managers and which are incurred by the Managers for the purpose of providing an efficient and economic management service and, without prejudice to the generality of the foregoing, shall include the cost of crew standby pay, training schemes for officers and ratings, cadet training schemes, sick pay, study pay, recruitment and interviews.

"Flag State" means the State whose flag the Vessel is flying.

"ISM Code" means the International Management Code for the Safe Operation of Ships and for Pollution Prevention and any amendment thereto or substitution therefor.

"ISPS Code" means the International Code for the Security of Ships and Port Facilities and the relevant amendments to Chapter XI of SOLAS and any amendment thereto or substitution therefor.

"Managers" means the party identified in **Box 4**.

"Management Services" means the services specified in SECTION 2 - Services (Clauses 4 through 7) as indicated affirmatively in **Boxes 6** through **8, 10 and 11,** and all other functions performed by the Managers under the terms of this Agreement.

"Owners" means the party identified in **Box 3**.

"Severance Costs" means the costs which are legally required to be paid to the Crew as a result of the early termination of any contracts for service on the Vessel.

"SMS" means the Safety Management System (as defined by the ISM Code).

"STCW 95" means the International Convention on Standards of Training, Certification and Watchkeeping for Seafarers, 1978, as amended in 1995 and any amendment thereto or substitution therefor.

"Vessel" means the vessel or vessels details of which are set out in Annex "A" attached hereto.

2. Commencement and Appointment

With effect from the date stated in **Box 2** for the commencement of the Management Services and continuing unless and until terminated as provided herein, the Owners hereby appoint the Managers and the Managers hereby agree to act as the Managers of the Vessel in respect of the Management Services.

3. Authority of the Managers

Subject to the terms and conditions herein provided, during the period of this Agreement the Managers shall carry out the Management Services in respect of the Vessel as agents for and on behalf of the Owners. The Managers shall have authority to take such actions as they may from time to time in their absolute discretion consider to be necessary to enable them to perform the Management Services in accordance with sound ship management practice, including but not limited to compliance with all relevant rules and regulations.

PART II
SHIPMAN 2009
Standard ship management agreement

4.   Technical Management   43
*(only applicable if agreed according to **Box 6**).*   44
The Managers shall provide technical management which includes, but is not limited to, the following   45
services: 46

    (a) ensuring that the Vessel complies with the requirements of the law of the Flag State;   47

    (b) ensuring compliance with the ISM Code;   48

    (c) ensuring compliance with the ISPS Code;   49

    (d) providing competent personnel to supervise the maintenance and general efficiency of the Vessel;   50

    (e) arranging and supervising dry dockings, repairs, alterations and the maintenance of the Vessel to the   51
standards agreed with the Owners provided that the Managers shall be entitled to incur the necessary   52
expenditure to ensure that the Vessel will comply with all requirements and recommendations of the   53
classification society, and with the law of the Flag State and of the places where the Vessel is required to   54
trade;   55

    (f) arranging the supply of necessary stores, spares and lubricating oil;   56

    (g) appointing surveyors and technical consultants as the Managers may consider from time to time to be   57
necessary;   58

    (h) in accordance with the Owners' instructions, supervising the sale and physical delivery of the Vessel   59
under the sale agreement. However services under this Sub-clause 4(h) shall not include negotiation of the   60
sale agreement or transfer of ownership of the Vessel;   61

    (i) arranging for the supply of provisions unless provided by the Owners; and   62

    (j) arranging for the sampling and testing of bunkers.   63

5.   Crew Management and Crew Insurances   64
    (a) *Crew Management*   65
*(only applicable if agreed according to **Box 7**)*   66
The Managers shall provide suitably qualified Crew who shall comply with the requirements of STCW 95.   67
The provision of such crew management services includes, but is not limited to, the following services: 68

    (i)   selecting, engaging and providing for the administration of the Crew, including, as applicable, payroll   69
arrangements, pension arrangements, tax, social security contributions and other mandatory dues related   70
to their employment payable in each Crew member's country of domicile;   71

    (ii)   ensuring that the applicable requirements of the law of the Flag State in respect of rank, qualification   72
and certification of the Crew and employment regulations, such as Crew's tax and social insurance, are   73
satisfied;   74

    (iii) ensuring that all Crew have passed a medical examination with a qualified doctor certifying that they are   75
fit for the duties for which they are engaged and are in possession of valid medical certificates issued in   76
accordance with appropriate Flag State requirements or such higher standard of medical examination   77
as may be agreed with the Owners. In the absence of applicable Flag State requirements the medical   78
certificate shall be valid at the time when the respective Crew member arrives on board the Vessel and   79
shall be maintained for the duration of the service on board the Vessel;   80

    (iv) ensuring that the Crew shall have a common working language and a command of the English language   81
of a sufficient standard to enable them to perform their duties safely;   82

    (v)   arranging transportation of the Crew, including repatriation;   83

    (vi) training of the Crew;   84

**PART II
SHIPMAN 2009
Standard ship management agreement**

(vii) conducting union negotiations; and 85

(viii) if the Managers are the Company, ensuring that the Crew, on joining the Vessel, are given proper 86
familiarisation with their duties in relation to the Vessel's SMS and that instructions which are essential 87
to the SMS are identified, documented and given to the Crew prior to sailing. 88

(ix) if the Managers are **not** the Company: 89

(1) ensuring that the Crew, before joining the Vessel, are given proper familiarisation with their duties 90
in relation to the ISM Code; and 91

(2) instructing the Crew to obey all reasonable orders of the Company in connection with the operation 92
of the SMS. 93

(x) Where Managers are **not** providing technical management services in accordance with Clause 4 94
(Technical Management): 95

(1) ensuring that no person connected to the provision and the performance of the crew management 96
services shall proceed to sea on board the Vessel without the prior consent of the Owners (such consent 97
not to be unreasonably withheld); and 98

(2) ensuring that in the event that the Owners' drug and alcohol policy requires measures to be taken 99
prior to the Crew joining the Vessel, implementing such measures; 100

(b) Crew Insurances 101
(only applicable if Sub-clause 5(a) applies **and** if agreed according to **Box 10**) 102
The Managers shall throughout the period of this Agreement provide the following services: 103

(i) arranging Crew Insurances in accordance with the best practice of prudent managers of vessels of a 104
similar type to the Vessel, with sound and reputable insurance companies, underwriters or associations. 105
Insurances for any other persons proceeding to sea onboard the Vessel may be separately agreed by 106
the Owners and the Managers (see **Box 10**); 107

(ii) ensuring that the Owners are aware of the terms, conditions, exceptions and limits of liability of the 108
insurances in Sub-clause 5(b)(i); 109

(iii) ensuring that all premiums or calls in respect of the insurances in Sub-clause 5(b)(i) are paid by their 110
due date; 111

(iv) if obtainable at no additional cost, ensuring that insurances in Sub-clause 5(b)(i) name the Owners as 112
a joint assured with full cover and, unless otherwise agreed, on terms such that Owners shall be under 113
no liability in respect of premiums or calls arising in connection with such insurances. 114

(v) providing written evidence, to the reasonable satisfaction of the Owners, of the Managers' compliance with 115
their obligations under Sub-clauses 5(b)(ii), and 5(b)(iii) within a reasonable time of the commencement 116
of this Agreement, and of each renewal date and, if specifically requested, of each payment date of the 117
insurances in Sub-clause 5(b)(i). 118

6. Commercial Management 119
(only applicable if agreed according to **Box 8**). 120
The Managers shall provide the following services for the Vessel in accordance with the Owners' instructions, 121
which shall include but not be limited to: 122

(a) seeking and negotiating employment for the Vessel and the conclusion (including the execution thereof) 123
of charter parties or other contracts relating to the employment of the Vessel. If such a contract exceeds the 124
period stated in **Box 9**, consent thereto in writing shall first be obtained from the Owners; 125

(b) arranging for the provision of bunker fuels of the quality specified by the Owners as required for the 126
Vessel's trade; 127

PART II
SHIPMAN 2009
Standard ship management agreement

(c) voyage estimating and accounting and calculation of hire, freights, demurrage and/or despatch monies 128
due from or due to the charterers of the Vessel; assisting in the collection of any sums due to the Owners 129
related to the commercial operation of the Vessel in accordance with Clause 11 (Income Collected and 130
Expenses Paid on Behalf of Owners); 131

If any of the services under Sub-clauses 6(a), 6(b) and 6(c) are to be excluded from the Management Fee, remuneration 132
for these services must be stated in Annex E (Fee Schedule). See Sub-clause 12(e). 133

(d) issuing voyage instructions; 134

(e) appointing agents; 135

(f) appointing stevedores; and 136

(g) arranging surveys associated with the commercial operation of the Vessel. 137

7. **Insurance Arrangements** 138
*(only applicable if agreed according to **Box 11**).* 139
The Managers shall arrange insurances in accordance with Clause 10 (Insurance Policies), on such terms as 140
the Owners shall have instructed or agreed, in particular regarding conditions, insured values, deductibles, 141
franchises and limits of liability. 142

PART II
SHIPMAN 2009
Standard ship management agreement

SECTION 3 – Obligations

8. **Managers' Obligations**   143
    (a) The Managers undertake to use their best endeavours to provide the Management Services as agents   144
    for and on behalf of the Owners in accordance with sound ship management practice and to protect and   145
    promote the interests of the Owners in all matters relating to the provision of services hereunder.   146

    Provided however, that in the performance of their management responsibilities under this Agreement, the   147
    Managers shall be entitled to have regard to their overall responsibility in relation to all vessels as may from   148
    time to time be entrusted to their management and in particular, but without prejudice to the generality of   149
    the foregoing, the Managers shall be entitled to allocate available supplies, manpower and services in such   150
    manner as in the prevailing circumstances the Managers in their absolute discretion consider to be fair and   151
    reasonable.   152

    (b) Where the Managers are providing technical management services in accordance with Clause 4 (Technical   153
    Management), they shall procure that the requirements of the Flag State are satisfied and they shall agree   154
    to be appointed as the Company, assuming the responsibility for the operation of the Vessel and taking over   155
    the duties and responsibilities imposed by the ISM Code and the ISPS Code, if applicable.   156

9. **Owners' Obligations**   157
    (a) The Owners shall pay all sums due to the Managers punctually in accordance with the terms of this   158
    Agreement. In the event of payment after the due date of any outstanding sums the Manager shall be entitled   159
    to charge interest at the rate stated in **Box 13**.   160

    (b) Where the Managers are providing technical management services in accordance with Clause 4 (Technical   161
    Management), the Owners shall: 162

    (i)   report (or where the Owners are not the registered owners of the Vessel procure that the registered   163
           owners report) to the Flag State administration the details of the Managers as the Company as required   164
           to comply with the ISM and ISPS Codes;   165

    (ii)   procure that any officers and ratings supplied by them or on their behalf comply with the requirements   166
           of STCW 95; and   167

    (iii) instruct such officers and ratings to obey all reasonable orders of the Managers (in their capacity as the   168
           Company) in connection with the operation of the Managers' safety management system.   169

    (c) Where the Managers are **not** providing technical management services in accordance with Clause 4   170
    (Technical Management), the Owners shall: 171

    (i)   procure that the requirements of the Flag State are satisfied and notify the Managers upon execution of   172
           this Agreement of the name and contact details of the organization that will be the Company by completing   173
           Box 5;   174

    (ii)   if the Company changes at any time during this Agreement, notify the Managers in a timely manner of   175
           the name and contact details of the new organization;   176

    (iii) procure that the details of the Company, including any change thereof, are reported to the Flag State   177
           administration as required to comply with the ISM and ISPS Codes. The Owners shall advise the Managers   178
           in a timely manner when the Flag State administration has approved the Company; and   179

    (iv)   unless otherwise agreed, arrange for the supply of provisions at their own expense.   180

    (d) Where the Managers are providing crew management services in accordance with Sub-clause 5(a) the   181
    Owners shall: 182

    (i)   inform the Managers prior to ordering the Vessel to any excluded or additional premium area under   183
           any of the Owners' Insurances by reason of war risks and/or piracy or like perils and pay whatever   184
           additional costs may properly be incurred by the Managers as a consequence of such orders including,   185
           if necessary, the costs of replacing any member of the Crew. Any delays resulting from negotiation   186
           with or replacement of any member of the Crew as a result of the Vessel being ordered to such an area   187

PART II
SHIPMAN 2009
Standard ship management agreement

shall be for the Owners' account. Should the Vessel be within an area which becomes an excluded or 188
additional premium area the above provisions relating to cost and delay shall apply; 189

(ii) agree with the Managers prior to any change of flag of the Vessel and pay whatever additional costs 190
may properly be incurred by the Managers as a consequence of such change. If agreement cannot be 191
reached then either party may terminate this Agreement in accordance with Sub-clause 22(e); and 192

(iii) provide, at no cost to the Managers, in accordance with the requirements of the law of the Flag State, 193
or higher standard, as mutually agreed, adequate Crew accommodation and living standards. 194

(e) Where the Managers are **not** the Company, the Owners shall ensure that Crew are properly familiarised 195
with their duties in accordance with the Vessel's SMS and that instructions which are essential to the SMS 196
are identified, documented and given to the Crew prior to sailing. 197

PART II
SHIPMAN 2009
Standard ship management agreement

SECTION 4 – Insurance, Budgets, Income, Expenses and Fees

10. Insurance Policies   198

The Owners shall procure, whether by instructing the Managers under Clause 7 (Insurance Arrangements)   199
or otherwise, that throughout the period of this Agreement: 200

(a) at the Owners' expense, the Vessel is insured for not less than its sound market value or entered for its   201
full gross tonnage, as the case may be for: 202

(i)   hull and machinery marine risks (including but not limited to crew negligence) and excess liabilities;   203

(ii) protection and indemnity risks (including but not limited to pollution risks, diversion expenses and,   204
except to the extent insured separately by the Managers in accordance with Sub-clause 5(b)(i), Crew   205
Insurances;   206

NOTE: If the Managers are not providing crew management services under Sub-clause 5(a) (Crew   207
Management) or have agreed not to provide Crew Insurances separately in accordance with Sub-clause   208
5(b)(i), then such insurances must be included in the protection and indemnity risks cover for the Vessel (see   209
Sub-clause 10(a)(ii) above).   210

(iii) war risks (including but not limited to blocking and trapping, protection and indemnity, terrorism and crew   211
risks); and   212

(iv) such optional insurances as may be agreed (such as piracy, kidnap and ransom, loss of hire and FD &   213
D) (see **Box 12**)   214

Sub-clauses 10(a)(i) through 10(a)(iv) all in accordance with the best practice of prudent owners of vessels   215
of a similar type to the Vessel, with sound and reputable insurance companies, underwriters or associations   216
("the Owners' Insurances");   217

(b) all premiums and calls on the Owners' Insurances are paid by their due date;   218

(c) the Owners' Insurances name the Managers and, subject to underwriters' agreement, any third party   219
designated by the Managers as a joint assured, with full cover. It is understood that in some cases, such as   220
protection and indemnity, the normal terms for such cover may impose on the Managers and any such third   221
party a liability in respect of premiums or calls arising in connection with the Owners' Insurances.   222

If obtainable at no additional cost, however, the Owners shall procure such insurances on terms such that   223
neither the Managers nor any such third party shall be under any liability in respect of premiums or calls arising   224
in connection with the Owners' Insurances. In any event, on termination of this Agreement in accordance   225
with Clause 21 (Duration of the Agreement) and Clause 22 (Termination), the Owners shall procure that the   226
Managers and any third party designated by the Managers as joint assured shall cease to be joint assured   227
and, if reasonably achievable, that they shall be released from any and all liability for premiums and calls   228
that may arise in relation to the period of this Agreement; and   229

(d) written evidence is provided, to the reasonable satisfaction of the Managers, of the Owners' compliance   230
with their obligations under this Clause 10 within a reasonable time of the commencement of the Agreement,   231
and of each renewal date and, if specifically requested, of each payment date of the Owners' Insurances.   232

11. Income Collected and Expenses Paid on Behalf of Owners   233

(a) Except as provided in Sub-clause 11(c) all monies collected by the Managers under the terms of this   234
Agreement (other than monies payable by the Owners to the Managers) and any interest thereon shall be   235
held to the credit of the Owners in a separate bank account.   236

(b) All expenses incurred by the Managers under the terms of this Agreement on behalf of the Owners   237
(including expenses as provided in Clause 12(c)) may be debited against the Owners in the account referred to   238
under Sub-clause 11(a) but shall in any event remain payable by the Owners to the Managers on demand.   239

(c) All monies collected by the Managers under Clause 6 (Commercial Management) shall be paid into a   240
bank account in the name of the Owners or as may be otherwise advised by the Owners in writing.   241

PART II
SHIPMAN 2009
Standard ship management agreement

12. **Management Fee and Expenses**   242
    (a) The Owners shall pay to the Managers an annual management fee as stated in **Box 14** for their services   243
    as Managers under this Agreement, which shall be payable in equal monthly instalments in advance, the first   244
    instalment (pro rata if appropriate) being payable on the commencement of this Agreement (see Clause 2   245
    (Commencement and Appointment) and **Box 2**) and subsequent instalments being payable at the beginning   246
    of every calendar month. The management fee shall be payable to the Managers' nominated account stated   247
    in **Box 15**.   248

    (b) The management fee shall be subject to an annual review and the proposed fee shall be presented in   249
    the annual budget in accordance with Sub-clause 13(a).   250

    (c) The Managers shall, at no extra cost to the Owners, provide their own office accommodation, office staff,   251
    facilities and stationery. Without limiting the generality of this Clause 12 (Management Fee and Expenses) the   252
    Owners shall reimburse the Managers for postage and communication expenses, travelling expenses, and   253
    other out of pocket expenses properly incurred by the Managers in pursuance of the Management Services.   254
    Any days used by the Managers' personnel travelling to or from or attending on the Vessel or otherwise used   255
    in connection with the Management Services in excess of those agreed in the budget shall be charged at   256
    the daily rate stated in **Box 16**.   257

    (d) If the Owners decide to layup the Vessel and such layup lasts for more than the number of months   258
    stated in **Box 17**, an appropriate reduction of the Management Fee for the period exceeding such period   259
    until one month before the Vessel is again put into service shall be mutually agreed between the parties. If   260
    the Managers are providing crew management services in accordance with Sub-clause 5(a), consequential   261
    costs of reduction and reinstatement of the Crew shall be for the Owners' account. If agreement cannot be   262
    reached then either party may terminate this Agreement in accordance with Sub-clause 22(e).   263

    (e) Save as otherwise provided in this Agreement, all discounts and commissions obtained by the Managers   264
    in the course of the performance of the Management Services shall be credited to the Owners.   265

13. **Budgets and Management of Funds**   266
    (a) The Managers' initial budget is set out in Annex "C" hereto. Subsequent budgets shall be for twelve   267
    month periods and shall be prepared by the Managers and presented to the Owners not less than three   268
    months before the end of the budget year.   269

    (b) The Owners shall state to the Managers in a timely manner, but in any event within one month of   270
    presentation, whether or not they agree to each proposed annual budget. The parties shall negotiate in good   271
    faith and if they fail to agree on the annual budget, including the management fee, either party may terminate   272
    this Agreement in accordance with Sub-clause 22(e).   273

    (c) Following the agreement of the budget, the Managers shall prepare and present to the Owners their   274
    estimate of the working capital requirement for the Vessel and shall each month request the Owners in writing   275
    to pay the funds required to run the Vessel for the ensuing month, including the payment of any occasional or   276
    extraordinary item of expenditure, such as emergency repair costs, additional insurance premiums, bunkers   277
    or provisions. Such funds shall be received by the Managers within ten running days after the receipt by the   278
    Owners of the Managers' written request and shall be held to the credit of the Owners in a separate bank   279
    account.   280

    (d) The Managers shall at all times maintain and keep true and correct accounts in respect of the Management   281
    Services in accordance with the relevant International Financial Reporting Standards or such other standard   282
    as the parties may agree, including records of all costs and expenditure incurred, and produce a comparison   283
    between budgeted and actual income and expenditure of the Vessel in such form and at such intervals as   284
    shall be mutually agreed.   285

    The Managers shall make such accounts available for inspection and auditing by the Owners and/or their   286
    representatives in the Managers' offices or by electronic means, provided reasonable notice is given by the   287
    Owners.   288

    (e) Notwithstanding anything contained herein, the Managers shall in no circumstances be required to use   289
    or commit their own funds to finance the provision of the Management Services.   290

PART II
SHIPMAN 2009
Standard ship management agreement

14. Trading Restrictions
If the Managers are providing crew management services in accordance with Sub-clause 5(a) (Crew Management), the Owners and the Managers will, prior to the commencement of this Agreement, agree on any trading restrictions to the Vessel that may result from the terms and conditions of the Crew's employment.

15. Replacement
If the Managers are providing crew management services in accordance with Sub-clause 5(a) (Crew Management), the Owners may require the replacement, at their own expense, at the next reasonable opportunity, of any member of the Crew found on reasonable grounds to be unsuitable for service. If the Managers have failed to fulfil their obligations in providing suitable qualified Crew within the meaning of Sub-clause 5(a) (Crew Management), then such replacement shall be at the Managers' expense.

16. Managers' Right to Sub-Contract
The Managers shall not subcontract any of their obligations hereunder without the prior written consent of the Owners which shall not be unreasonably withheld. In the event of such a sub-contract the Managers shall remain fully liable for the due performance of their obligations under this Agreement.

17. Responsibilities
(a) *Force Majeure* - Neither party shall be liable for any loss, damage or delay due to any of the following force majeure events and/or conditions to the extent that the party invoking force majeure is prevented or hindered from performing any or all of their obligations under this Agreement, provided they have made all reasonable efforts to avoid, minimise or prevent the effect of such events and/or conditions:

(i) acts of God;

(ii) any Government requisition, control, intervention, requirement or interference;

(iii) any circumstances arising out of war, threatened act of war or warlike operations, acts of terrorism, sabotage or piracy, or the consequences thereof;

(iv) riots, civil commotion, blockades or embargoes;

(v) epidemics;

(vi) earthquakes, landslides, floods or other extraordinary weather conditions;

(vii) strikes, lockouts or other industrial action, unless limited to the employees (which shall not include the Crew) of the party seeking to invoke force majeure;

(viii) fire, accident, explosion except where caused by negligence of the party seeking to invoke force majeure; and

(ix) any other similar cause beyond the reasonable control of either party.

(b) *Liability to Owners*
(i) Without prejudice to Sub-clause 17(a), the Managers shall be under no liability whatsoever to the Owners for any loss, damage, delay or expense of whatsoever nature, whether direct or indirect, (including but not limited to loss of profit arising out of or in connection with detention of or delay to the Vessel) and howsoever arising in the course of performance of the Management Services **UNLESS** same is proved to have resulted solely from the negligence, gross negligence or wilful default of the Managers or their employees or agents, or sub-contractors employed by them in connection with the Vessel, in which case (save where loss, damage, delay or expense has resulted from the Managers' personal act or omission committed with the intent to cause same or recklessly and with knowledge that such loss, damage, delay or expense would probably result) the Managers' liability for each incident or series of incidents giving rise to a claim or claims shall never exceed a total of ten (10) times the annual management fee payable hereunder.

(ii) *Acts or omissions of the Crew* - Notwithstanding anything that may appear to the contrary in this Agreement, the Managers shall not be liable for any acts or omissions of the Crew, even if such acts

PART II
SHIPMAN 2009
Standard ship management agreement

or omissions are negligent, grossly negligent or wilful, except only to the extent that they are shown to   336
have resulted from a failure by the Managers to discharge their obligations under Clause 5(a) (Crew   337
Management), in which case their liability shall be limited in accordance with the terms of this Clause   338
17 (Responsibilities).   339

(c) *Indemnity* - Except to the extent and solely for the amount therein set out that the Managers would be   340
liable under Sub-clause 17(b), the Owners hereby undertake to keep the Managers and their employees,   341
agents and sub-contractors indemnified and to hold them harmless against all actions, proceedings, claims,   342
demands or liabilities whatsoever or howsoever arising which may be brought against them or incurred or   343
suffered by them arising out of or in connection with the performance of this Agreement, and against and in   344
respect of all costs, loss, damages and expenses (including legal costs and expenses on a full indemnity   345
basis) which the Managers may suffer or incur (either directly or indirectly) in the course of the performance   346
of this Agreement.   347

(d) *"Himalaya"* - It is hereby expressly agreed that no employee or agent of the Managers (including every   348
sub-contractor from time to time employed by the Managers) shall in any circumstances whatsoever be   349
under any liability whatsoever to the Owners for any loss, damage or delay of whatsoever kind arising or   350
resulting directly or indirectly from any act, neglect or default on his part while acting in the course of or in   351
connection with his employment and, without prejudice to the generality of the foregoing provisions in this   352
Clause 17 (Responsibilities), every exemption, limitation, condition and liberty herein contained and every   353
right, exemption from liability, defence and immunity of whatsoever nature applicable to the Managers or to   354
which the Managers are entitled hereunder shall also be available and shall extend to protect every such   355
employee or agent of the Managers acting as aforesaid and for the purpose of all the foregoing provisions   356
of this Clause 17 (Responsibilities) the Managers are or shall be deemed to be acting as agent or trustee   357
on behalf of and for the benefit of all persons who are or might be their servants or agents from time to time   358
(including sub-contractors as aforesaid) and all such persons shall to this extent be or be deemed to be   359
parties to this Agreement.   360

18. **General Administration**   361
(a) The Managers shall keep the Owners and, if appropriate, the Company informed in a timely manner of   362
any incident of which the Managers become aware which gives or may give rise to delay to the Vessel or   363
claims or disputes involving third parties.   364

(b) The Managers shall handle and settle all claims and disputes arising out of the Management Services   365
hereunder, unless the Owners instruct the Managers otherwise. The Managers shall keep the Owners   366
appropriately informed in a timely manner throughout the handling of such claims and disputes.   367

(c) The Owners may request the Managers to bring or defend other actions, suits or proceedings related   368
to the Management Services, on terms to be agreed.   369

(d) The Managers shall have power to obtain appropriate legal or technical or other outside expert advice in   370
relation to the handling and settlement of claims in relation to Sub-clauses 18(a) and 18(b) and disputes and   371
any other matters affecting the interests of the Owners in respect of the Vessel, unless the Owners instruct   372
the Managers otherwise.   373

(e) On giving reasonable notice, the Owners may request, and the Managers shall in a timely manner make   374
available, all documentation, information and records in respect of the matters covered by this Agreement   375
either related to mandatory rules or regulations or other obligations applying to the Owners in respect of   376
the Vessel (including but not limited to STCW 95, the ISM Code and ISPS Code) to the extent permitted by   377
relevant legislation.   378

On giving reasonable notice, the Managers may request, and the Owners shall in a timely manner make   379
available, all documentation, information and records reasonably required by the Managers to enable them   380
to perform the Management Services.   381

(f) The Owners shall arrange for the provision of any necessary guarantee bond or other security.   382

(g) Any costs incurred by the Managers in carrying out their obligations according to this Clause 18 (General   383
Administration) shall be reimbursed by the Owners.   384

PART II
SHIPMAN 2009
Standard ship management agreement

19. **Inspection of Vessel** 385
The Owners may at any time after giving reasonable notice to the Managers inspect the Vessel for any reason 386
they consider necessary. 387

20. **Compliance with Laws and Regulations** 388
The parties will not do or permit to be done anything which might cause any breach or infringement of the 389
laws and regulations of the Flag State, or of the places where the Vessel trades. 390

21. **Duration of the Agreement** 391
(a) This Agreement shall come into effect at the date stated in **Box 2** and shall continue until terminated by 392
either party by giving notice to the other; in which event this Agreement shall terminate upon the expiration 393
of the later of the number of months stated in **Box 18** or a period of two (2) months from the date on which 394
such notice is received, unless terminated earlier in accordance with Clause 22 (Termination). 395

(b) Where the Vessel is not at a mutually convenient port or place on the expiry of such period, this Agreement 396
shall terminate on the subsequent arrival of the Vessel at the next mutually convenient port or place. 397

22. **Termination** 398
(a) *Owners' or Managers' default.* 399
If either party fails to meet their obligations under this Agreement, the other party may give notice to the 400
party in default requiring them to remedy it. In the event that the party in default fails to remedy it within a 401
reasonable time to the reasonable satisfaction of the other party, that party shall be entitled to terminate this 402
Agreement with immediate effect by giving notice to the party in default. 403

(b) Notwithstanding Sub-clause 22(a): 404

(i) The Managers shall be entitled to terminate the Agreement with immediate effect by giving notice to the 405
Owners if any monies payable by the Owners and/or the owners of any associated vessel, details of 406
which are listed in Annex "D", shall not have been received in the Managers' nominated account within 407
ten days of receipt by the Owners of the Managers' written request, or if the Vessel is repossessed by 408
the Mortgagee(s). 409

(ii) If the Owners proceed with the employment of or continue to employ the Vessel in the carriage of 410
contraband, blockade running, or in an unlawful trade, or on a voyage which in the reasonable opinion 411
of the Managers is unduly hazardous or improper, the Managers may give notice of the default to the 412
Owners, requiring them to remedy it as soon as practically possible. In the event that the Owners fail to 413
remedy it within a reasonable time to the satisfaction of the Managers, the Managers shall be entitled 414
to terminate the Agreement with immediate effect by notice. 415

(iii) If either party fails to meet their respective obligations under Sub-clause 5(b) (Crew Insurances) and 416
Clause 10 (Insurance Policies), the other party may give notice to the party in default requiring them to 417
remedy it within ten (10) days, failing which the other party may terminate this Agreement with immediate 418
effect by giving notice to the party in default. 419

(c) *Extraordinary Termination* 420
This Agreement shall be deemed to be terminated in the case of the sale of the Vessel or, if the Vessel 421
becomes a total loss or is declared as a constructive or compromised or arranged total loss or is requisitioned 422
or has been declared missing or, if bareboat chartered, unless otherwise agreed, when the bareboat charter 423
comes to an end. 424

(d) For the purpose of Sub-clause 22(c) hereof: 425

(i) the date upon which the Vessel is to be treated as having been sold or otherwise disposed of shall be 426
the date on which the Vessel's owners cease to be the registered owners of the Vessel; 427

(ii) the Vessel shall be deemed to be lost either when it has become an actual total loss or agreement has 428
been reached with the Vessel's underwriters in respect of its constructive total loss or if such agreement 429
with the Vessel's underwriters is not reached it is adjudged by a competent tribunal that a constructive 430
loss of the Vessel has occurred; and 431

(iii) the date upon which the Vessel is to be treated as declared missing shall be ten (10) days after the Vessel 432

PART II
SHIPMAN 2009
Standard ship management agreement

was last reported or when the Vessel is recorded as missing by the Vessel's underwriters, whichever 433
occurs first. A missing vessel shall be deemed lost in accordance with the provisions of Sub-clause 22(d) 434
(ii). 435

(e) In the event the parties fail to agree the annual budget in accordance with Sub-clause 13(b), or to agree 436
a change of flag in accordance with Sub-clause 9(d)(ii), or to agree to a reduction in the Management Fee in 437
accordance with Sub-clause 12(d), either party may terminate this Agreement by giving the other party not 438
less than one month's notice, the result of which will be the expiry of the Agreement at the end of the current 439
budget period or on expiry of the notice period, whichever is the later. 440

(f) This Agreement shall terminate forthwith in the event of an order being made or resolution passed 441
for the winding up, dissolution, liquidation or bankruptcy of either party (otherwise than for the purpose of 442
reconstruction or amalgamation) or if a receiver or administrator is appointed, or if it suspends payment, 443
ceases to carry on business or makes any special arrangement or composition with its creditors. 444

(g) In the event of the termination of this Agreement for any reason other than default by the Managers the 445
management fee payable to the Managers according to the provisions of Clause 12 (Management Fee and 446
Expenses), shall continue to be payable for a further period of the number of months stated in **Box 19** as 447
from the effective date of termination. If **Box 19** is left blank then ninety (90) days shall apply. 448

(h) In addition, where the Managers provide Crew for the Vessel in accordance with Clause 5(a) (Crew 449
Management): 450

(i) the Owners shall continue to pay Crew Support Costs during the said further period of the number of 451
months stated in **Box 19**; and 452

(ii) the Owners shall pay an equitable proportion of any Severance Costs which may be incurred, not 453
exceeding the amount stated in **Box 20**. The Managers shall use their reasonable endeavours to minimise 454
such Severance Costs. 455

(i) On the termination, for whatever reason, of this Agreement, the Managers shall release to the Owners, 456
if so requested, the originals where possible, or otherwise certified copies, of all accounts and all documents 457
specifically relating to the Vessel and its operation. 458

(j) The termination of this Agreement shall be without prejudice to all rights accrued due between the parties 459
prior to the date of termination. 460

23. BIMCO Dispute Resolution Clause 461
(a) This Agreement shall be governed by and construed in accordance with English law and any dispute 462
arising out of or in connection with this Agreement shall be referred to arbitration in London in accordance with 463
the Arbitration Act 1996 or any statutory modification or re-enactment thereof save to the extent necessary 464
to give effect to the provisions of this Clause. 465

The arbitration shall be conducted in accordance with the London Maritime Arbitrators Association (LMAA) 466
Terms current at the time when the arbitration proceedings are commenced. 467

The reference shall be to three arbitrators. A party wishing to refer a dispute to arbitration shall appoint its 468
arbitrator and send notice of such appointment in writing to the other party requiring the other party to appoint 469
its own arbitrator within 14 calendar days of that notice and stating that it will appoint its arbitrator as sole 470
arbitrator unless the other party appoints its own arbitrator and gives notice that it has done so within the 471
14 days specified. If the other party does not appoint its own arbitrator and give notice that it has done so 472
within the 14 days specified, the party referring a dispute to arbitration may, without the requirement of any 473
further prior notice to the other party, appoint its arbitrator as sole arbitrator and shall advise the other party 474
accordingly. The award of a sole arbitrator shall be binding on both parties as if he had been appointed by 475
agreement. 476

Nothing herein shall prevent the parties agreeing in writing to vary these provisions to provide for the 477
appointment of a sole arbitrator. 478

In cases where neither the claim nor any counterclaim exceeds the sum of USD50,000 (or such other sum 479
as the parties may agree) the arbitration shall be conducted in accordance with the LMAA Small Claims 480
Procedure current at the time when the arbitration proceedings are commenced. 481

PART II
SHIPMAN 2009
Standard ship management agreement

(b) This Agreement shall be governed by and construed in accordance with Title 9 of the United States Code | 482
and the Maritime Law of the United States and any dispute arising out of or in connection with this Agreement | 483
shall be referred to three persons at New York, one to be appointed by each of the parties hereto, and the | 484
third by the two so chosen; their decision or that of any two of them shall be final, and for the purposes of | 485
enforcing any award, judgment may be entered on an award by any court of competent jurisdiction. The | 486
proceedings shall be conducted in accordance with the rules of the Society of Maritime Arbitrators, Inc. | 487

In cases where neither the claim nor any counterclaim exceeds the sum of USD50,000 (or such other sum | 488
as the parties may agree) the arbitration shall be conducted in accordance with the Shortened Arbitration | 489
Procedure of the Society of Maritime Arbitrators, Inc. current at the time when the arbitration proceedings | 490
are commenced. | 491

(c) This Agreement shall be governed by and construed in accordance with the laws of the place mutually | 492
agreed by the parties and any dispute arising out of or in connection with this Agreement shall be referred | 493
to arbitration at a mutually agreed place, subject to the procedures applicable there. | 494

(d) Notwithstanding Sub-clauses 23(a), 23(b) or 23(c) above, the parties may agree at any time to refer to | 495
mediation any difference and/or dispute arising out of or in connection with this Agreement. | 496

(i) In the case of a dispute in respect of which arbitration has been commenced under Sub-clauses 23(a), | 497
23(b) or 23(c) above, the following shall apply: | 498

(ii) Either party may at any time and from time to time elect to refer the dispute or part of the dispute to | 499
mediation by service on the other party of a written notice (the "Mediation Notice") calling on the other | 500
party to agree to mediation. | 501

(iii) The other party shall thereupon within 14 calendar days of receipt of the Mediation Notice confirm that | 502
they agree to mediation, in which case the parties shall thereafter agree a mediator within a further 14 | 503
calendar days, failing which on the application of either party a mediator will be appointed promptly by | 504
the Arbitration Tribunal ("the Tribunal") or such person as the Tribunal may designate for that purpose. | 505
The mediation shall be conducted in such place and in accordance with such procedure and on such | 506
terms as the parties may agree or, in the event of disagreement, as may be set by the mediator. | 507

(iv) If the other party does not agree to mediate, that fact may be brought to the attention of the Tribunal | 508
and may be taken into account by the Tribunal when allocating the costs of the arbitration as between | 509
the parties. | 510

(v) The mediation shall not affect the right of either party to seek such relief or take such steps as it considers | 511
necessary to protect its interest. | 512

(vi) Either party may advise the Tribunal that they have agreed to mediation. The arbitration procedure shall | 513
continue during the conduct of the mediation but the Tribunal may take the mediation timetable into | 514
account when setting the timetable for steps in the arbitration. | 515

(vii) Unless otherwise agreed or specified in the mediation terms, each party shall bear its own costs incurred | 516
in the mediation and the parties shall share equally the mediator's costs and expenses. | 517

(viii) The mediation process shall be without prejudice and confidential and no information or documents | 518
disclosed during it shall be revealed to the Tribunal except to the extent that they are disclosable under | 519
the law and procedure governing the arbitration. | 520

(Note: The parties should be aware that the mediation process may not necessarily interrupt time limits.) | 521

(e) If **Box 21** in Part I is not appropriately filled in, Sub-clause 23(a) of this Clause shall apply. | 522

*Note: Sub-clauses 23(a), 23(b) and 23(c) are alternatives; indicate alternative agreed in **Box 21**. Sub-clause* | 523
23(d) shall apply in all cases. | 524

24. Notices | 525
(a) All notices given by either party or their agents to the other party or their agents in accordance with the | 526
provisions of this Agreement shall be in writing and shall, unless specifically provided in this Agreement to | 527

PART II
SHIPMAN 2009
Standard ship management agreement

the contrary, be sent to the address for that other party as set out in **Boxes 22** and **23** or as appropriate or to such other address as the other party may designate in writing. 528 529

A notice may be sent by registered or recorded mail, facsimile, electronically or delivered by hand in accordance with this Sub-clause 24(a). 530 531

(b) Any notice given under this Agreement shall take effect on receipt by the other party and shall be deemed to have been received: 532 533

(i)   if posted, on the seventh (7ᵗʰ) day after posting; 534

(ii) if sent by facsimile or electronically, on the day of transmission; and 535

(iii) if delivered by hand, on the day of delivery. 536

And in each case proof of posting, handing in or transmission shall be proof that notice has been given, unless proven to the contrary. 537 538

25. Entire Agreement 539
This Agreement constitutes the entire agreement between the parties and no promise, undertaking, representation, warranty or statement by either party prior to the date stated in **Box 2** shall affect this Agreement. Any modification of this Agreement shall not be of any effect unless in writing signed by or on behalf of the parties. 540 541 542 543

26. Third Party Rights 544
Except to the extent provided in Sub-clauses 17(c) (Indemnity) and 17(d) (Himalaya), no third parties may enforce any term of this Agreement. 545 546

27. Partial Validity 547
If any provision of this Agreement is or becomes or is held by any arbitrator or other competent body to be illegal, invalid or unenforceable in any respect under any law or jurisdiction, the provision shall be deemed to be amended to the extent necessary to avoid such illegality, invalidity or unenforceability, or, if such amendment is not possible, the provision shall be deemed to be deleted from this Agreement to the extent of such illegality, invalidity or unenforceability, and the remaining provisions shall continue in full force and effect and shall not in any way be affected or impaired thereby. 548 549 550 551 552 553

28. Interpretation 554
In this Agreement: 555

(a) *Singular/Plural* 556
The singular includes the plural and vice versa as the context admits or requires. 557

(b) *Headings* 558
The index and headings to the clauses and appendices to this Agreement are for convenience only and shall not affect its construction or interpretation. 559 560

(c) Day 561
"Day" means a calendar day unless expressly stated to the contrary. 562

ANNEX "A" (DETAILS OF VESSEL OR VESSELS)
TO THE BIMCO STANDARD SHIP MANAGEMENT AGREEMENT
CODE NAME: SHIPMAN 2009

Date of Agreement:

Name of Vessel(s):

Particulars of Vessel(s):

ANNEX "A" (DETAILS OF VESSEL OR VESSELS)
TO THE BIMCO STANDARD SHIP MANAGEMENT AGREEMENT
CODE NAME: SHIPMAN 2009

ANNEX "B" (DETAILS OF CREW)
TO THE BIMCO STANDARD SHIP MANAGEMENT AGREEMENT
CODE NAME: SHIPMAN 2009

Date of Agreement:

Details of Crew:

Numbers   Rank   Nationality

ANNEX "C" (BUDGET)
TO THE BIMCO STANDARD SHIP MANAGEMENT AGREEMENT
CODE NAME: SHIPMAN 2009

Date of Agreement:

Managers´ initial budget with effect from the commencement date of this Agreement (see **Box 2**):

ANNEX "D" (ASSOCIATED VESSELS)
TO THE BIMCO STANDARD SHIP MANAGEMENT AGREEMENT
CODE NAME: SHIPMAN 2009

NOTE: PARTIES SHOULD BE AWARE THAT BY COMPLETING THIS ANNEX "D" THEY WILL BE SUBJECT TO THE PROVISIONS OF SUB-CLAUSE 22(b)(i) OF THIS AGREEMENT.

Date of Agreement:

Details of Associated Vessels:

ANNEX "D" (ASSOCIATED VESSELS)
TO THE BIMCO STANDARD SHIP MANAGEMENT AGREEMENT

ANNEX "E" (FEE SCHEDULE)
TO THE BIMCO STANDARD SHIP MANAGEMENT AGREEMENT
CODE NAME: SHIPMAN 2009

1. Agents		STANDARD STATEMENT OF FACTS (SHORT FORM)

RECOMMENDED BY
THE BALTIC AND INTERNATIONAL MARITIME CONFERENCE (BIMCO)
AND THE FEDERATION OF NATIONAL ASSOCIATIONS
OF SHIP BROKERS AND AGENTS (FONASBA)

2. Vessel's name	3. Port	
4. Owners/Disponent Owners	5. Vessel berthed	
	6. Loading commenced	7. Loading completed
8. Cargo	9. Discharging commenced	10. Discharging completed
	11. Cargo documents on board	12. Vessel sailed
13. Charter Party*	14. Working hours/meal hours of the port*	
15. Bill of Lading weight/quantity 16. Outturn weight/quantity		
17. Vessel arrived on roads	18.	
19. Notice of readiness tendered	20.	
21. Next tide available	22.	

DETAILS OF DAILY WORKING*

Date	Day	Hours worked		Hours stopped		No. of gangs	Quantity load./disch.	Remarks*
		From	to	From	to			

General remarks*

Place and date	Name and signature (Master)*
Name and signature (Agents)*	Name and signature (for the Charterers/Shippers/Receivers)*

* See Explanatory Notes overleaf for filling in the boxes

INSTRUCTIONS FOR FILLING IN THE BOXES

General

It is recommended to fill in the boxes with a short text. When it is a matter of figures to be inserted as is the case in most of the boxes, this should be done as follows:

> 6. Loading commenced
> 1975-03-15-0800

the figures being mentioned in the following order: year–month–date–time.

Boxes Calling for Special Attention

Charter Party*:

Insert name and date of charter, for instance, "Gencon" dated 1975-03-01.

Working hours/meal hours of the port*:

Indicate normal working hours/meal hours of the port and not the actual hours worked on board the vessel which may be longer or shorter than the hours normally worked in the port. Such day-by-day figures should be indicated in the box provided for under "Details of Daily Working".

Some empty boxes are made available in which other relevant information applying to the particular port or vessel could be inserted, such as, time of granting free pratique, if applicable, etc.

Details of Daily Working*:

Insert day-by-day figures and indicate in the vertical column marked "Remarks*" all relevant details as to reasons for stoppages such as bad weather, strikes, breakdown of winches/cranes, shortage of cargo, etc.

General Remarks*:

This box should be used for insertion of such general observations which are not covered in any of the boxes provided for in the first main group of boxes, for instance, reasons for berthing delay or other general observations.

Signatures*:

It is of importance that the boxes provided for signatures are duly signed by the parties concerned.

Disbursement Account

* See Explanatory Notes overleaf for filling in the boxes

GIANT SHIPPING LTD

Suite 216 Giant's Tower
TILBURY
Essex RM99 1AA

Tel: +44 1375 888444
Fax: +44 1375 888555
email: Tilbury@giantgroup.com

Master & Owners of
mv "I.C.S. VENTURE"
Ocean House
Harbour Road
117000 SINGAPORE

DISBURSEMENT ACCOUNT

Vessel:	I.C.S. VENTURE		
Voy No:	031/03	Disch: Containers	Invoice No: 02005/03
Port:	Tilbury	Sailed: 17.03.2004	Date: 31.03.2004
Arrived:	15.03.2003	To: Rotterdam	Ref: T1460
From:	Hamburg	Loaded: Containers	

Detail	Voucher No	Item	Total
		£	£
Port Charges			
Conservancy Dues	1	6,588.00	
Pilotage – River	2 & 3	4,224.50	
Pilotage – Dock	4 & 5	2,149.00	
Towage	6 & 7	3,985.00	
Light Dues	8	3,208.00	20,154.50
Cargo Handling Charges			
Stevedoring	9 to 17	35,216.30	
Landing & Terminal Charges	18 to 22	5,204.00	
Sundry	23	274.00	40,694.30
Ship's Expenses			
Cash to Master	24	4,500.00	
Cash returned by Master	25	−650.00	
Crew Expenses – Hotels	26 & 27	654.32	
Crew Expenses – Travel	28 to 36	1,059.46	
Supply of Fresh Water	37	78.92	
Deck Stores – Chandlery	38 & 39	1,026.15	
Agency Fee		600.00	7,256.85
Total Disbursements			68,117.65
Less: Received on Account			60,000.00
Balance due to us			£8,117.65
VAT: Zero Rate			

Giant Shipping Ltd	Bankers:	Bank of Toyland plc
VAT Reg. GB 999 8888 77		Throgmorton Street LONDON EC3 1AA
A member of the Giant Group plc		Sortcode: 10-11-12
Registered in England No. 1075849		Account: 12 34 56 78

Appendix 11 Disbursement Account

The Federation of National Associations of Ship Brokers and Agents

STANDARD LINER AND GENERAL AGENCY AGREEMENT

Revised and adopted 2001

Approved by BIMCO 2001

It is hereby agreed between:

....of...(hereinafter referred to as the Principal)

and

....of...(hereinafter referred to as the Agent)

on the ....day of ....20..........

that:

1.00   The Principal hereby appoints the Agent as its Liner Agent for all its owned and/or chartered vessels including any space or slot charter agreement serving the trade between ....
and ....

1.01   This Agreement shall come into effect on ....and shall continue until.................
Thereafter it shall continue until terminated by either party giving to the other notice in writing, in which event the Agreement shall terminate upon the expiration of a period of .....months from the date upon which such notice was given.

1.02   The territory in which the Agent shall perform its duties under the Agreement shall be...............
hereinafter referred to as the "Territory".

1.03   This Agreement covers the activities described in section 3..............................

1.04   The Agent undertakes not to accept the representation of other shipping companies nor to engage in NVOCC or such freight forwarding activities in the Territory, which are in direct competition to any of the Principal's transportation activities, without prior written consent, which shall not unreasonably be withheld.

1.05   The Principal undertakes not to appoint any other party in the Agent's Territory for the services defined in this Agreement.

1.06   The established custom of the trade and/or port shall apply and form part of this Agreement.

1.07   In countries where the position of the agent is in any way legally protected or regulated, the Agent shall have the benefit of such protection or regulation.

1.08   All aspects of the Principal's business are to be treated confidentially and all files and records pertaining to this business are the property of the Principal.

2.0   Duties of the Agent

2.01   To represent the Principal in the Territory, using his best endeavours to comply at all times with any reasonable specific instructions which the Principal may give, including the use of Principal's documentation, terms and conditions.

2.02   In consultation with the Principal to recommend and/or appoint on the Principal's behalf and account, Sub-Agents.

2.03   In consultation with the Principal to recommend and/or to appoint on the Principal's behalf and account, Stevedores, Watchmen, Tallymen, Terminal Operators, Hauliers and all kinds of suppliers.

2.04   The Agent will not be responsible for the negligent acts or defaults of the Sub-Agent or Sub-Contractor unless the Agent fails to exercise due care in the appointment and supervision of such Sub-Agent or Sub- Contractor. Notwithstanding the foregoing the Agent shall be responsible for the acts of his subsidiary companies appointed within the context of this Clause.

2.05   The Agent will always strictly observe the shipping laws and regulations of the country and will indemnify the Principal for fines, penalties, expenses or restrictions that may arise due to the failure of the Agent to comply herewith.

3.0   **Activities of Agent** (Delete those which do not apply)

    3.1   **Marketing and Sales**

    3.11   To provide marketing and sales activities in the Territory, in accordance with general guidelines laid down by the Principal, to canvass and book cargo, to publicise the services and to maintain contact with Shippers, Consignees, Forwarding Agents, Port and other Authorities and Trade Organisations.

    3.12   To provide statistics and information and to report on cargo bookings and use of space allotments. To announce sailing and/or arrivals, and to quote freight rates and announce freight tariffs and amendments.

    3.13   To arrange for public relations work (including advertising, press releases, sailing schedules and general promotional material) in accordance with the budget agreed with the Principal and for his account.

    3.14   To attend to conference, consortia and /or alliance matters on behalf of the Principal and for the Principal's account.

    3.15   To issue on behalf of the Principal Bills of Landing and Manifests, delivery orders, certificates and such other documents.

    3.2   **Port Agency**

    3.21   To arrange for berthing of vessels, loading and discharging of the cargo, in accordance with the local custom and conditions.

    3.22   To arrange and co-ordinate all activities of the Terminal Operators, Stevedores, Tallymen and all other Contractors, in the interest of obtaining the best possible operation and despatch of the Principal's vessel.

    3.23   To arrange for calling forward, reception and loading of outward cargo and discharge and release of inward cargo and to attend to the transhipment of through cargo.

    3.24   To arrange for bunkering, repairs, husbandry, crew changes, passengers, ship's stores, spare parts, technical and nautical assistance and medical assistance.

    3.25   To carry out the Principal's requirements concerning claims handling, P & I matters, General Average and/or insurance, and the appointment of Surveyors.

    3.26   To attend to all necessary documentation and to attend to consular requirements.

    3.27   To arrange for and attend to the clearance of the vessel and to arrange for all other services appertaining to the vessel's movements through the port.

    3.28   To report to the Principal the vessel's position and to prepare a statement of facts of the call and/or a port log.

    3.29   To keep the Principal regularly and timely informed on Port and working conditions likely to affect the despatch of the Principal's vessels.

    3.3   **Container and Ro/Ro Traffic**

        Where "equipment" is referred to in the following section it shall comprise container, flat racks, trailers or similar cargo carrying devices, owned, leased or otherwise controlled by the Principal.

    3.31   To arrange for the booking of equipment on the vessel.

    3.32   To arrange for the stuffing and unstuffing of LCL cargo at the port and to arrange for the provision of inland LCL terminals.

    3.33   To provide and administer a proper system, or to comply with the principal's system for the control and registration of equipment. To organise equipment stock within the Territory and make provision for storage, positioning and repositioning of the equipment.

    3.34   To comply with Customs requirements and arrange for equipment interchange documents in respect of the movements for which the Agent is responsible and to control the supply and use of locks, seals and labels.

    3.35   To make equipment available and to arrange inland haulage.

    3.36   To undertake the leasing of equipment into and re-delivery out of the system.

    3.37   To operate an adequate equipment damage control system in compliance with the Principal's instructions. To arrange for equipment repairs and maintenance, when and where necessary and to report on the condition of equipment under the Agent's control.

General Agency

3.41 To supervise, activities and co-ordinate all marketing and sales activities of Port, Inland Agents and/or Sub-agents in the Territory, in accordance with general guidelines laid down by the Principal and to use every effort to obtain business from prospective clients and to consolidate the flow of statistics and information.

3.42 To supervise and co-ordinate all activities of Port, Inland Agents and/or Sub-agents as set forth in the agreement, in order to ensure the proper performance of all customary requirements for the best possible operation of the Principal's vessel in the G.A.'s Territory.

3.43 In consultation with the Principal to recommend and/or appoint on the Principal's behalf and account Port, Inland Agents, and/or Sub-Agents if required.

3.44 To provide Port, Inland Agents and/or Sub-agents with space allocations in accordance with the Principal's requirements.

3.45 To arrange for an efficient rotation of vessels within the Territory, in compliance with the Principal's instructions and to arrange for the most economical despatch in the ports of its area within the scope of the sailing schedule.

3.46 To liaise with Port Agents and/or Sub-agents if and where required, in the Territory in arranging for such matters as bunkering, repairs, crew changes, ship's stores, spare parts, technical, nautical, medical assistance and consular requirements

3.47 To instruct and supervise Port, Inland Agents and/or Sub-Agents regarding the Principal's requirements concerning claims handling. P & I matters and/or insurance, and the appointment of Surveyors. All expenses involved with claims handling other than routine claims are for Principal's account.

3.5 Accounting and Finance

3.51 To provide for appropriate records of the Principal's financial position to be maintained in the Agent's books, which shall be available for inspection and to prepare periodic financial statements.

3.52 To check all vouchers received for services rendered and to prepare a proper disbursement account in respect of each voyage or accounting period.

3.53 To advise the Principal of all amendments to port tariffs and other charges as they become known.

3.54 To calculate freight and other charges according to Tariffs supplied by the Principal and exercise every care and diligence in applying all terms and conditions of such Tariffs or other freight agreements. If the Principal organises or employs an organisation for checking freight calculations and documentation the costs for such checking to be entirely for the Principal's account.

3.55 To collect freight and related accounts and remit to the Principal all freights and other monies belonging to the Principal at such periodic intervals as the Principal may require. All bank charges to be for the Principal's account. The Agent shall advise the Principal of the customary credit terms and arrangements. If the Agent is required to grant credit to customers due to commercial reasons, the risk in respect of outstanding collections is for the Principal's account unless the Agent has granted credit without the knowledge and prior consent of the Principal.

3.56 The Agent shall have authority to retain money from the freight collected to cover all past and current disbursements, subject to providing regular cash position statements to the Principal.

3.57 The Agent in carrying out his duties under this Agreement shall not be responsible to the Principal for loss or damage caused by any Banker, Broker or other person, instructed by the Agent in good faith unless the same happens by or through the wilful neglect or default of the Agent. The burden of proving the wilful neglect of the Agent shall be on the Principal.

4.0 Principal's Duties

4.01 To provide all documentation, necessary to fulfil the Agent's task together with any stationery specifically required by the Principal.

4.02 To give full and timely information regarding the vessel's schedules, ports of call and line policy insofar as it affects the port and sales agency activities.

4.03 To provide the Agents immediately upon request with all necessary funds to cover advance disbursements unless the Agent shall have sufficient funds from the freights collected.

4.04 The Principal shall at all times indemnify the Agent against all claims, charges, losses, damages and expenses which the Agent may incur in connection with the fulfilment of his duties under this Agreement. Such indemnity shall extend to all acts, matters and things done, suffered or incurred by the Agent during the duration of this Agreement, notwithstanding any termination thereof, provided always, that this indemnity shall not extend to matters arising by reason of the wilful misconduct or negligence of the Agent.

4.05   Where the Agent provides bonds, guarantees and any other forms of security to Customs or other statutory authorities then the Principal shall indemnify and reimburse the Agent immediately such claims are made, provided they do not arise by reason of the wilful misconduct or the negligence of the Agent.

4.06   If mutually agreed the Principal shall take over the conduct of any dispute which may arise between the Agent and any third party as a result of the performance of the Agent's duties.

5.0   Remuneration

5.01   The Principal agrees to pay the agent and the Agent accepts, as consideration for the services rendered, the commissions and fees set forth on the schedule attached to this Agreement. Any fees specified in monetary units in the attached schedule shall be reviewed every 12 months and if necessary adjusted in accordance with such recognised cost of living index as is published in the country of the Agent.

5.02   Should the Principal require the Agent to undertake full processing and settlement of claims, then the Agent is entitled to a separate remuneration as agreed with the Principal and commensurate with the work involved.

5.03   The remuneration specified in the schedule attached is in respect of the ordinary and anticipated duties of the Agent within the scope of this Agreement. Should the Agent be required to perform duties beyond the scope of this Agreement then the terms on which the Agent may agree to perform such duties will be subject to express agreement between the parties. Without prejudice to the generality of the foregoing such duties may include e.g. participating in conference activities on behalf of the Principal, booking fare-paying passengers, sending out general average notices and making collections under average bonds insofar as these duties are not performed by the average adjuster.

5.04   If the Tariff currency varies in value against the local currency by more than 10% after consideration of any currency adjustment factor existing in the trade the basis for calculation of remuneration shall be adjusted accordingly.

5.05   Any extra expenses occasioned by specific additional requirements of the Principal in the use of computer equipment and systems for the performance of the Agent's duties to the Principal shall be borne by the Principal.

5.06   The Principal is responsible for all additional expenses incurred by the Agent in connecting its computers to any national or local port community system.

6.0   Duration

6.01   This agreement shall remain in force as specified in clause 1.01 of this Agreement. Any notice of termination shall be sent by registered or recorded mail.

6.02   If the Agreement for any reason other than negligence or wilful misconduct of the Agent should by cancelled at an earlier date than on the expiry of the notice given under clause 1.01 hereof, the Principal shall compensate the Agent. The compensation payable by the Principal to the agent shall be determined in accordance with clause 6.04 below.

6.03   If for any reason the Principal withdraws or suspends the service, the Agent may withdraw from this agreement forthwith, without prejudice to its claim for compensation.

6.04   The basis of compensation shall be the monthly average of the commission and fees earned during the previous 12 months or if less than 12 months have passed then a reasonable estimate of the same, multiplied by the number of months from the date of cancellation until the contract would have been terminated in accordance with clause 1.01 above. Furthermore the gross redundancy payments, which the Agent and/or Sub-Agent(s) is compelled to make to employees made redundant by reason of the withdrawal or suspension of the Principal's service, or termination of this Agreement, shall also be taken into account.

6.05   The Agent shall have a general lien on amounts payable to the Principal in respect of any undisputed sums due and owing to the Agent including but not limited to commissions, disbursements and duties.

7.0   Jurisdiction

7.01   a) This Agreement shall be governed by and construed in accordance with the laws of the country in which the Agent has its principle place of business and any dispute arising out of or in connection with this Agreement shall be referred to arbitration in that country subject to the procedures applicable there.

b) This Agreement shall be governed by and construed in accordance with the laws of .... and any dispute arising out of or in connection with this Agreement shall be referred to arbitration at ...., subject to the procedures applicable there.

c) Any dispute arising out of this Agreement shall be referred to arbitration at....................subject to the law and procedures applicable there.

(subclauses [a] [b] & [c] are options. If [b] or [c] are not filled in then [a] shall apply.)

REMUNERATION SCHEDULE BELONGING TO STANDARD LINER AND GENERAL AGENCY AGREEMENT

Between...and...date............................

    (As Principal)   (As Agent)

The Agent is entitled to the following remuneration based on all total freight earnings (including any surcharges,(eg BAF, CAF) handling charges (eg THC) and freight additionals including inland transport which may be agreed) of the Principal's liner service to and from the Territory to be paid in Agent's local currency. The total remuneration per call shall not in any case be lower than the local fee applicable

I   A.   Where the Agent provides all the services enumerated in this Agreement the Commission shall be:

               Services outward.......................%   [Min .... per cont or tonne/cbm]   } MIN

                   inward.......................%   [Min .... per cont or tonne/cbm]   } LUMP SUM

      2.   ....% for cargo when only booking is involved. [Min .... per cont] } PER

      3.   ....% for cargo when only handling is involved. [Min......... per cont] } CALL ....

          ("only handling" in the remuneration schedule is so defined that the duties of an Agent are to call forward and otherwise arrange for the cargo to be loaded on board, where the specific booking has been made elsewhere and acknowledged as such by the shipper as nominated for the Principal's service.

      4.   In respect of movements of cargo outside the Agent's Territory...............% of the gross total freight is payable in cases where only collection of freight is involved.

      5.   An additional fee for containers and/or units entering or leaving the inventory control system of the Agent a fee of....................... per unit.

II   A.   ....% for cargo loaded on board in bulk [Min .... per tonne / cbm]

      2.   ....% for cargo discharged in bulk. [Min .... per tonne / cbm]

III   Where the Agent provides only the services as non-port agent the remuneration shall be:

   When actually booked/originating from this area:

      1.   Services outward ....% [Min .... per cont or tonne / cbm]

               inward ....% [Min .... per cont or tonne / cbm]

      2.   An additional fee for containers and/or units entering or leaving the inventory control system of the Agent a fee of .... per unit.

IV   Where the Agent provides only the services as non-port agent the remuneration shall be:

      1.   ....% for cargo loaded on board in bulk. [Min .... per tonne / cbm]

      2.   ....% for cargo discharged in bulk. [Min .... per tonne / cbm]

5.   Clearance and ship's husbandry fee shall be as agreed.

6.   A Commission of .... % shall be paid on all ancillary charges collected by the Agent on behalf of the Principal such as Depot Charges, Container Demurrage, Container Damage etc.

7.   Communications: The Principal will either pay actual communication expenses on a cost plus basis or pay a lumpsum monthly on an average cost plus basis, to be review able.

8.   Travelling expenses: When the Agent is requested by the Principal to undertake journeys of any significant distance and/or duration, all travel expenses including accommodation and other expenses will be for the Principal's account.

9.   Documentary and Administrative Charges: Such charges to be levied as appropriate by the Agent to cargo interests and to remain with the Agent even if related to the trade of the principal.

10. In case of Transhipment Cargo, a transhipment fee of .... per cont / tonne / cbm is charged by the Agent.

....

    PRINCIPAL   **AGENT**

Original

CARGO UNDERWRITING AGENCY LTD

2nd Floor, 72 High Street,
Sevenoaks, Kent TN13 1JR
Tel: +44 (0) 1732 452020
Fax: +44 (0) 1732 464950
www.aciscargoinsurance.com

Specimen Reference

CERTIFICATE OF MARINE INSURANCE NO. 15002

This is to Certify that the Underwriters have insured the goods specified below

under Policy No.

subject to the Policy Terms, Conditions and other details shown hereon

In favour of

Conveyance	From (Commencement of transit)	
Via to	To (final destination)	Insured Value and Currency
Marks and Numbers	Interest	

SURVEYS

In the event of loss or damage for which the Underwriters may be liable, immediate application must be made by the INSURED or his agents or the consignee to the UNDERWRITERS or the following agents to arrange for a Surveyor to be appointed:-

Cancelled
Specimen Copy Only

CLAIMS payable at

by

Please refer to instructions printed overleaf

Failure to comply with these instructions may prejudice any claim.

If the insured shall make any claim knowing the same to be false or fraudulent, as regards amount or otherwise, this insurance shall become void and all claims hereunder shall be forfeited.

SHIPPED UNDER DECK BUT CONTAINER SHIPMENTS ON OR UNDER DECK

CONDITIONS OF INSURANCE:
Subject to the conditions printed overleaf, as applicable to the type of interest shown above

Signed for the Underwriters by

Underwriter
ACIS Cargo Underwriting Agency Limited

(The Institute Clauses referred to are those current at time of commencement of transit or risk)

THIS CERTIFICATE REQUIRES ENDORSEMENT BY THE INSURED.

This certificate is not valid unless countersigned by an authorised person

Place and Date of Issue

Authorised Signatory

AUTHORISED AND REGULATED BY THE FINANCIAL SERVICES AUTHORITY (FSA) AND ENTERED IN THE FSA REGISTER UNDER FIRM REFERENCE No 311294

Appendix 13 Certificate of Insurance for Cargo

BIMCO

CONGENBILL 2007

BILL OF LADING
To be used with charter parties
Page I

Shipper	Bill of Lading No.	Reference No.

| Consignee | Vessel | |

| Notify address | Port of loading | |
| | Port of discharge | |

Shipper's description of goods | Gross weight

(of which   on deck at shipper's risk; the Carrier not being responsible for loss or damage howsoever arising)

Freight payable as per
CHARTER PARTY dated:

SHIPPED at the Port of Loading in apparent good order and condition on the Vessel for carriage to the Port of Discharge or so near thereto as the Vessel may safely get the goods specified above.

FREIGHT ADVANCE
Received on account of freight:

Weight, measure, quality, quantity, condition, contents and value unknown.

IN WITNESS whereof the Master or Agent of the said vessel has signed the number of Bills of Lading indicated below all of this tenor and date, any one of which being accomplished the others shall be void.

FOR CONDITIONS OF CARRIAGE SEE OVERLEAF.

Date shipped on board	Place and date of issue	Number of original Bills of Lading

Signature:

(i) ....Master
Master's name and signature

Or

(ii) ....as Agent for the Master
Agent's name and signature

Or

(iii) ....as Agent for the Owner*
Agent's name and signature

.... Owner
*if option (iii) filled in, state Owner's name above

CONGENBILL 2007
BILL OF LADING
To be used with charter parties
Page 2

Conditions of Carriage

(1) All terms and conditions, liberties and exceptions of the Charter Party, dated as overleaf, including the Law and Arbitration Clause/Dispute Resolution Clause, are herewith incorporated.

(2) **General Paramount Clause**
The International Convention for the Unification of Certain Rules of Law relating to Bills of Lading signed at Brussels on 25 August 1924 ("the Hague Rules") as amended by the Protocol signed at Brussels on 23 February 1968 ("the Hague-Visby Rules") and as enacted in the country of shipment shall apply to this Contract. When the Hague-Visby Rules are not enacted in the country of shipment, the corresponding legislation of the country of destination shall apply, irrespective of whether such legislation may only regulate outbound shipments.

When there is no enactment of the Hague-Visby Rules in either the country of shipment or in the country of destination, the Hague-Visby Rules shall apply to this Contract save where the Hague Rules as enacted in the country of shipment or if no such enactment is in place, the Hague Rules as enacted in the country of destination apply compulsorily to this Contract.

The Protocol signed at Brussels on 21 December 1979 ("the SDR Protocol 1979") shall apply where the Hague-Visby Rules apply, whether mandatorily or by this Contract.

The Carrier shall in no case be responsible for loss of or damage to cargo arising prior to loading, after discharging, or while the cargo is in the charge of another carrier, or with respect to deck cargo and live animals.

(3) **General Average**
General Average shall be adjusted, stated and settled according to York-Antwerp Rules 1994 in London unless another place is agreed in the Charter Party.

Cargo's contribution to General Average shall be paid to the Carrier even when such average is the result of a fault, neglect or error of the Master, Pilot or Crew.

(4) **New Jason Clause**
In the event of accident, danger, damage or disaster before or after the commencement of the voyage, resulting from any cause whatsoever, whether due to negligence or not, for which, or for the consequence of which, the Carrier is not responsible, by statute, contract or otherwise, the cargo, shippers, consignees or the owners of the cargo shall contribute with the Carrier in General Average to the payment of any sacrifices, losses or expenses of a General Average nature that may be made or incurred and shall pay salvage and special charges incurred in respect of the cargo. If a salving vessel is owned or operated by the Carrier, salvage shall be paid for as fully as if the said salving vessel or vessels belonged to strangers. Such deposit as the Carrier, or his agents, may deem sufficient to cover the estimated contribution of the goods and any salvage and special charges thereon shall, if required, be made by the cargo, shippers, consignees or owners of the goods to the Carrier before delivery.

(5) **Both-to-Blame Collision Clause**
If the Vessel comes into collision with another vessel as a result of the negligence of the other vessel and any act, neglect or default of the Master, Mariner, Pilot or the servants of the Carrier in the navigation or in the management of the Vessel, the owners of the cargo carried hereunder will indemnify the Carrier against all loss or liability to the other or non-carrying vessel or her owners in so far as such loss or liability represents loss of, or damage to, or any claim whatsoever of the owners of said cargo, paid or payable by the other or non-carrying vessel or her owners to the owners of said cargo and set-off, recouped or recovered by the other or non-carrying vessel or her owners as part of their claim against the carrying Vessel or the Carrier.
The foregoing provisions shall also apply where the owners, operators or those in charge of any vessel or vessels or objects other than, or in addition to, the colliding vessels or objects are at fault in respect of a collision or contact.

For particulars of cargo, freight, destination, etc., see overleaf